editorial

The production of an *Intervention* volume never follows a linear path from conception through to publication. It is invariably an improvised process in which order emerges only at the end. The apparent harmony of the finished product is the outcome of a disharmonic progression which picks up a theme here, a chord there, while it finds new players and forms new attachments along the way. This volume has been no different. However, while the rhythm of production has been slow, almost inaudible at times, all these volumes have contributed to the introduction of new values into local left culture. It is tempting to suggest that it is precisely this nomadic process of free self-constitution which has enabled *Intervention* to provide a space for theoretical and political innovation. In any case, the process continues: plans are well advanced for Volume 20, *New Left/New Writing*. The particularly successful *Media Interventions* will shortly be followed by *Media Interventions II*; and a volume on 'The Body Politic', titled *Flesh* is currently in production.

Two years after the publication of *Beyond Marxism ?*, the radical left felt compelled to call a conference in recognition of the changed cultural environment. It is in response to just this context of the loss of theoretical certainties that we have attempted to define a role for *Intervention*: that of an open space in which new forms of political analysis may be developed and critically contrasted with old; or in which older approaches might find new objects of concern. In this project, one of our aims has been to demonstrate the futility of the polarisation which has grown up between those enthusiasts of 'foreign' theory and those who share an implacably 'local' hostility towards it. In Australia of all places, today's indigenous intellectuals are only yesterday's students of North Atlantic Literature. There is no point in denying that much of the theory which informs local intellectual activity comes from overseas, nor anything to be gained from indulging in angst about the problems raised by its importation. Adopting a more pragmatic approach, we have sought to demonstrate the relevance for progressive politics of the seemingly esoteric concerns of post-structuralists and semioticians. At the same time, we have tried to avoid the simple reproduction of fashionable theory for its own sake, or for the sake of its purely symbolic exchange-value in the cultural marketplace. Instead, we have sought to encourage the expanded reproduction of the insights contained in such theory; the kind of knowledge-effect which only comes from its application to some particular object.

The present volume contains examples of this kind of work. Its coherence derives from the deployment of a wide variety of styles of writing upon a narrow field of related issues. Ranging over political economy and the analysis of male desire, its theoretical references place Clausewitz and classical Marxism alongside Virilio and Deleuze. In the process, it addresses some of the cultural support-structures which maintain the global military apparatus and Australia's place in it, such as the capitalist economy and the politico-discursive history of American bases in Australia. It is signficant, however, that what began as a strategy for a collection of articles dealing with aspects of war and the current opposition to its nuclear form, has emerged with such an emphasis on masculinity. This shouldn't be surprising, since historically, feminist activity within the peace movement has emphasised the importance of this particular support for militarism. In the present volume, masculinity becomes problematised as one of the central, sustaining codes of our culture — informing not only its modalities of exploitation and violence, but also the very forms of its political constitution. Feminism has proved a more powerful lever of cultural criticism than some older, left traditions suspected. Its effects will continue to be felt in future *Intervention* publications.

All correspondence, subscriptions, submissions, send to Intervention Publications.

INTERVENTION is published by —
Intervention Publications.
P.O. Box 395
Leichhardt 2040,
SYDNEY NSW
AUSTRALIA.

War/Masculinity

Editors: Paul Patton, Ross Poole
Co-ordinator: Jose Borghino
Design: Ken Wark, Jose Borghino
Cover Design: Mary Temelovski, Ken Wark
Cover Photo: Steve Cummins
Word-processing: Roberta Blake
Production Collective: Kurt Brereton, Jose Borghino, Gary Campbell, Brigitte Carcenac, Mick Carter, Marc Gration, Gavin Harris, Gregory Harvey, Peter Hutchings, Rosemary Johnson, Peter Krockenberger, Daniel Luscombe, John O'Brien, Paul Patton, Ross Poole, Kim Raschepkin, Alastair Walton, Ken Wark, Leigh Raymond.

Printed in Australia by Social Literacy,
87 Clarendon Road, Stanmore. (02) 569-1057.

Typesetting: Rochester Photosetting

© 1985, Intervention Publications
ISSN 0311 1989
ISBN 0 959 3460 2 3

1985/86 SUBSCRIPTIONS
Rates per 3 issues
Australia:
Individuals — $20.00
Institutions — $40.00
Overseas:
Individuals — $A25.00
Institutions — $A45.00

Future Intervention issues:
"New Left ... New Writing"
"Media Interventions II"
"Flesh"

Bill Bonney died on July 19 1985, after a 10 month battle with cancer.

Born in Tasmania, and educated (several times) at Oxford, Bill nevertheless had about him defining (but yet elusive) qualities that made him uniquely a 'Sydney' identity. Feisty, trenchant, very lovable, slightly obsessive (about his work, his workplace, his work-mates and friends) and always ready to entertain contradiction both in himself and others, Bill spanned one of the most feverish periods in the emergence of new political and philosophical thinking in Sydney, and Australia as a whole.

Bill's teaching in Philosophy at Sydney University was renowned, and he spoke with equal pride of former students who had become taxi-drivers as he did of those who followed him into the education industry. His work at the NSW Institute of Technology from the early 70s until his death saw him intimately involved with emergent studies in Australian media and culture that drew not only on a background of philosophical scholarship and disputation, but also on a political Marxism to which he clung tenaciously but cultivated broadly.

Bill was a fine friend, an inspiring mentor and a tireless battler and struggler against the forces of oppression, inequality and authority. We, along with many, many others, miss him deeply.
        Ross Poole
        Noel Sanders

WAR/MASCULINITY

edited by
Paul Patton and Ross Poole

Bob Connell	*Masculinity, Violence and War*	4
Terry Smith	*A State of Seeing, Unsighted ...: Notes on the Visual in Nazi War Culture*	11
Noel Sanders	*Staging the Bases: Scenarios for Destruction 1963-74*	26
Jocelyn Dunphy	*Thinking New Thoughts: Australian Responses to the Question of Nuclear Armaments*	36
Gavin Harris and Leigh Raymond	*Men at War in Sydney Suburbs*	46
Adam Farrar	*War: Machining Male Desire*	59
Ross Poole	*Structures of Identity: Gender and Nationalism*	71
Chris Cunneen	*Working Class Boys and Crime: Theorising the Class/Gender Mix*	80
Brian Martin	*The Social Construction of Australian Peace Movement Demands*	87
Brian Pinkstone	*The Political Economy of Arms and Disarmament*	100

4 WAR/MASCULINITY

MASCULINITY, VIOLENCE AND WAR

Bob Connell

One

In 1976 there were 22 million people under arms in the world's 130-odd standing armies. The figure today may be a little higher. Probably 20 million of them are men. I have not seen any global totals by sex, but there are figures for particular countries which serve as pointers. In the major NATO forces in 1979-80, for instance, 92% of the US military forces were men; 95% of the French and British; 99.93% of the German. From what is commonly known about other countries, these are not likely to be exceptional figures. The vast majority of the world's soldiers are men. So are most of the police, most of the prison warders, and almost all the generals, admirals, bureaucrats and politicians who control the apparatus of coercion and collective violence. Most murderers are men. Almost all bandits, armed robbers, and muggers are men; all rapists, most domestic bashers; and most people involved in street brawls, riots and the like.

The same story, then, appears for both organised and unorganised violence. It seems there is some connection between being violent and being male. What is it? And what light can an analysis of masculinity, apparently a question of individual psychology, throw on the question of violence on a world scale?

There is a surprisingly widespread belief that this is all 'natural'. Human males are genetically programmed to be hunters and killers, the argument runs. The reason is that ape-man aggression was a survival need in the prehistoric dawn, while the ape-women clustered passively round their campfires suckling and breeding.

Right-wing inflections of this argument thus explain and justify aggression, competition, hierarchy, territoriality, patriarchy, and by inference private property, national rivalry, armies and war. Crude versions of this doctrine are part of the stock rhetoric of modern fascism. More sophisticated versions are developed by 'sociobiologists' in the universities.

Remarkably, there is now a feminist version of this argument too. The line of thought is that human males are naturally predatory and violent; patriarchal power is thus an expression of men's inner nature. Rape and war become synonymous. A poster slogan reads: RAPE IS WAR, WAR IS RAPE. Even serious and thoughtful attempts to reckon with the connection between sexual dominance and war, like Penny Strange's pamphlet *It'll Make a Man of You*, talk freely of 'male cosmology', 'male violence', 'male values' and so on.

Two things have gone wrong here. One is that biological speculation has substituted for hard analysis. A critical examination shows practically no grounding in evidence. The sociobiologists' pre-history is speculative, their anthropology highly selective, and their mechanisms of selection and inheritance simply imaginary. By equally convincing evolutionary speculation one can 'prove' that men are naturally co-operative and peaceful. In fact it has been done, by Kropotkin in *Mutual Aid*.

More important, perhaps, is the confusion of concepts in phrases like 'male power', 'male violence', 'male culture', 'malestream thought', 'male authority'. In each of these phrases a **social** fact or process is coupled with, and implicitly attributed to, a **biological** fact. The result is not only to collapse together a rather heterogeneous group (do gays suffer from 'male cosmology', for instance; or boys?). It also, curiously, takes the heat off the open opponents of feminism. The hard-line male chauvinist is now less liable to be thought personally responsible for what he says or does in particular circumstances, since what he says or does is attributable to the general fatality of being male.

That this is a point where argument and emotion have got tangled is not accidental. There is a basic theoretical problem here. The social categories of gender are quite unlike other categories of social analysis, such as class, in being firmly and visibly connected to biological difference. It is therefore both tempting and easy to fall back on biological explanation of any gender pattern. This naturalisation of social processes is without question the commonest mechanism of sexual ideologies. That biological difference underpins and explains the social supremacy of men over women is the prized belief of enormous numbers of men, and a useful excuse for resisting equality. Academic or pseudo-academic versions of this argument, male-supremacist 'sociobiology' from Tiger's *Men in Groups* through Goldberg's *The Inevitability of Patriarchy* to the present, find a never-failing audience.

If we cannot do better than this in getting to grips with the connection between masculinity and violence, then the left might as well pack its bags and go home, turn on the VCR and play *Threads* until the missiles arrive. For if it all stems from the biological fact of **maleness**, there is nothing that can be done.

We can do better, and the basis for doing so is well known. It is to recognise that war, murder, rape and masculinity are **social and cultural** facts, not settled by biology. The patterns we have to deal with as issues of current politics have been produced within human society by the processes of history. It is the shape of social relations, not the shape of genes, that is the effective cause. 'Male' and 'masculine' are very different things. Masculinity is implanted in the male body, it does not grow out of it.

This argument implies a very different approach to the nature of gender from the natural categories appealed to by both sociobiology and cultural (or eco-) feminism. Such an understanding has been emerging from the work of other groups of feminists (in Australia, research such as Game and Pringle's *Gender at Work* and Burton's *Subordination*), theorists of gay liberation (such as Fernbach's *The Spiral*

Path), and others. Broadly, gender is seen as a structure of social practice, related in complex ways to biological sex but with a powerful historical dynamic of its own.

That general framework suggests two lines of approach to the question of masculinity and war. One is to investigate the social construction of masculinity. The other is to undertake a social analysis of war. In what follows I'll suggest some points about both.

Two

Given a framework of social analysis, we can look at the familiar images and archetypes of manliness in a clearer light. They are parts of the cultural process of producing particular types of masculinity. What messages they convey are important because they help to shape new generations.

One of the central images of masculinity in the Western cultural tradition is the murderous hero, the supreme specialist in violence. A string of warrior-heroes — Achilles, Siegfried, Lancelot and so on — populate European literature from its origins. The twentieth century has steadfastly produced new fictional heroes of this type: Tarzan, Conan, James Bond, the Jackal, the Bruce Lee characters. If you walk into a shop selling comics you will find a stunning array of violent heroes: cops, cowboys, supermen, infantry sergeants, fighter pilots, boxers and so on. The best of the Good Guys, it seems, are those who pay evil-doers back in their own coin.

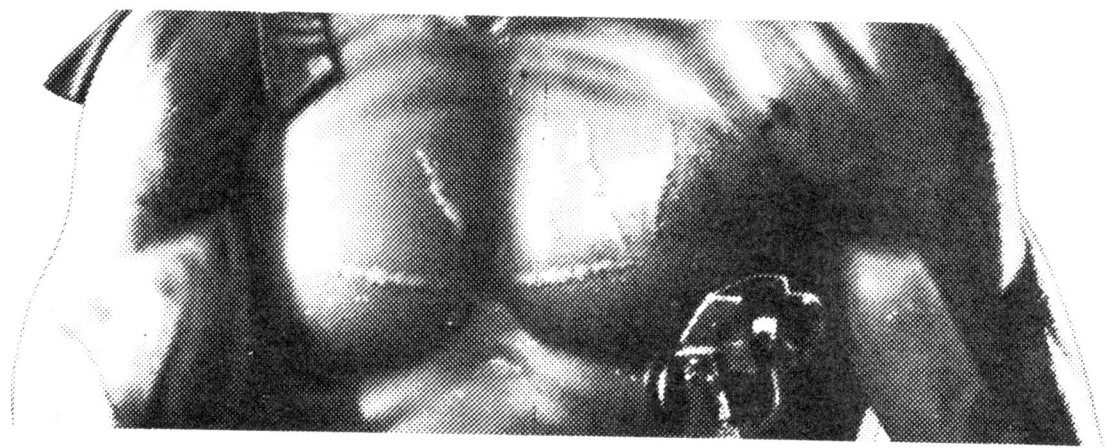

This connection between admired masculinity and violent response to threat is a resource that governments can use to mobilise support for war. The most systematic case in modern history was the Nazis' cult of Nordic manhood, reaching its peak in the propaganda image of the SS-man during World War II. In a different context, a cult of masculinity and toughness flourished in the Kennedy and Johnson administrations in the USA, and helped commit that country to war in Vietnam. Fasteau documents this in one of the early books to come out of the American 'men's movement', *The Male Machine*. I can remember the process operating on young men of my generation in Australia, whose conservative government sent troops to support the Americans in Vietnam. Involvement in the war was presented as standing up to threat, and opponents were smeared as lily-livered effeminates. In the fullness of time support for napalm raids and carpet bombing by B-52s became the test of manliness. In the aftermath of the TWA jet hijacking, Reagan has been playing this tune again, trying to rouse American feeling against the threat of terrorism to provide a cover for his own military operations in central America.

Yet there is a good deal of scepticism in response to Reagan. And in the previous case, Western opposition to the Vietnam war did grow. Together with the Vietnamese resistance it eventually forced the American military to withdraw. The cult of masculine toughness is not all-powerful. This should alert us to some complexities in masculinity and its cultural images.

It is striking that the *Iliad* centres not on Achilles' supremacy in violence, but on his refusal to use it. And what changes his mind is not his reaction to threat, but his tenderness — his love for his friend Patroclus. Siegfried and Lancelot, not exactly gentle characters, are likewise full of hesitations, affection, and divided loyalties.

The image of heroism in modern figures like Tarzan and James Bond is a degraded one. The capacity for tenderness, emotional complexity, aesthetic feeling and so on has been deleted. More exactly, they are split off and assigned only to women, or to other, inferior types of men — such as the wimps, poofters and effeminates who evaded the Vietnamese war. (Part of the legend of Achilles was that he put on a dress and lived among women in order to evade the Trojan war.)

We know very little of the history of masculinity as distinct from the history of men; the detailed research has not been done. We know enough to understand that such changes in images of heroism are part of the historical process by which different kinds of masculinity are separated from each other, some exalted and some spurned. A crucial fact about men is that masculinity is not all of a piece. There have always been different kinds, some more closely associated with violence than others. This is why one should not talk of 'male violence' or of 'males' doing this and that — phrasing which smuggles back in the idea of a biological uniformity in social behaviour.

At any given moment some forms of masculinity will be hegemonic — that is, most honoured and most influential — and other forms will be marginalized or subordinated. The evidence about these forms is very scattered, as the question is only just coming into focus as a research issue. Some points are clear. Modern hegemonic masculinity is defined as heterosexual (not true of all societies or all periods of history), and sharply contrasted with homosexual masculinity (in our society the type case of **subordinated** masculinity). Some other forms of subordinated masculinity are temporary — like that of apprentices in a strongly-masculinized trade. There are kinds of masculinity that are not directly subordinated but rather **marginalized** by a process of social change that undermines their cultural presuppositions — the patriarchal masculinity of many immigrant men from Mediterranean countries is an important case in Australia at present. And there are struggles about what form of masculinity should be **hegemonic** — for instance the contest going on in the ruling classes of the capitalist world between professional/managerial and entrepreneurial/authoritarian masculinities. (The victory of Reaganism in the US is an important shift in the style of American patriarchy as well as in the precise locus of class power.)

Three

In some civilisations the hegemonic forms of masculinity stress restraint and responsibility rather than violence. I believe that was true, for instance, of Confucian China. In contemporary Western society, hegemonic masculinity is strongly associated with aggressiveness and the capacity for violence. Modern feminism has shown us one of the bases for this: the assertion of men's power over women. This relationship itself has a strong component of violence. Wife-bashing, intimidation of women in the street, rape, jealousy-murder, and other patterns of violence against women are not accidental or incidental. They are widespread and systematic, arising from the tensions of a power struggle. This struggle has many turns and twists. Even in a society that defines a husband as the 'head of the household', there are many families where wives actually run the show. Bashings may then result from an attempt to re-assert a damaged masculine ego. In other cases domestic violence is a direct expression of the husband's power, his belief that he can get away with anything, and his contempt for women in general or his wife in particular.

So there are many complexities and contradictions. The main axis, however, remains the social subordination of women, and men's general interest in maintaining it. The masculinity built on that bedrock is not necessarily violent — most men in fact do not bash women — but it is constructed, so to speak, with a door open towards violence.

Gay liberation has shown us another dimension: hegemonic masculinity is aggressively heterosexual. It defines itself in part by a vehement rejection of homosexuality. This rejection very often takes violent forms: arrests, frequent bashings, and occasional murders. Homosexual men seem to arouse particular fear and loathing among tough 'macho' men. This fact has led many to think the violence is an attempt to purge the world of what one suspects in oneself. In psychoanalytic terms, there is a current of repressed homosexual feeling buried somewhere in hegemonic masculinity. This, again, suggests the importance of the tensions and contradictions within masculinity. It is by no means a neat package.

In much of the writing about men produced by the 'men's liberation movement' of the 1970s it was assumed that violence was simply an expression of conventional masculinity. Change the macho image, stop giving little boys toy guns, and violence would be reduced. We can now see that the connection of masculinity and violence is both deeper and more complex than that. Violence is not just an expression; it is a part of the process that divides different masculinities from each other. There is violence within masculinity; it is constitutive. Once again, this is not to imply that it is universal. Real men don't necessarily bash three poofters before breakfast every day. For one thing, TV does it for them. Part of the pattern of contemporary masculinity is the commercial production of symbolic violence on an unprecedented scale, from Tarzan movies to Star Wars, Space Invaders, World Series Cricket, and now Rambo.

Four

It is very important that much of the actual violence is not isolated and individual action, but is institutional. Much of the poofter-bashing is done by the police; much of the world's rape is done by soldiers. These actions grow readily out of the 'legitimate' violence for which police forces and armies are set up. The state is an instrument of coercion; this remains true whatever else about it varies. It uses one of the great discoveries of modern history, rational bureaucratic organization, to have policy-making centralized and execution down the line fairly uniform. Given this, the state can become the vehicle of calculated violence based on and using hegemonic masculinity. Armies are a kind of hybrid between bureaucracy and masculinity.

But to make this connection with an undifferentiated 'masculine violence' — as, say, Fernbach does in *The Spiral Path* — is to misunderstand the way armies work. Generals, notoriously, die in bed. They are not themselves 'violent men', and would be bad generals if they were. Of course they need violent men under their command as front-line troops, or at least as organisers of front-line troops — men like the grim Sergeant Croft of *The Naked and the Dead* (a novel that strikingly makes the point about different masculinities).

It is the *relationship* between forms of masculinity — physically violent but subordinate to orders on the one hand, dominating and organisationally competent on the other — that is the basis of military organisation. The two need not overlap at all. Heinrich Himmler, the commander of one of the most brutal military organisations in recent history, never killed anyone personally. When present at an execution where some brains splattered on his neat SS uniform, he threw a screaming fit.

Even this is to understate the matter. In modern armies the majority of soldiers are not combatants at all. Most are in support services, as transport workers, administrators, technicians, maintenance workers, cooks, etc, and have no competence as fighters at all. The proportion of this kind of worker in armies has grown markedly over the last century and a half with the increasing technologisation of warfare, as several major developments have reduced the need for cannon-fodder and increased the need for supply workers. The US made two great contributions to the art of war in the 1940s — nuclear weapons and logistics. Logistics was certainly more militarily effective at the time. And you don't want Rambo types driving your jeeps and supply trucks.

Automatic weapons (machine-guns and quick-firing artillery), self-propelled military vehicles (tanks and aircraft), and ultimately long-distance weapons that eliminate the 'front' (strategic bombers, nuclear missiles) have successively intensified the trend. They have made more and more important in military organisations a third kind of masculinity, the professionalised, calculative rationality of the technical specialist.

The first stage of this was the rise of the 'General Staff' to a central position in European military organisation by the early twentieth century. The idea of a General Staff was a group of planners, separate from the command of combat units, who worked out overall strategies as well as technical issues of supply. The 'Schlieffen Plan' for the German attack on France in 1914 marked the ascendancy of staff over line commanders. In no sense did this mean a shift away from violence — the violence of war was growing on an unprecedented scale. The man who was the 20th century's most successful general, the Soviet Chief of Staff Georgi Zhukov, was notorious for his disregard for human life. He accepted huge casualties in order to gain advantage in battles of attrition at Moscow, Stalingrad and Kursk (the battles responsible for the ultimate defeat of Hitler).

The second stage was the mobilisation of physical scientists on a large scale into weapons research, culminating in the Manhattan Project. The friction within the Manhattan Project, and the crisis of conscience suffered by the nuclear physicists immediately after the explosion of the Hiroshima and Nagasaki bombs, are measures of the difficulty of integrating this kind of worker into the military. But the huge growth of nuclear weapons research establishments in the USA and USSR since then shows that the initial difficulties have been overcome. The end of the world has been made technically possible by this achievement in human relations.

Five

In the past, as well as being the main actors of war, men have also been the main victims. Napoleon's wars killed mainly soldiers. The harnessing of high technology to the bureaucratic state has steadily changed this. Hitler's mass extermination campaigns, and the Anglo-American firebombing of Hamburg, Dresden and Tokyo, were an organised turning of conventional weapons to the killing of whole populations. The nuclear arsenal has been directed against whole populations from the start.

It has thus become a matter of urgency for humans as a group to undo the tangle of relationships that sustains the nuclear arms race. Masculinity is part of this tangle. It will not be easy to alter. The pattern of an arms race, i.e. mutual threat, itself helps sustain an aggressive masculinity.

Nor can the hegemonic pattern of masculinity be rejected totally. To achieve disarmament in reality means conducting a long and difficult struggle against an entrenched power structure. This calls for some of the qualities hegemonic masculinity exalts — toughness, endurance, determination and the like. It is no accident that hegemonic masculinity has been important in radical movements in the past: in unionism, in national liberation movements, and in socialist parties.

Yet we know masculinity is not fixed. It is at least conceivable that we can re-work masculinity in a way that sustains a struggle without reproducing the enemy. In much this sense feminism has been re-working femininity. In doing this it will be useful to remember the hidden riches of masculinity, as well as its horrors. There are cultural resources in subordinated masculinities, and in patterns lost or by-passed in recent history.

References

Burton, C., *Subordination: Feminism and Social Theory*, Sydney, Allen and Unwin, 1985.

Carrigan, T., Connell, R.W. & Lee, J., 'Hard and Heavy Phenomena: the Sociology of Masculinity', *Theory & Society*, forthcoming.

Chapkis, W., Ed., *Loaded Questions: Women in the Military*, Amsterdam, Transnational Institute, 1981.

Clark, A., *Barbarossa: The Russian-German Conflict 1941-1945*, Harmondsworth, Penguin, 1966.

Connell, R.W., 'Men's bodies' in *Which Way Is Up?*, Sydney, Allen and Unwin, 1983.

Fernbach, D., *The Spiral Path: A Gay Contribution to Human Survival*, London, Gay Mens' Press, 1981.

Fasteau, M.F., *The Male Machine*, New York, McGraw-Hill, 1974.

Game, A. & Pringle, R., *Gender at Work*, Sydney, Allen & Unwin, 1983.

Goldberg, S., *The Inevitability of Patriarchy*, New York, William Morrow, 1973.

Irving, D.J.C., *The Destruction of Dresden*, London, Kimber, 1963.

Kropotkin, P., *Mutual Aid* (1902), Boston, Extending Horizons, n.d.

Mailer, N., *The Naked and the Dead* (1949), London, Deutsch, 1964.

Strange, P., *It'll Make a Man of You: A Feminist View of the Arms Race*, Nottingham, Peace News/Mushroom, 1983.

Tiger, L., *Men in Groups*, New York, Random House, 1969.

Zhukov, G.K., *Marshal Zhukov's Greatest battles*, London, Sphere, 1971.

A STATE OF SEEING, UNSIGHTED ... :
NOTES ON THE VISUAL IN NAZI WAR CULTURE

Terry Smith

Yoshiwara ... a shell-shaped auditorium where a crowd shares a common narcotic delusion in which one of them becomes 'the embodied conception of the intoxication of them all ... Each of the thousands of others in ecstasy lives the thousand-fold ecstasy which embodies itself in him'.
         Thea von Harbou, Metropolis (Berlin, 1924).

The Nazi state freshly exerts the powerful horror of fascination ... not so much an early warning example of aberrant excess, more as a prefiguration of some aspects of the global state of pure war which multinational capital now so desperately seeks. These notes read the operations of the visual in Nazi war culture in the names of three theoretical perspectives: class, the spectacle and power.

Kidding, Mr. Hitler

We need to put aside the usual beginning in Hitler's personal interest in art, architecture and things visual. To see Nazi art, and the Nazi emphasis on the visual, as the systematisation of the personal inclinations of Hitler and perhaps other leaders such as Goebbels is a mistake. Moreover, it is a mistake with important ideological consequences. It is a particularisation of the tendency to regard Nazism as aberrant, a detour in the history of Germany, as a sudden, extremist, uncharacteristic eruption within European history caused by a set of unrepeatable circumstances, particularly the devilish cunning of certain individuals. Similarly, Nazi art is often dismissed as the work of artists under direct pressure by a watchful

state, a distortion of German art, something 'alien', found only under totalitarian regimes, such as the Soviet Union. The same exceptionality is attributed to Nazi architecture, the other arts and to public festivals, such as the parades and rallies. Since the pleas of 'not guilty' by the Nazi leadership during the Nuremberg trials, there has been a massive effort to disassociate values and practices which remain of use to some powerful interests from their role during the Nazi period. For example, medicine's objectivity and scientificity is maintained by labelling 'insane' medical practices in concentration camps. Similarly with the law, religion, and bureaucracy where the 'excesses' of the regime are centred on minor bureaucrats ('tin Hitlers') who proved unable to handle the powers given them.

In the case of art and architecture, the 'moral purity' of avant-garde modernism is preserved by citing the demonstrable Nazi hatred for certain aspects of it and pointing to the stylistically 'reactionary' character of officially-approved art. The ideological aim of such readings is, of course, to exempt all but a few from guilt for their actions during this period and, more importantly, to obscure the kind of analysis which shows that fascism was, and remains (although it is transformed) the kind of social system most suited to the defence of monopoly capital when it goes — as it constantly and so variously must — into crisis. Nazi war culture was novel in that a key means by which it sought to maintain itself was specific to visual imagery; and in that the ultimate 'moment', the purest form, the ideal figure of the Nazi state was the Nuremberg mass rally. Something like this was, I think, in Benjamin's mind when he wrote that mankind's 'self-alienation has reached such a degree that it can experience its own destruction as an aesthetic pleasure of the first order', this being 'the situation of politics which Fascism is rendering aesthetic'. That this attempt meets resistance, that it does not ever succeed in achieving the coherence or dominance it aims for, is recognised in his next sentence: 'Communism responds by politicising art'.[1] Nonetheless, we will examine the claim that this process of aestheticisation was of central importance to the Nazi state. How might this have been so, and, particularly, how close does such an account square with the relationships between Nazism, monopoly capital and the German petit-bourgeoisie? We will first explore the nature of Nazi propaganda in general, and then gradually develop a reading of the rallies by probing each of their constituent elements in turn and in relation to each other.

Propaganda: The Total Mirror of Production

Reportedly impressed by the use of propaganda against German soldiers by the British army in a campaign led by Lord Northcliffe during World War I, Hitler, himself a 'political officer' during 1919, devoted a chapter of Mein Kampf to the subject. He set a record early attendance at a Nazi Party (NSDAP) meeting when, in 1920, he conducted a 'brilliant advertising campaign' to attract over 2,000 people to the Munich Hofbrauhaus to hear him deliver his '25 Theses'.[2] He remained party propaganda officer until 1925, when Gregor Strassner took over, to be replaced by Goebbels in 1929. Other reported models for Nazi propaganda were the rituals and spectacles of the Catholic church, and the public recruitment campaigns of working class organisations such as the Communist Party, particularly during the 1920s when the NSDAP was fighting on the streets for the allegiance of the petit-bourgeoisie and disaffected workers.

Hitler and Goebbels held general and personal views on their propaganda, as we would expect from people who are both organising a propaganda machine and are principal actors within it. Hitler, in Mein Kampf, asserted that 'by clever and continuous use of propaganda a people can even be made to mistake heaven for hell, and vice versa, the most miserable life for Paradise'.[3] Goebbels, in a speech from the Berlin period:

That propaganda is good which leads to success, and that is bad which fails to achieve the desired result, however intelligent it is, for it is not propaganda's task to be intelligent, its task is to lead to success.[4]

---

1. 'The Work of Art in the Age of Mechanical Production', (1936) in *Illuminations* (New York: Schocken, 1969), p. 242.

2. Ward Rutherford, *Hitler's Propaganda Machine* (London: Bison, 1978), p. 8, p. 18.

3. *Mein Kampf* (New ed. Boston: Houghton Misslin, 1962).

4. Cited in Joachim C. Fest, *The Face of the Third Reich*, (Penguin, 1970), p. 141.

Goebbels boasted that he could play upon the national psyche 'as on a piano', and Hitler, not surprisingly, saw his own skills as crucial to the enterprise:

I am conscious that I have no equal in the art of swaying the masses, not even Goebbels. Everything that can be learnt with the intelligence, everything that can be achieved by the aid of clever ideas, Goebbels can do, but real leadership of the masses cannot be learnt.[5]

Indeed, if it cannot be learnt, it can only be imposed: shaped by a propagandist as brilliant as Goebbels and enforced by the detailed exercise of power, in fact, of terror: 'A sharp sword must always stand behind propaganda if it is to be really effective'.[6]

Upon taking power in 1933, the NSDAP added to its party propaganda agencies a number of smaller ones, such as Hitler's press office led by Otto Dietrich, and Foreign Minister Ribbentrop's press corps. As well, there were propaganda centres/sources in the SS, in the Army and in the newspaper *Volkischer Beobachter* (edited by Alfred Rosenberg). But above all was the large Propaganda Ministry, with 12 departments, the first devoted to administration, the second to special campaigns, and the others to particular media, such as broadcasting, the press, etc. Both party and government agencies were careful to develop precise advance profiles for their efforts through the use of questionnaires, statistical measurement of reactions, details of ticket sales, as well as the development of predictive skills among surveillance officers — careful comparisons are made between predicted and 'actual' responses to publications, broadcasts, etc., and causes of failure actively sought. The various media were rated in order of importance vis-a-vis each other, and then internally, so that efforts at censorship/surveillance could be rationalised (the press had priority and within it, newspapers; newsreels were the important aspect of cinema; news and commentaries the key to newspapers and radio).[7]

Equal effort was expended on developing a national network of public speakers — orators were selected and intensively trained, then distributed through a hierarchy which stretched from the local area, through regions, to specialists who would travel anywhere, then shock troop speakers (trouble shooters) and, finally, the *Reichs* speakers (extremely well-paid star performers). Above these, of course, were the party leaders. Most NSDAP and Government organisations were similarly sorted: total, sectionalised, hierarchical and centralised. Paralleling the party and the Government organisations were the chambers which co-ordinated all production and distribution within each field. The Press Chamber, for example, drew all representative organisations into itself, issued licences to publish, controlled the distribution of paper sales down to news-stands, and, through the Association of the German Press, acted as a labour exchange. It also operated internal censorship, paralleling that imposed by both the NSDAP and the Ministry for Propaganda. (Goebbels was head of the propaganda section of the Ministry and of the Press Chamber). The organisational ideal here is one in which all production, distribution and consumption is regulated in both form and content according to the principle of it being utterly open to the scrutiny which exactly matches it. (The party watches the government and both watch the producer/distributor/consumer).

This Kafkaesque/Orwellian nightmare in which every act by any citizen is matched by a bureaucratic response, was never achieved, and may have been the expression as much of the necessity for the conflicting tendencies within the Nazi party, government and state to keep each other's powers in check as it was of a need to control those formally 'outside' the party. Nonetheless, this was the ideal, the 'rational' aim of the Nazi restructuring of all these social relations of production. You are watched by those above you and, ultimately, by the Fuhrer. Visibility is the principle of position, being seen to be in place. You **are** the state just in the continuous activity of watching others to see if they deviate. But they can only deviate from a full-hearted acceptance of being watched as they go about designated tasks. In this 'going about' of designated work, you are one of **the people**. If you were to, simultaneously, watch yourself as you worked, you would magically fuse the gap between the people and the state and become the state, the German people. But, usually, this privileged moment was only possible under the gaze of the leader.

5. Ibid., p. 499.

6. Luis P. Lochner *Die Goebbels Tagebuecher 1942-1943* (Zurich; Atlantis Verlag, 1948), 20 September, 1943.

7. Rutherford, pp. 23-6.

WAR/MASCULINITY

Simplicity and Saturation

During the 'time of struggle' (1920-1933), when the major task of the NSDAP was to persuade voters to support the party against rival claimants for legitimacy, particularly the huge Communist party, the major visual form through which the party introduced itself was the poster. Outstanding poster artists, designers and cartoonists did work for the Nazis. 'Mjolnir' (Hans Schweitzer), who specialised in images of unbeatable Aryan youth, became head of the section of the Reich Art Chamber responsible for the design of NSDAP symbols. Nonetheless, the effectiveness of NSDAP posters and visible public imagery, such as the ubiquitous black and white on red, depended on its simplicity and saturation. Their main function was to declare the existence of a totally Nazi environment: to declare it to party members, to those undecided, and to opponents alike. This was the purpose of NSDAP meetings during the 'time of struggle' — to engender a crisis with marches beforehand, a hall hung with simple, repetitive banners, the regalia of the SA, the chorus of *Heils*, the singing, the ritualised violence of ejecting protestors, the orator saying the usually unsayable, the forbidden — to demonstrate what it would be like were the NSDAP actually in power. From 1933 this effort to create a totally managed environment was an all-out one, and the centrepiece of it all was the catharsis of the public rally, particularly those of the party itself — annually, in Nuremberg, from 1923 to 1938:

> ... Vast agglomerations of shapes which excited the senses — flags, banners, flaming torches, all forming regular but moving patterns in the hands which held them; the tramp of thousands of feet, the goose-step rattling on the hard granite of the arena, the clatter of hooves or the clank and squeals of tanks as they manoeuvred; parades, drills, gymnastic displays. All, in some way, acting on the minds of the spectators like voodoo drums, rousing them to frenzies until they are in a trance.[8]

Even unsympathetic spectators are reported to have been stunned by the 'grandiose beauty' of the spectacles.[9]

8. Rutherford, pp. 142-5.

9. Sir Neville Henderson, cited in Rutherford, p. 142; William L. Shirer, cited in Fest, p. 145.

Goebbels had overall responsibility for the rallies but they were planned by a specific office within the Propaganda Ministry headed by Robert Ley. His council organised the program, which grew from one day celebrating the electoral victory of 1933 to eight days of events surrounding the NSDAP congress meeting of 1938, from the staging of the rallies down to accommodation and railway timetables. Art exhibitions, musical festivals (particularly Wagner and Bruckner), fireworks and gymnastic displays accompanied the ceaseless round of party business — all of these fed into the stadia spectacles in important, although indirect, ways. During the 'period of struggle', the NSDAP had developed a surprisingly limited iconography: the swastika, the head of Hitler, the eagle. Sometimes these would be combined, or braided, or a specifying symbol added: the Iron Cross, the skull, the slogan 'Germany Awake!'. But that is all: this is the range of Nazi imagery, it was never added to significantly. The point, however, is that it was repeated constantly in an astonishing variety of forms: the swastika not only as flag, bunting, armband (as expected), but also as altar cloth, silver paperweight, fan decoration, cover of sheet music for the Horst Wessell song, on goblets, cutlery, children's swapcards and books, embroidered pillows, toys, mantelpiece and wall decorations, wall paper and decals etc. Hitler's head and the eagle are used in the same and similar situations, as were images of the Hitler youth, the SA, the SS and the various branches of the army.

Again, the impulse is towards totality via saturation/repetition but, in the case of these examples, not abstractly: the propaganda aims of the party are continuous with the normal operations of small business, for example, the souvenir trade. These have been documented in the case of postcards in Germany and Italy.[10]

The widespread dissemination of Nazi imagery tends to domesticate it — yet the party early forbade *Kitsch* representations of its major symbols, confining them to slightly upmarket situations, such as cutlery, to educational purposes and to the controlled public media and spaces. The photograph of Hitler, the copy of *Mein Kampf* and the salute seem to have been enough in the domestic situation to support the consent-seeking via discursive argument, default and force. The consent sought by NSDAP seems always to have retained an edge of internal aggression, a fear-effect, which too much domestication, ordinariness, for-grantedness would belie. There was no Nazi 'style' in, say, the ambience of interior decoration, in dress fashions, in styles of speech, or public behaviour (how 'real' is the brownshirt-macho-redneck straightforwardness? A pseudo-aristocratic snobbery towards the social stylelessness of the 'plebeian' petty bourgeoisie in government?).

10. Umberto Silva, *Ideologia e Arte del Fascismo* (Milan: Mazzotta, 1973); and John Fraser, 'Propaganda on the Picture Postcard', *Oxford Art Journal*, 3 (October, 1980).

This implies that the direction of Nazi imagery was from the private to the public; its impulse was to reconstitute the private in the public by a saturation of the private with visions of its participation in the public. This supports the view that the Nazi state had no economic, political, social or even ideological program coherent enough to propagate to the people. Thus what it propagated was **propaganda itself**, the process of its self-propagation: winning consent became an end-in-itself, consent not to a program, an ideal, a form of the state, a vision of the future, but a consent to conviction as such, to **consent itself**. If this is so, then the disparate, random visuality of the domestic Nazi imagery is of little consequence. What is important is the movement towards the public, towards the public domains in which all visual forms are controlled by the party.

Less is More

Settings for the rallies: as noted, the range of imagery is exceedingly restricted. The swastika and the eagle, along with the presence of Hitler are the three central images, which were elaborated slightly by certain details and colours in the SA and SS uniforms and insignia — but no more. The 1933 rally sported flags, but the only other imagery was a gargantuan eagle behind the party leaders. In the following year Speer went further, creating a spatial context often cited for its overwhelming beauty: Hitler's speech was timed to end at nightfall as 130 spotlights spaced 40ft apart threw their beams upwards. Speer aimed for the effect of 'a vast room with the beams serving as mighty pillars of infinitely high outer walls'. On other occasions he managed to produce the effect of being inside a light-dome. Gradually, year by year, the stadia were clad with granite and marble, new 'temples', 'urns' and other paraphernalia added on a larger and larger scale. Nuremberg, 'the city of rallies', was blessed with four specially-built arenas: between the Luitpoldheim and the Marzfeld a straight, broad avenue stretched for 16 miles. On either side of it

16 WAR/MASCULINITY

was the Zeppelinweise — with a capacity greater than the population of its host city (400,000) — and the German stadium.

These structures, and implied structures, carried little ornament, but their symbolic purposes were nonetheless unambiguous and strong. Their message was understood to be carried by their form and by their use. Let me immediately point to an irony — or is it? These phrases are the slogans not just of the builders of the Thousand-year Reich, but also of the pioneers and promoters of the Modern Movement in European and U.S. architecture. The rally buildings at Nuremberg, whatever other significations they have, conform closely to such precepts as "Form follows function", "Meaning is use", "Less is more". Usually read in the context of the grandiose excesses of the plan to rebuild central Berlin, and compared (with boring regularity) to the winning wedding-cake design for the Palace of the Soviets in 1932, these buildings might be more closely related to the immediate context from which their architects came: from a profession excitingly led by the industry-serving simplicities of the *Werkbund*, and by the taming, regularizing, planed-down yet gargantuan and imposing, heavy 'classicism' of Peter Behrens and Mies Van Der Rohe. This latter conservatism clearly oversees Speer's buildings; indeed, both Behrens and Mies continued to build for the new State — the former throughout, the latter until he was (reluctantly) obliged to leave. Speer's 'lightbuildings' may be conceptually closer to nothing more than Mies' first essays in glass skyscrapers in 1920 — although the 'dome' might relate to Bruno Taut's glasshouse at the *Werkbund* exhibition of 1914 — both archetypal modernist structures.[11]

There is a photograph of Hitler standing before five microphones on the tribune of the Luitpold Arena at Nuremberg. It shows a repoussoir, right-angled, unusually unveiled swastika on the massive, granite-covered tribune. Behind, to the left, a glimpse of rows of banner-bearers and above them a huge eagle with wings outspread. Both eagle and banner-bearers look at Hitler. But these are apparently minor elements, merely finessing the focus of the image: the breathtaking division between the empty sky in the top half of the image, and the structures below and, within the bottom half, the turning of the tribune at such an angle that an opposition of full, glaring light on the front of the tribune and deepest black shadow at its side becomes a visual drama of a high order, engulfing the banner-bearers, reducing the eagle to a silhouette and *Der Fuhrer* to a tiny, still figure, split like the podium into a shape and a silhouette, positioned at the very top edge of that dramatic division. It is an image whose energy is got by its line, and by the specifically photographic ways in which line — that is, light contrast — becomes a content which dominates its ostensible subject matter, reducing Hitler to (powerless) isolation, the party to the shadows/wings, the eagle to a manicured hedge (an urn in the background looks like a minaret/toy Roman temple) — all subservient to the cutting edge of the internal composition of the 'shot'.

It is an extraordinary image of stillness, of silence — yet probably taken at a moment when the sensual overload described above was at its height. It may have been an effort by a dissident camera-person to express his/her personal distance from the event. It may have been a sympathetic camera-person's effort to give a specifically visual form to the 'heroic isolation' of a god-like leader. It may have been intended to picture that aspect of public speaking when the orator, having swayed the crowd, steps back into exhausted removal. Or it may have been, finally, a chance result, a

11. See, for example, Lucius Burckhardt (ed.), *The Werkbund, Studies in the History and the Ideology of the Deutscher Werkbund* (La Biennale di Venezia, 1977; London: Design Council, 1980); Albert Speer, *Inside the Third Reich* (New York: Macmillan, 1970); Bernhard Leitner, 'Architecture as a Weapon; Hitler's Speer', *Artforum* (December 1970), pp. 51-55 and his interview, 'Albert Speer, the Architect', *October*, 20 (Spring 1982), pp. 14-50. See also E. Hochman, 'Mies van der Rohe and the Third Reich', *Oppositions*, 18 (Fall, 1979), pp. 45-49.

by-product of the efforts of a photographer, trained in the company of such modernists as Renger-Patzsch, to take as straightforward a documentary image as possible — his/her *Neue Sachlichkeit* 'aesthetics', however, irresistably tending to prioritise the formal.

Are these all of the possible readings of the image's genesis? Could it not, ultimately, be an intentional image of the moment, a modernist image to be sure, and one quite fitting the aesthetics of its subject? Is there no parallel to Speer's own 'unpolitical', technocratic 'neutrality', the professional doing the most competent job according to the most advanced means available? Could not the priorities of modernism be at the heart of Nazi aesthetics/politics of the visual? Not unaccompanied, as we shall see, but not separate either. Was not the first, great official Nazi rally with Speer's lights on May 1 1933 at the functionalist Tempelhof airfield — and did not the Nazis continue to use 'functionalist'/modernist buildings for industrial and military purposes? Is not this image a more devastatingly fitting one — with its bold contrasts, its essentialist simplicity, its regularity, its subjugation of time, space, motion, human intention, physical space, natural phenomena to its exploration of how light and absence of light form edges? Is not this obsessive, unequivocal directness of concern with its own means of visualisation an exact visual parallel to the structure of Nazi propaganda itself? Is this not the most accurate conceivable image of the Nazi state itself? How does this square with the notoriously anti-art, anti-modernist Nazis?[12]

Other aspects of the photograph are significant. The implied freedom of movement of the photographer: the closeness to this remote hill of power — a point of view physically possible for one of the front-line of parading troops, but the photographer's ability to move elsewhere is not shared by them. In fact only the leadership and the cameras did have freedom of movement in these precise displays, only they had the point of view which could see all — and only they could decide how to relay the spectacle through film to those not present.

But this particular image denies this movement by its own struggles for monumental stillness. It is exceptional as a photograph of a Nazi rally. Mostly, they seem to be newspaper-reportage-type images of a massive crowd, overfilling the frame, somewhat violently organised within it, shaped by the photographer into rows, or diagonals or edges, usually tied fully to a descriptive account of a moment, descriptive of time and place; inviting such captions as '*Der Fuhrer* takes the salute from SA troops during Party Day'. The photograph under analysis is, however, very like two other sorts of imagery which are definitive of Nazi propaganda: NSDAP films, such as *Triumph of Will*, and photographs of architecture.

Nazi Architecture and the Photomodern

Most of the buildings which the German public and other audiences believed were typical of Nazi architecture exist only in the form of photographs of models and of actual-size mock-up details. There were less than twenty major structures actually built, and these — with obvious exceptions such as the Autobahn — were not primarily used for their declared purposes. The New Reich Chancellery in Berlin was rarely used as a seat of government — rather, Hitler received visitors in the famous 'mile-long' hall, but officials rarely occupied the building. Rather, its function was to provide images of its exterior and interior for reproduction in the mass media as a symbol of a new kind of power. The style of photography: stark, spare, closely descriptive yet generously scaled, employing sharp and bold light/dark contrasts, expunging all from the image except the 'thing itself', an animistic aesthetic which saw the 'life' of objects/things/phenomena immanently expressed in their form. This is the style of Albert Renger-Patzsch's *The World is Beautiful* 1928 (first title: *Things*), and the style of the official NSDAP architectural photography. It is also, partly, the style of the architecture itself.

That architecture played a special role within the Nazi state is attested to by Hitler's frequent statements to this effect, such as 'Never in German history were greater and nobler buildings planned, begun and completed than in our time', and in the constant metaphor to Hitler as a builder, 'Architect of the Thousand-year Reich'. Goebbel's birthday panegyric of 20 April 1937 is instructive: a sycophantic

12. The orthodox view of the Nazis as anti-modernist barbarians (held, for example, by Lehmann-Haupt) has given way to the view that they attempted to evolve a unique 'Art of the Third Reich', deploying mostly traditional and archaic aesthetics (Berthold Hinz, *Art in the Third Reich*, New York: Pantheon, 1979). The view closest to mine is that the regime supported both modernist *and* archaic aesthetics, according to political and ideological exigencies (John Heskett, 'Modernism and Archaism in Design in the Third Reich', *Block*, 3, 1980, pp. 13-24). In the September 1942 issue of the official Nazi art magazine *Die Kunst des Dritten Reich* Particles on modern industrial architecture and the significance of engineer-architects appear alongside the presentation of Speer's plans for the new Reich Chancellery.

monstrosity, yet revealing in its arcane formality, of an ordering of powers:

> May the Fuhrer remain with us for many years yet, in power, health and strength as the standard-bearer of the people, as the first among many millions of workers, soldiers, peasants and townspeople, as the friend and protector of the young, the architect of the new unified nation.

The organisation — the ordering and spacing — of these roles is significant: it becomes inscribed in the program/schedule of the Nuremberg rallies and in the script of *Triumph of the Will*. Thus the high rhetoric of Fritz Erler's *Portrait of the Fuhrer* 1939: Hitler stands in formal pose, his hands crossed before him, modestly holding his hat and gloves, 'at ease' in his military uniform. Beneath him the stonecutter/mason/sculptor's tools of trade lie on dressed marble blocks; in the distance a colonnade at the left and, at the right, the roof of an ancient building with statuary spaced along it (the new classicism echoes the old, a Nazi colonnade paralleling a device of Roman architecture, and of, for example, Michelangelo's Campidoglio). Above Hitler stands a large sculpture of a young male athlete/warrior, sword half-raised in one hand, the eagle taking off, falcon-like, from the other. Both Fuhrer and sculpture stare out resolutely, as a new dawn breaks behind them. The fictions of the painting are not only the assimilation of Hitler to the Aryan ideal of the sculpture but also the grasping at eternity — as if Hitler could become the ideal carved above him, lasting as long as classical statuary, indeed, become a secular god; as if the new architecture of the Reich could itself be an architecture for a millenium, beautiful in a thousand years like Roman ruins are today; as if these buildings, this sculpture, this leader could lay the foundations for a permanent state, one existing in such monumental dignity forever; as if, finally, the viewer of this image could, through viewing it, through Hitler, aspire to become part of the new, eternal Reich. The irony is that the formal vocabulary of the artist (and of the NSDAP itself) is so limited that for an imagery of eternity he has chosen forms which are also the imagery of death (ancient structures devoid of people, the bird-soul departs, the statue over a tomb), that the imagery of the future here is entirely based on the imagery of the past. It is a sepulchral vision, as if the only content of the future Nazi utopia was embalmment in a permanent, very distant, past — the emptiness of a filled, unoriginal, totally unknown death.

Working Art: Purity of Surplus Value

Two elements persistently recur, suggesting chains of explanation/speculation. This statement by Hitler at Nuremberg in 1936: 'Art is the only truly enduring investment of human labour'. And a report on building methods at Nuremberg: because of the colossal size of the buildings and the relative lack of time to actually do the work, at least one of the stadia was built by means of workers following instructions issued from a loudspeaker situated in a tower specially constructed for the supervisors in the centre of the arena.[13] Is this a logical extension of Taylorist supervision of assembly-line manufacture to the building of stadia or a simple transposition of the prison and concentration camp conditions from which at least some of the workers (and nearly all of the marble and granite) came? Or is it an actualisation to an extreme of the 'modern' conception of work — work as a sequence of isolated acts, each act observed, the whole known only to management, that is work aestheticised, work as 'pure value'?

In the last chapter of his *Art in the Third Reich*, Berthold Hinz takes this up as the key to understanding Nazi aesthetics. The Nazi building program did not focus on housing, schools, not even athletic fields for the German people — rather, its major purpose was to change the appearance of the central areas of major German cities. These new buildings were meant to transcend the interest of particular groups, including the capitalists; they aimed to express the 'communality' of the German people. Few of the buildings served any useful social purpose, many were 'commemorative' (of 'German soldiers', of 'the dead', of 'early Germany' and other abstractions). All of the buildings conspicuously consumed expensive materials and entailed considerable hard labour in their construction — anachronistic, uneconomic practices hailed as securing the building's 'dignity'. In this way, Hitler pointed out, 'the people' could learn 'what community means and why their own

13. Rutherford, p. 145.

personal interests should be subordinated to a higher purpose'.[14] This points to the Nazi conception of work: in a classic capitalist move, the exchange value of work on such projects was reduced by severely restricting the wages involved. This was part of the overall restriction of both wages and consumption in the economy as a whole, which produced 'full' employment and the production of absolute surplus value.

But, at the same time, because mainly forced labour was used to procure the building materials and to construct the buildings, both the buildings and the materials in them represented direct creation of value.[15]

The cost of such labour was nowhere publicly listed or accounted: it embodied work as such, a value in itself to the Nazi State — an ideologically useful belief to those extracting surplus value from its exercise.

Accordingly, the products of such work could only be regarded as products in themselves, as monuments that were not tainted by utilitarian considerations and that only commemorated the self-realising, self-identifying labour invested in them ... The productive labour force, working in total heteronomy, was to receive the economic equivalence of its labour in the manifest autonomy symbolised by art.[16]

To return to Hitler's statement above: we now see it to mean that the consumption of individuals in labour, their self-denial/'realisation', their being consumed by the purifying ritual of labour for its own sake, was a gesture of supreme beauty, creating a state of supreme beauty — from the point of view of the controller. No wonder Hitler liked Fritz Lang's *Metropolis* — the Behemoth of the productive machinery could serve all if the Ruler and the Workers were united 'by the heart'. The 'investment' is financial, honorific and entombing — productive, ennobling and eternal/fatal. (Thus Benjamin's remarks on fascism's ability to secure the masses' aesthetic pleasure at their own death.) It was a committal of labour to work in and for itself: to which the resultant building stood as a commemoration. If the building were to have any other use, this transcendant value would be in some way compromised. Thus Nazi architecture converges with extremist, avant-garde modernism, not just in sharing a preference for lack of ornament, not only in that both regarded geometric forms as 'absolute' and 'basic', but also in allowing nothing to obscure the purity of 'art'. Hinz cites modern movement pioneer Adolf Loos:

Only a small segment of architecture can be properly classified as art: the tomb and the monument. Everything else, everything that serves a function, has no place in the realm of art.[17]

14. Nuremberg speech, September 7, 1937, cited in A. Teut, *Architektur im Dritten Reich 1933-1945* (Berlin, 1967), p. 188.

15. Hinz, p. 195; see also Jochen Thies, 'Nazi Architecture — A Blueprint for World Domination: the Last Aims of Adolf Hitler', in David Welch (ed.), *Nazi Propaganda, the Power and the Limitations* (Beckenham, Kent: Croom Helm, 1983), p. 58.

16. Hinz, p. 198.

17. 1910, in *Gesammelte Schriften* (ed. F. Gluck), volume 1, (Vienna, 1962), p. 315.

18. Hinz, p. 198.

The ultimate symbolisation in both cases is an extreme symbolism of the central life of capitalism itself: work as 'pure value', the wage-slave ascends to heaven, consumed in the purifying fire of his/her labour.

Is this the truly shocking aspect of Nazism in the realms of representation, in the arts, the aesthetic, the visual — does it constitute a pure form of the core of a major thrust in twentieth century artistic practices, does it reveal to us something shocking about the modernist quest for artistic autonomy, something usually unsayable about the 'regime of form'? Or was Hitler, and the entire Nazi public imagery enterprise, simply making a category mistake by transposing onto all work the value of the creative work of artists? Is there not a defence in the claim that the work of 'mere workers' is not at all like the work of the inspired, superlatively skilful artist? (What else is entailed by such an assumption, what is its class bias?) Modernism celebrates a certain range of imagery which may be consonant with Nazi stylistics (except that few modernists would accept the references to ancient, classical styles: although it was certainly not the **total** rejection of past styles often claimed). It celebrates the autonomy of creativity, the social separatedness of art, but it retains a Romantic emphasis on the essentiality of the inspired, individual creator. It is set against the lemming-like mass self-consumption of the Nazi program. Does its individualism save it? While the individualism of the artist-creator-leader was maintained, modernism conceived of those 'subject' to art and architecture less as individuals than had any designers, officials, etc. since the early Middle Ages. The modulor, the average, the economically predictable user are all part of its conceptual vocabulary. The difference is more that the modern movement sought an architecture which would rationalise, cohere, co-ordinate the rest of the functions performed by numbers of individuals conceived atomistically, whereas the Nazi architecture sought a similar control over numbers of individuals conceived as masses. It is not, at the time and place, a significant difference.

The Social Work of the Spectacle

We can now see the stylistic characteristics of Nazi buildings as either direct visualisations of the ideological drives we have been exploring or as means to an end of securing effectiveness. Hinz argues that the major determinant in the relatively uniform style was the first Nazi buildings themselves, such as those of Troost and Speer, implying that, in such a closed regime, the approved prototypes dominate all else.[18] But this rigidity is not so evident elsewhere in the Nazi system: rather, the approach seems to have been to purge all forms of work that did not serve the ends dimly glimpsed as central to the New Order, but, within the approved forms, some considerable energy was concentrated. Lack of plurality is not the same as uniformity.

It was the embodiment, the valorisation of work which determined the shapes, look, size, layout of the buildings. This valorisation, we can see at Nuremberg, and in the Konigsplatz in Munich. The monuments to the dead there and elsewhere, took the form of demanding a surrender to an ideal of work, of ideal work. In fact — and here I want to bring together the concepts (argued above) of the valorisation of work and of the centrality of propaganda to the Nazi state — what seems to have occurred at these heightened moments when the individual member of 'the masses', the individual 'worker', 'soldier', 'housewife', 'peasant' or whatever, **becomes** the Nazi state under the gaze of the Fuhrer is a **substitution** in which the idea of ideal work takes the place of work itself. That is, the representation becomes the highest form of that which it represents. (Hitler only sees the representation). When you are seen to represent the type who you are, when you surrender yourself to that gaze, then you 'become' the type of what you are.

This (or something like this, because it could not be **stated** as this) was recognised, indeed celebrated at the time by the aesthetician, writer on art and architecture, Schrader, in 1937:

The political soldiers focus their gaze on it [the building]. Standing together in the same posture, in the same uniform, intent on the same goal, they are bound to perceive the straight lines of the columns as an expression of the order to which they have submitted themselves. They find, expressed in stone, the same will to order that has taken possession of them as living human beings. They feel a total harmony between themselves and this architecture.[19]

Another such writer observed of the 'work soldiers', that they came to Nuremberg ... to stand before the Fuhrer. The simple precision of the white columns on the Nuremberg parade ground extended over into the orderly columns of men assembled there.[20]

Hinz acutely observes that this relationship between the buildings and the military formations drawn up before them, massed around them, passing through them, was an 'ornamental' one.[21] This was the key reason why Nazi buildings were internally unelaborated; they were conceived as part of an ensemble which was attempting a total visuality. All of the soldiers, SA and SS, 'work soldiers', peasants, youth, etc. were obliged to experience the buildings 'ornamentally', they were obliged to become ornament itself. A kind of ornamentation so simple and repetitive that anyone could substitute for them, as long as that person could 'look right' in the ensemble.

Yet this destabilising possibility was obviated by another: none of the participants could, in fact, see the spectacle as a whole. Participants could only see those around them, sense themselves as part of a multiplication of thousands of others like themselves, perhaps sense a fragment of a pattern, or feel that they might look like some reproduction of a rally seen on a postcard, poster, newsphoto or newsreel. Everybody else sees equally little — except Hitler, some of the leadership and all those who would watch the film of the rally. Film audiences include, of course, those who had been at the rally — the point being, however, that they could only see it reproduced as an edited representation. It is a surrender of point-of-view, of visibility itself, to the leader.

It is in the reproducibility of Nazi rallies, parades, meetings, monuments, architecture and insignia imagery that their deepest meaning lies. They were made to be reproduced and repeated so as to secure a mass following. The huge buildings meant to stand for a widespread, triumphal society; the marching masses and rituals of the spectacles were meant to represent the total mass of the German population. As constantly reproduced through the mass media, this message seemed more and more to define reality. But, crucially, the consent being sought and reinforced was consent to the idea of being part of the Nazi spectacle, part of this fictive, propaganda representation of the 'Nazi state'. A fiction which could only be maintained by constant repetition, reproduction, by ever more elaborated, more aesthetic representations.

Such a regime — constantly under pressure from the demands of the monopolists it chiefly served, the demands of the petty bourgeoisie who most wholeheartedly supported it, the constant threat of working class agitation, the uncertainty about the loyalty of the army, the doubts of the liberals and (some) technocrats, pressure from other nations as well as internal contradictions in all aspects of policy — such a regime is clearly both illegitimate and unstable. It was also criminal in its repression of workers, minority groups and dissidents. Illegitimacy and criminality were perpetuated primarily through closing down options, more terror and by external aggression, but the chief means of their ideological covering was aesthetic. We are asking just how central was this process of aestheticisation, and what was the role of visual media within it. Let us go, then, to the central point of vision within the Nazi regime and ask: what did Hitler see?

What the Leader Saw

The later Nazi parades and rallies were prodigiously controlled, neat, lucid — their visual clarity, co-ordinated by Speer, was a sophistication of what tended to be a more crowded, teeming, overwhelming accumulation of numbers in earlier Nazi rallies. It is the visual clarity of abstract, non-objective painting — a constructivist geometry. A massing of colours, line and shape into a compositional form of which

19. H. Schrader, *Bauten des Dritten Reich* (Leipzig 1937), p. 19.

20. H. Fischer, in *Kunst im Dritten Reich*, 7 (1943), p. 77.

21. Hinz, p. 199. The originator of this observation is Siegfried Kracauer in *From Caligari to Hitler* (Princeton University Press, 1947), pp. 94-95, 301-302, 'The Mass Ornament', *Frankfurter Zeitung*, July 9 and 10, 1927 (translation in *New German Critique*, 5, Spring 1975, pp. 67-76), and an unpublished report of 1936 to the Frankfurt Institute for Social Research 'Masse und Propaganda' (see Karsten Witte, 'Introduction to Kracauer', *New German Critique*, ibid. p. 62). This last contains the key ideas presented here.

22 WAR/MASCULINITY

Hitler could see himself as the artist. It was the compressing of men and women into the shapes required by visual clarity, by artistic logic, by lucidity. It was the organisation of people so that they could be seen. But how? And by whom?

There are, in fact, surprisingly few records of rallies taken from Hitler's point-of-view. One photograph of a rally of the SA at Dortmund in 1933 is taken from behind Hitler, showing him leaning casually on the railing as the troops settle into place on the sportsground below.[22] It seems to be a snapshot by a member of the official party — a rarely repeated occurrence. Some photographs are clearly from the reviewing stand but most are near, at the side or, most often, looking up towards the reviewing stand. How many and which of the point-of-view shots in *Triumph of the Will* were shots 'through Hitler's eyes'? They are few but significant. Near the beginning of the film, the dark clouds part, light floods the sky and Hitler's plane appears. Then, 'we' look down upon the ancient city of Nuremberg, 'we' cast a friendly eye over the crowds lining the streets below, 'we' see a city looking up in homage. The camera eye becomes 'ours', and then — 'breathless clearing!' — we see what Hitler sees! Then the sequence of swift shots of close-ups of the waiting crowds, running the usual range of types (old and young, men and women, soldiers, workers, peasants, etc.) restores the audience to where they 'are' (their primary definition in the film) so that they can properly greet the figure of Hitler as he steps out of the plane[23]

22. Rutherford, p. 129. This snap precedes the decimation of the SA, just as *Triumph of the Will* succeeds that moment.

23. See the 'Outline' in Richard A. Maynard, *Propaganda on Film: A Nation at War* (Rochelle Park, N.J.: Hayden, 1975), p. 29.

In an important sense, it does not matter precisely what Adolf Hitler himself saw at these rallies. He may have been dazzled by them, and, in a way, have seen 'nothing'. This would match the limited field of vision of the massed participants. Both are instances of a kind of blindness at the point of apparently total visibility — a tremendous, detailed, totalising effort to fill the senses (especially the visual) results in sensual deprivation: the paradox of such fierce reductions, such rigid singularity. The rallies, the heights of an entirely constructed vitality, become a case

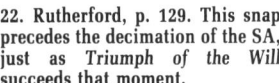

of the blind seeing the blind. And we can generalise this result for the cinema audiences of the weekly newsfilms, and *Triumph of the Will* and *Olympia*: the hypnotic rejection of a saturated visual environment, after the excitement or the terror subsides, induces a sense of solemn drift (for the committed) or impatient boredom (for the uncommitted).

In another sense, what Adolf Hitler saw is inconsequential: the entire ensemble achieves its logic as long as there is someone looking out from the rostrum. Not, of course, anyone, but rather a Seer, a leader, an eye of power: some idea/ideal/god/presence/thing with power over the lives of all those looking back. This is not implied surveillance, this is seeing and being seen in the full glare of conditions of the utmost visibility, with an unprecedented amount of electric light (the Nuremberg rallies were reportedly visible at Frankfurt, over 100 miles away), and an unprecedented audience through the media. The exchange seems to have been something like: the power of these people assembled, concentrated and co-ordinated, focused upon the leader, empowering (charging) him to a condition of . . . translucency, so bright that he could light up everybody present. Hitler was also the least 'decorated', least 'uniformed' of those present — also the only hatless one: the very paucity of signifying codes in the figure who was the central focus of all eyes implied that their presence invested/dressed him with their colouration.

What Hitler actually said on these occasions was probably not heard by most (although the rhythms of his speech were perceptible) and what the participants **did**, was minimal. What was crucial was that both Hitler and 'the people' **saw** each other, and that they were seen to be doing so by all those not present who saw a newsreel, photograph or film, or heard it described on a radio broadcast. The crystal-clear structure, the hierarchy (a bottom layer divided according to loyalty, productivity and region; middle layers of officialdom, party functionaries, army officers, etc., up to the pinnacle) was visibly laid out on these occasions, like a design in the centre of a carpet, a map, a pyramid. Hitler's power was symbolised in the very layout of the rally: he was the visual focus of all the events ('eyes right' during the marches past, 'eyes forward' during the rallies) and he could see more than anybody else, he could see **over** everyone — in fact, oversee them, see **all**. And he spoke of his vision, the Seer, the Artist-Fuhrer.

WAR/MASCULINITY

24. H. Rauschning, *Voice of Destruction*, (NY 1940: London, 1939 as *Hitler Speaks*); cited in Fest, p. 447.

One final structural feature of these rallies: the simplicity of the imagery and its repetition, the division of the masses into simple sections, the lucid, step-by-step pyramid of power from the individuals at the base to the single individual at the top, all of these structures operated to include certain people within the Nazi state, to energize their devotion to it, to stimulate their work for it as well as to make its structure visible to them. But all of these structures also served to exclude certain people, attitudes, beliefs, behaviours, and representations from the Nazi state. This meant excluding them from the Nazi-defined 'German people' and, as the regime developed its power on the streets and internationally, it meant excluding certain workers, Communists, Jews, homosexuals, dissidents, peoples from the Central European states, as well as those beaten in war or terrorised during occupation, not only from the State, the 'German people' but from 'humanity' itself. Those defined outside commitment, productivity or region were enslaved, dead.

Thus Hitler's other global image of the future — the four 'classes': the National Socialist high aristocracy 'tempered by battle'; the hierarchy of party members forming 'the new middle class'; then 'the great mass of the anonymous, the serving collective, the eternally disenfranchised'; and finally 'the class of subject alien races; we need not hesitate to call them the modern slave class'.[24] This 'vision' takes the absolute division of mental and manual labour stratified in Lang's *Metropolis* but then elaborates it. Not through an imaginary 'harmony' of capital and labour, but through an ideological ('Spiritual') resolution, ostensibly above economics. The 'mental' is divided into those with the 'vision', the 'purity' to transcend the manual through 'battle' and 'will'; and those who would carry out the running of the state. The 'manual' is divided between those who 'consent' to work within this system, those who seem to be 'just there' but are nonetheless Germans, entitled to be part of the state; and the excluded, the foreign, the racially inferior, the sub-human. It is a vision unspecific about the role of capital (presumably party-controlled, a 'middle-class' function); in it men are the only means of production; and it is anti-bourgeois in that it is essentially static.

Hitler's vision is a layout, a stratification which lies at the basis of the actual design of the Nazi rallies. It is what their form points to: arranged before the eyes of the leadership (itself set out across the vision of those before it) were the party functionaries, then 'the great mass of the anonymous, the serving collective', all sorted out and uniformed according to their function, their location, their degree of belief. Excluded from the rallies, from the sight of the German people, were the 'alien races' labouring in hidden, 'subterranean' places. When the Fuhrer speaks, the whole ensemble stops moving, all its relationships laid bare, open to the sight of the leader and the camera, all locked into place, forever. Until 'he' energises it through his own speech, movements, look — it moves until it can be brought again before him, in stasis, the 'ideal' sight — a quintessential (single) visual image.

Hitler's insight, that 'the most brilliant propaganda technique must confine itself to a few points and repeat them over and over' (*Mein Kampf*), was applied to the way the Nazi State was organised. Indeed, I have argued that it was — or, at least during its many points of self-representation such as the rallies, became for a time — a political constitution of propaganda itself. The aim of this argument is not to reduce the complexities of effect during this period to a single bogey, a disease which can be isolated and destroyed. It is to underscore the centrality of (particularly visual) propaganda as a means which the Nazi regime used to further its ends in the service of German monopoly capital. It is to say that, to an unusual degree, the Nazi state was substantively present in the minds of its controllers and its subjects as a self-signifying system; that participation in it often amounted to little more than participation in various concrete processes of propagating the NSDAP and the 'Third Reich', in disseminating, witnessing, being part of the representations of the Nazi state and ideology; that the dictates of the effective visual propaganda influenced Nazi policy more and more; that the particular forms of Nazi propaganda — its quest for a simple, unified, glorious and 'German' totality — obliterated complexities and contradictions in the perception of both Nazi leadership and its subjects, enabling them to practice their exclusions, persecutions and genocides with impunity.

Throughout the 'days of struggle', during early 1933, at those moments when the NSDAP was at its weakest and most vulnerable, its superior propaganda held the day, yielding results inconceivable without it. The remarks of Hitler, but especially Goebbels, during this period are replete with exultant, gloating surprise that they have 'gotten away with' a risky, dangerously provocative lie. This sort of success clearly fed on itself, especially when institutionalised in the ways already described. Controlling representation usually meant controlling reality — especially if you had the force to insist on the accuracy of your definition and were evidently prepared to use it. Controlling the representations of itself, of all the social relations within itself, and of how they related to other representations and other states, became a major, definitive function of the Nazi state.

Simplicity and repetition, saturation and totality, clarity and lucidity: the values of social control, capitalist labour, propaganda and modern art meet. The Nuremberg rally, the newsreel, and *Triumph of the Will* become the most apt symbolisations, the clearest expressions, the most typical images of the Nazi state. And, for those who submit themselves to them, the rallies and films become the Nazi state itself — for a moment, an oft-remembered definitive moment, a moment which positions one as a participant, a victim or an opponent of the Nazi state.

A number of questions about Nazi war culture remain. A whole range of questions concerning the social construction of visual representation have been provoked by this analysis. There are, for example, questions about sites of ideological negotiation which Nazi imagery seems to render relatively subsidiary: the family; the factory; relations between city work and agricultural work. These are sites with which Nazi imagery was crucially concerned, but the sign systems through which it negotiated them were public in a different way to the rallies or were sourced differently: for example, the 'New Aryan Body' was sited in the athletics arena, the camp, the youth league and in the more restricted audiences for art. Here, too, sexuality was reshaped, unleashed and stiffened again. Visually, this seems to have been figured most in art, and in the massively disseminated reproductions of paintings and sculptures. These have played a minor role in this account, because they have been studied by others, yet clearly they are of major significance, especially when articulated within the broader structure of social signing which I have been attempting to map. They play out the dramatics of a gendered sexuality being gradually de-gendered until it is available for transcendence through the larger signifying system sketched here. At the spiritual heart of masculine war culture — at the moment of the death of the hero — occurs a passage through the feminine, through adolescence, to . . .

Nazi *Totenturme* (memorial towers) and the arrested erotics of much Third Reich sculpture point this way. As does an extraordinary image at the heart of Australian war culture: the figure of *Sacrifice* at the core of the Anzac Memorial, Hyde Park, Sydney.

Thanks to Mick Carter for advice and encouragement.

SUBSCRIBE!

I would like to subscribe to six editions of ALR.

Name...

Address...

....Postcode...........

Australian Left Review, P.O. Box A247,
Sydney South. 2000.

Rates: *Six issues for $12 employed, $20 libraries and institutions and $8 low income earners.*

OUT NOW

STAGING THE BASES: SCENARIOS FOR DESTRUCTION 1963-74

Noel Sanders

Methods that have real expectations of success are classified, and methods that have little possibility of success are advertised.
　　　　　　　　　Edward Teller on Star Wars, 1985.

The strongest images we have of U.S. bases are of their peripheries. Footage of protests at Greenham Common or the recent **Pine Gap Images** alternately shows women weaving fabric into perimeter fences, or executing processions and graceful, ritualised movements as convoys leave the gates. Our view is from the sidelines, along the circumference of the central but centreless discourse called 'the bases'.

To the periphery, the incoherent glimpse or the visual props — the puffball radomes of Pine Gap, whose function is only to protect the equipment inside from the weather and from prying eyes, for instance — are *tableaux*: what we see is what **prevents** us from seeing. In all this stagecraft, the piece that most (or least) gives a hint of the bases' relationship to Australia is the one contained in Article 13 of the North West Cape Agreement of 7 May 1963, that

the Australian flag will be flown on a separate and adjacent flagstaff whenever the United States flag is flown at the station.[1]

The *mis en scene* of the bases, with their visible facades and invisible contents, confronts the spectator with a 'traditional' problem: the movement '*Per visibilia ad invisibilia*' (*Romans* i, 20). The bases' own technology, however, is in the newer tradition of radar or the high definition cameras of the satellites themselves: they are '**invisible weapons which (nevertheless) render visible**', as Paul Virilio[2] has it. Invisible as they (nevertheless) are, they conform to the technology of camouflage or the blackout. Spectators are, then, 'enemy', or explorers of alien territory — a *terra incognita* within *Terra Incognita*.

1. Millar, T.B., *Australia in Peace and War*, ANU, 1969, Appendix 9 (NW Cape Agreement), p. 475, also *SMH* July 2, 1969.

2. Virilio, P., 'Guerre et Cinema I: Logistique de la Perception', *Cahiers du Cinema*, Edition de l'Etoile, Paris, 1984, p. 125.

The Bases and their 'Theatre'

For a mountain to play the role of Mount Analogue, I concluded, its summit must be inaccessible, but its base accessible ... The door to the invisible must be visible.[3]

Mount Analogue, in Rene Daumal's 1944 *conte philosophique* of the same name, is an island 'perhaps as big as Australia'[4] that a group of *savants* and eccentrics set out to find. Because, they reason, 'everything takes place as if Mount Analogue did not exist', then it could not **not** exist. Such are the promises of their voyage of discovery. In the time (and space) warp of their *libido sciendi*, their mental map becomes that of a **spiritual** journey: entering through the 'door of the visible', they attain to invisible spaces — heights, summits.

On the one hand, the mode of approach to the visible takes in the time-proven logistical desires of the 'commander' of former times: the person who understands quantities, forces and materials. On the other hand, the commander transcends these by an **interior** (akin to spiritual) vision: in the words of a military strategist of the 20s, J. Holland Rose:

The warrior's foresight is merely imagination raised to the nth degree by the fire of genius. It is never divorced from actuality; but working upon ascertained facts, it fuses them into an intellectual effort which soars above actuality.[5]

(In this sense, the diabolical inspiration of Reagan's harnessing of the Lucas *Star Wars* space opera to the 'Strategic Defense Initiatives' further reduces the spectator's view to that of cinema-goer, but taking in along the way an extension of the Duke of Wellington's desire to 'find out what the enemy is doing on the other side of the hill').

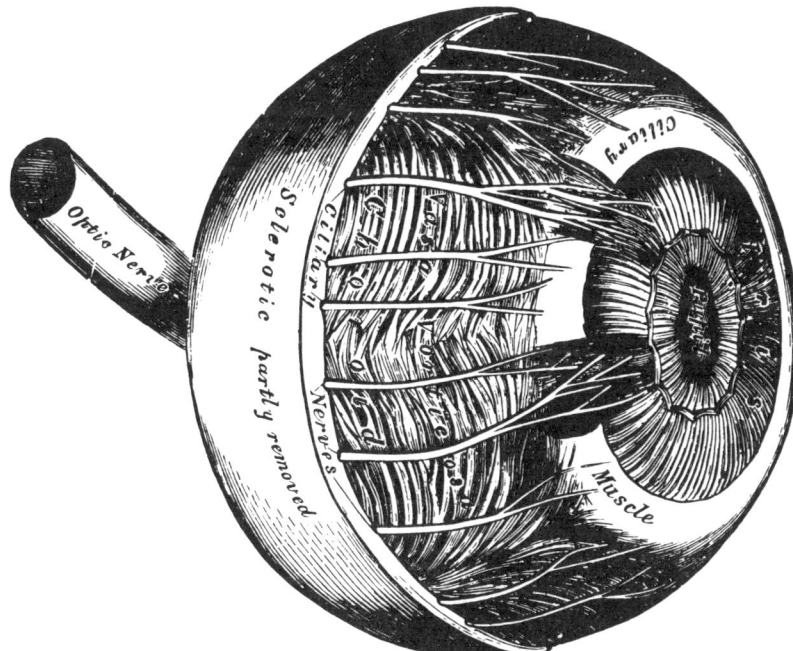

Traditional mythologies of seeing the invisible 'depths' from the visible heights are likewise as much the *pabulum* of military logistics as they are of Mosaic or Olympian 'divinity'. 'Seeing' attains, in both cases, to an excessive register: **of seeing what cannot be seen.** For a strategist like von Clausewitz, writing in the 1820s, the psychological component of height is essential:

Of these elements (advantage, elevation, view) is composed the power of dominating, overlooking, commanding; from these sources springs the sense of superiority and security which is felt in standing on the brow of a hill and looking at the enemy below, and the feeling of weakness and apprehension of those below.[6]

3. Daumal, R., *Mount Analogue*, Penguin, Baltimore, 1974, p. 46.

4. ibid, p. 62.

5. Rose, J.H., *The Indecisiveness of Modern War*, Kennikat, 1927, p. 154.

6. von Clausewitz, D., *On War*, RKP, 1968, Vol. 2, p. 127.

The strategy is not unfamiliar: it is as common to Keats' feeling in 'On first looking into Chapman's Homer' (1817), of being

> ... like some watcher out of the skies
> When a new planet swims into his ken;
> Or like stout Cortez when with eagle eyes
> He stared at the Pacific — and all his men
> Look'd at each other with a wild surmise —
> Silent, upon a peak in Darien

as it is for the modern-day TV viewer or film-goer similarly set in 'dominant specularity' (McCabe) over global and extraterrestial events (real or fictional). Invocations to viewers and readers to 'reach for the stars' through everything from science-fiction books and movies to Flying Doctor and Kingsford Smith telemegaseries have the same effect: the transformation of the temporary command of (fictional) heights into ersatz and momentary 'superiority', along the lines of von Clausewitz's 'commander'. But only under condition that the **actual** advantage commanded by the commander be traded in for an essentially **spiritual**, ideological and imaginary experience of such power.

Steven Spielberg's 'Neary' character in Close Encounters of the Third Kind is cast as a figure in these manoeuvres. Going off to Saturday work, he is 'trying to organise enough of himself to at least get the shaver working'. As he squirts the glob of Rapid Shave into his hand, he starts (unaccountably) to shape a mountain with the middle finger of his left hand:

'No, that's not right,' Neary said to himself, not really conscious of what he was doing or saying. But this image reminded him of something — something maddeningly out of mental reach — he knew this shape so well and yet it felt as if the connection was a million miles away. Neary blinked, a little distressed. Everybody experiences something like this he thought — a moment, an image that seems so familiar ...[7]

Perhaps an image of power, of himself exerting it in the work he is about to undertake (hence the shaving cream), the mountain takes on the form of the near-and-far-at-once or of the Vedantic vision (which also informs Daumal's text) of the descending divine meeting of the ascending human. Nearby (Neary is a Very Significant Name), Jillian is also drawing mountains, 'terribly tall and thin, needly and distorted like one of those desert spires formed when wind and sand have eaten away the softer stone to lay bare the **core spout of harder lava that formed the ancient throat of a volcano**'.[8]

7. Spielberg, S., *Close Encounters of the Third Kind*, Sphere Books, 1978, p. 89.

8. ibid, p. 108.

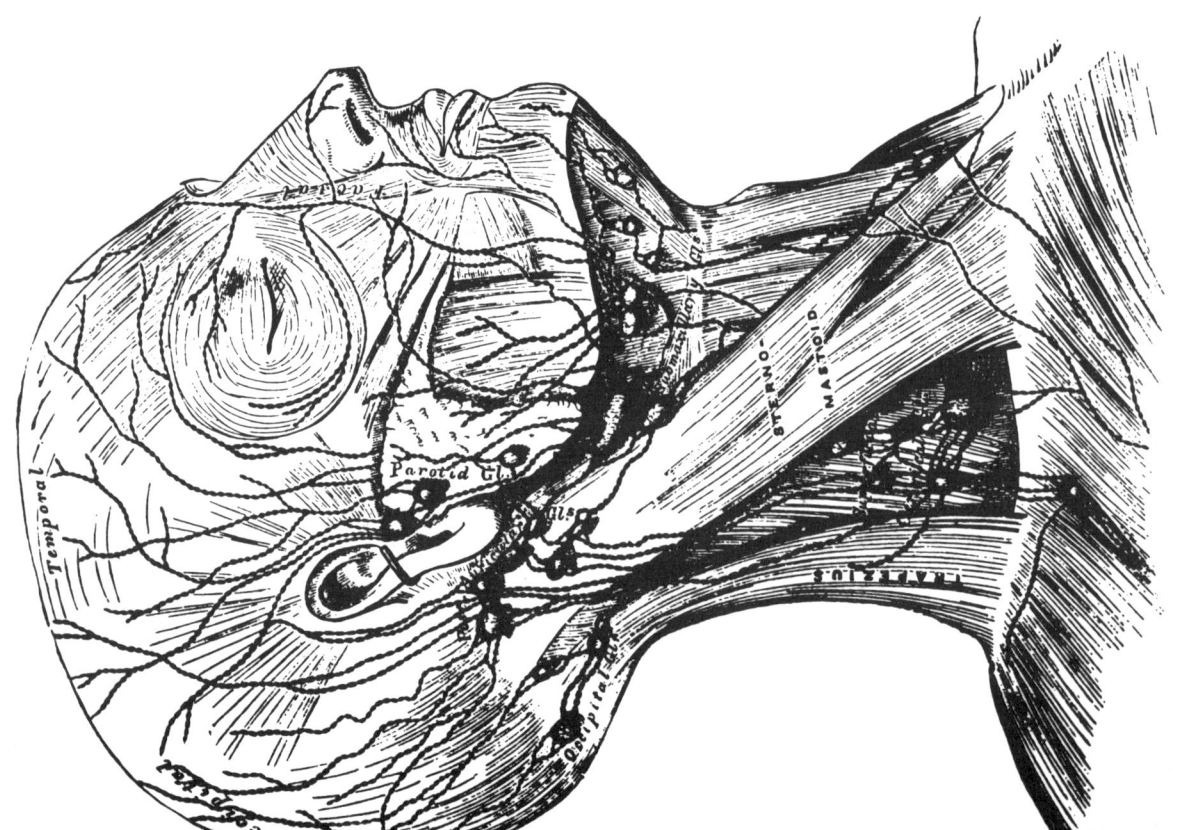

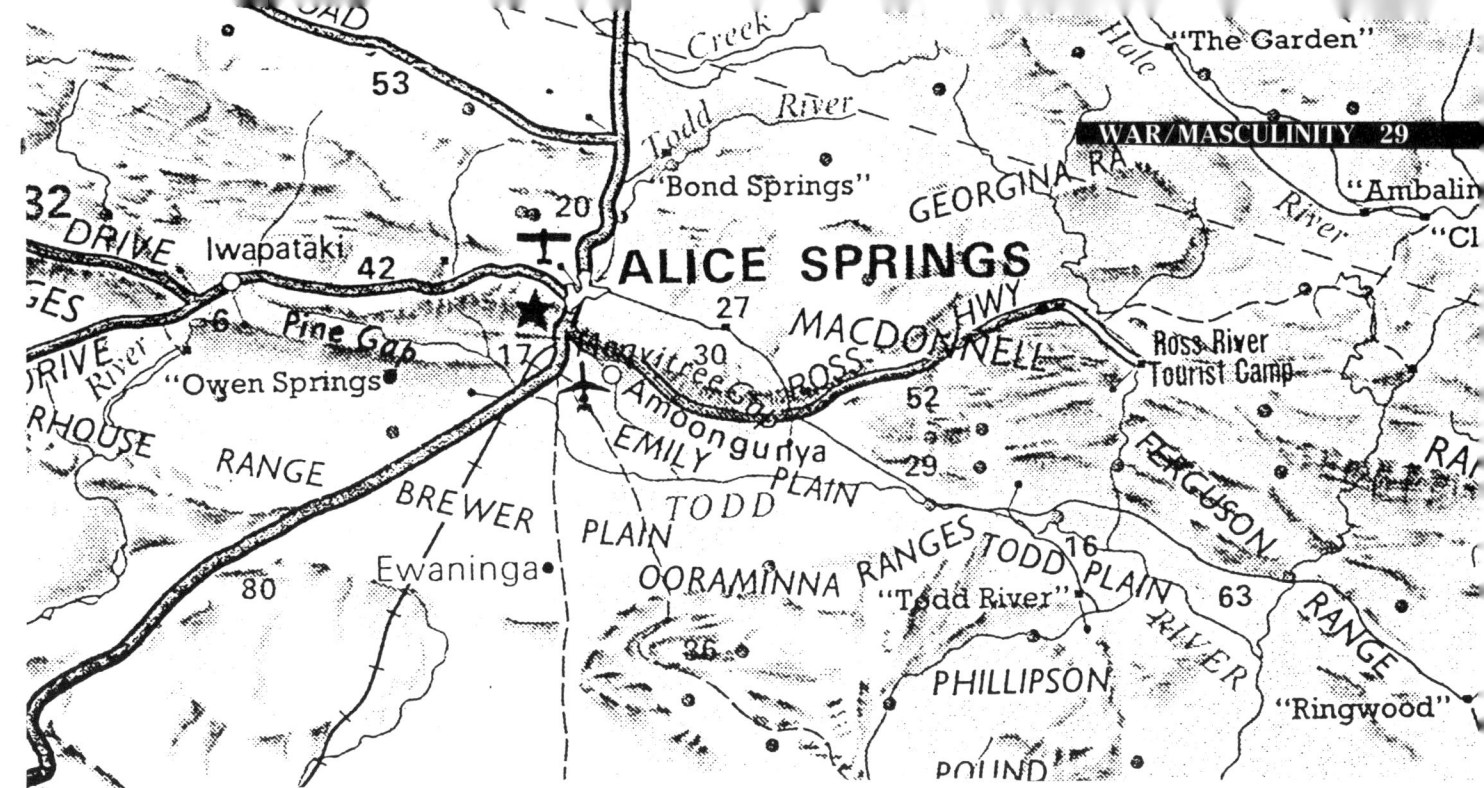

The mountain here is not just any old mountain, but a mountain that has depths — the core of a volcano spewing lava up through it, the image of source and the image of the visible (lava) through which the invisible can be traced (ancient power, ancient fire). In the recent film *The Falcon and The Snowman*, it is the Project Rhyolite information that Chris Boyce is most irked by. Project Rhyolite 'is a multi-purpose covert electronic surveillance system' operating through 'major ground stations in Australia'.[9] Along with another program that Boyce found operating in Australia (AR — Advanced Rhyolite, or Argus, which 'in Greek mythology ... was a giant with one hundred eyes ... a vigilant guardian'), Project Rhyolite suggests a vertical, mountain-creating geological process — a place of vantage created by igneous upwelling. The *OED* defines 'rhyolite' as 'fine-grained granite', from GK. *rhuax* lavastream plus *lithos* stone: just as Neary in *Close Encounters* piles mashed potatoes, shaving cream and plasticene into mountainous shapes in his 'need to ... to make this thing',[10] and as Jillian paints 'always the same picture over and over again ... A mountain, nor a range of mountains, with valleys and canyons, but just this one mountain ... with harshly grained sides',[11] so Chris Boyce is initiated into the 'black world' of surveillance with its 'birds' (satellites, falcons) feeding material down into Pine Gap, and, from his own subterranean, invisible place in the Black Vault, builds up his own 'picture'.

Mount Analogue, Daumal's *savants* think, is the antipode of where they plan their expedition:

'Wonderful,' cried Cicoria, the Hegelian tailor. 'I follow you now ... Mount Analogue is located at the antipodes of this region, which puts it ... wait a minute while I work it out ... here, southeast of Tasmania and southwest of New Zealand, west of the island of Auckland ...[12]

From their 'visible' place of entry into the quest for the 'invisible', they plan a catalepsis of which the bases are the Virilian reverse: the visible made so by invisible means.

Popular conspiracy theory like Stan and Louise Deyo's *Cosmic Conspiracy* makes much of the idea that the North American Air Defence Command (NORAD) is buried a mile under Cheyenne Mountain in Colorado, and then goes on to suggest that its antipode may be a VLF transmitter operated by the U.S. at the South Pole (making a huge Tesla transmitter):

[Furthermore] one wonders even more about the antipodes of the Pine Gap and North West Cape transmitters. The Pine Gap transmitter sits very near the Tropic of Capricorn and its antipode is directly in the middle of the Bermuda Triangle ...[13]

9. Lindsey, R., *The Falcon and The Snowman*, Penguin, 1981/5, p. 60.

10. Spielberg, op. cit., p. 151.

11. ibid, p. 128.

12. Daumal, op. cit., p. 70.

13. Deyo, S. and L., *The Cosmic Conspiracy*, West Australian Texas Trading, 1978, p. 42.

Pine Gap, in particular, inspires the Deyo's to conjecture that, *a la* Cheyenne Mountain, 'nearby to the obvious Pine Gap facility in an underground, man-made city of multiple levels ... [is] the real 'Pine Gap Facility'.[14] The Deyo's system of conjecture, whacky as it might be, is common to all forms of conjecture from the 'periphery' of the bases — to proliferate possible plausibilities, but at the same time endlessly re-arrange the *tableaux* that stage the bases' existence, thus ensuring both their intangibility and their seductiveness as 'secrets'. As with UFO's, the more spurious conjecture that surrounds them, the more the idea of their actual existence persists, aided by their visibility only as theatre. As the antipode of knowledge they perform one of the most mystical functions of hegemony — the 'refusal to confirm or deny' that produces Pine Gap (that 'picturesquely named spot', as Robert Cooksey[15] wrote in 1968) not as a mountain but, as its name metaphorically implies, a gap: a prevention of all discourses but the peripheral ones along the perimeters of the sort of 'knowing' that would give the bases the status of 'existence'. As with Mount Analogue, we know only what they cannot not be.

'Sovereignty', Culture and Control

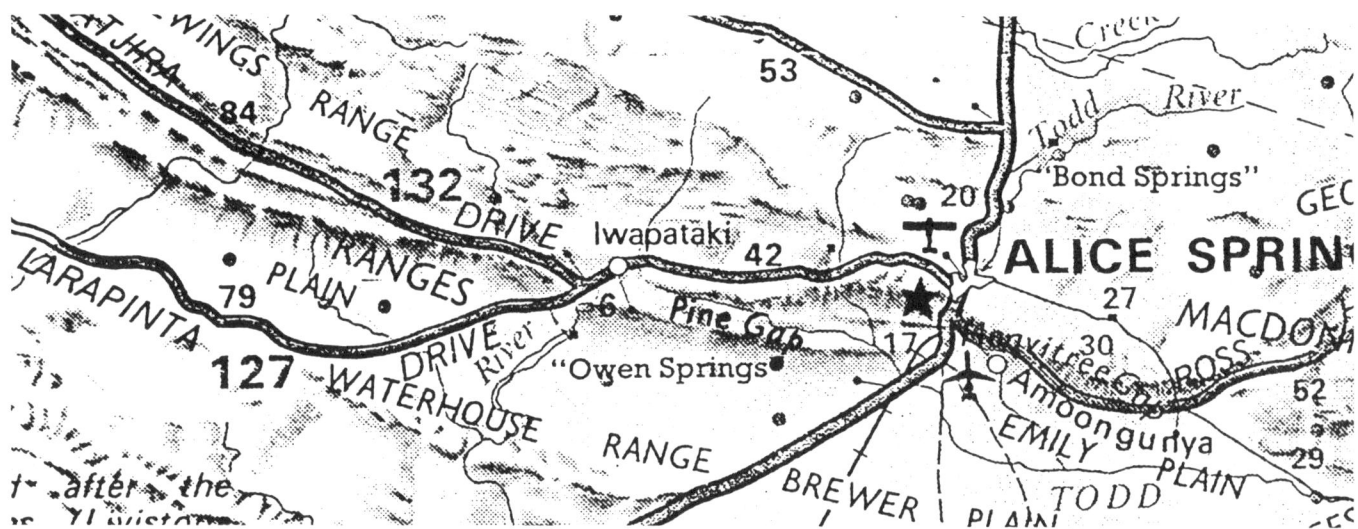

The film version of *The Falcon and The Snowman* has a scene that is not in Robert Lindsey's 1979 book of the same name: Hollywood's way of producing 'revelation' by referring to its own status as historical memory. The scene is of Chris Boyce's political epiphany, not in the seminary which he has renounced, but in a bar. On the TV news Boyce sees an item telling him that Whitlam has been sacked, and it is a moment that confirms his 'worst fears'. Yet these fears, for which Boyce in both the book and the film is the single historical source, had been a major topic in popular media and political discourses in Australia for the ten years intervening between Boyce's 'moment of truth' and the setting up of North West Cape in 1963. At the same time, Hollywood's mania for 'discovery' (its self-appointed role as explorer, historian or ethnographer) seems to be a weird apotheosis of the whole 'staging' process of the bases. In this sense alone, it is singularly apt for Hollywood to fulfil the ultimate fictionalising function. In the *Right Stuff*, a scene of sparks rising from the camp fire of a group of Aborigines sitting at night outside a U.S. observation base mystically signifies a propititious outcome for an American Space Flight as the space vehicle passes overhead. And in similar (but different) vein, it is the 'secret ' precincts of Aboriginal life and territory that are the catalysts for Boyce's political awakening:

The continual disclosures about the secret world fascinated Chris, and he was especially intrigued by what he saw as a bizarre contrast between the mechanical spies ... and the location of the ground stations. The Rhyolite earth stations had been placed as close as man could find now to The Stone Age; they were situated near Alice Springs in the harsh Outback of Australia, an oasis in a desert where Aborigines still lived much as Stone Age men did thousands of years ago.[16]

14. ibid, p. 24.

15. Cooksey, R., 'Pine Gap', *The Australian Quarterly*, December 1968.

16. Lindsey, op. cit., p. 68.

This uncanny alignment of cultural extremes comes up later too when Lindsey's text refers to satellites as having become 'as indispensable to modern generals as spears were to ancient warriors'.[17] The comparison is in the grand manner of popular historiography, and the elision it makes is familiar: since modern weapons technology is so 'secret', unthinkable both in its complexities and consequences, appropriately picturesque 'cosmic' metaphors of deterritorialisation (in the pop-sublime register) must be found to speak about the extraterrestrialisation of the nuclear weapons industry. (*Star Wars* with its revolt of the orphan Luke Skywalker against the Empire is one of many examples). In drawing on Aboriginal culture as the last post of the 'mystical' (rather than its political and social reality) Hollywood may be doing nothing more than what Virilio calls 'the militarisation of the hidden, the conscription of the unknown, [in which] the invisible is requisitioned in the service of the state'.[18]

The Hollywood rendition of the bases in Australia is, however, not just a determined outcome of its own practices, but the outcome also of (at least) two hundred years of the elaboration of the discourse on 'bases'. Against arguments that the U.S. installations in Australia are not really bases at all, it may be salutary to remember

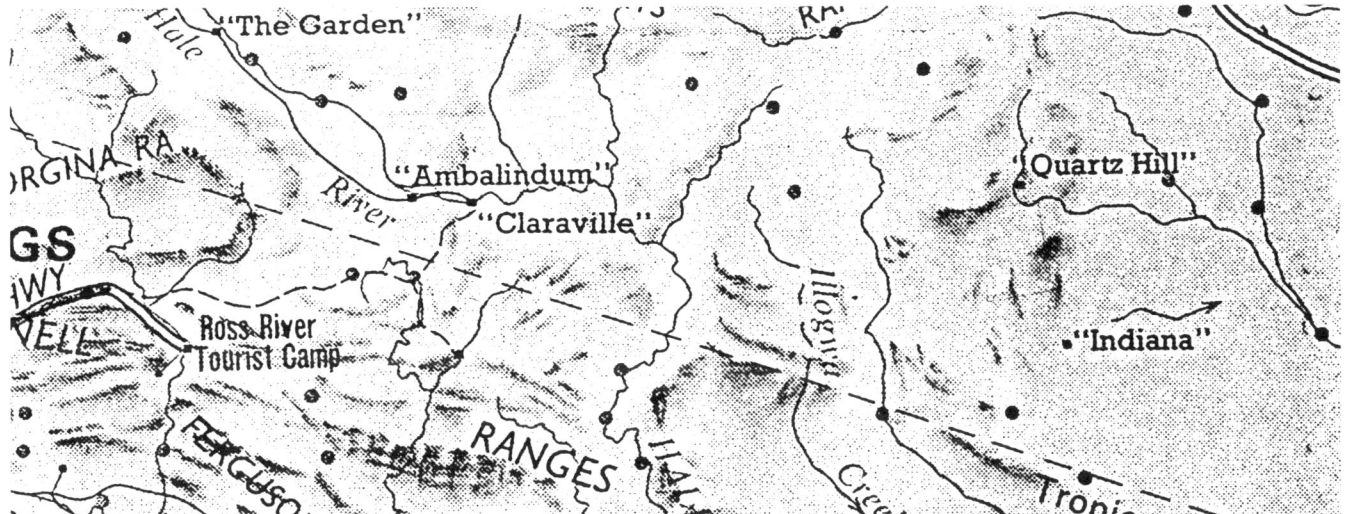

that at least since the Napoleonic wars, establishing a base has meant not only setting up a fortified outpost, an acquiescent government and assured lines of communication and supply from 'home-base', but also the **seduction of the culture** in which the base is situated.

In the modern history of bases, appeals to atrophied and sentimental notions of the 'host' culture's national self-respect, the recruitment of a 'national-popular' elite of 'organic' intellectuals to germinate 'discussion' on the bases' presence, and the cranking-up of discourses about 'sovereignty' all create the illusion that the host shares the interests of the parasite culture but places its own interests first — and hence that it is the host (rather than the parasite) that benefits most. One of the first perfectors of this strategy of interpretation of 'base' was Napoleon himself. Unlike the Roman Empire, the Napoleonic version sought to set up bases that were not geographically contingent with its territory, and where the problem then became to mine out a form of **ideological** contiguity as a substitute. At the height of his campaign into Egypt in 1798, Napoleon put his efforts into establishing Malta as a base using cultural, political and military means, considered as equally important. Malta was *le sud du sud*, backed up by the illusion of a defence of Maltese culture **via** a risky comparison with the allegiance to his own (French) roots in the declaration that 'I would rather see the British on the heights of Montmartre than in Malta'.[19]

All this sudden caring might have been a big surprise to the Maltese, had it not been

17. ibid, p. 76.

18. Virilio, P., 'The Aesthetic of Disappearance', *Frogger*, March 1985.

19. Hughes, Q., *Fortress: Architecture and Military History in Malta*, Lund Humphries, 1969, p. 230.

for the fact that Napoleon was intervening in an essentially **domestic** crisis. In 1798, Malta had been ruled for the last 270 years by the squattocratic Knights of Malta, and saw a possibility of liberation from them, under the aegis of the French revolutionary spirit. Yet the real winners were the British. By 1802, the French were ejected, and a new strategem in base establishment occurred with British occupation of the island in that year. As J. Holland Rose wrote:

> The outstanding fact is that the British government did not annex the island. It sought to restore the old order of things there (the Knights) and reform it from within while mapping it from without.[20]

It is not unthinkable that a similar scenario was played out in Australia in 1963. In 1963, employment and production were on the up, but it was still election year, and historiography usually converges on the opinion that Menzies managed to fight and win the 1963 election on letting our great and powerful ally in to set up North West Cape. But along the way Menzies, as well the U.S., was able to trigger off a discussion that has lasted now for twenty years — one which in the political arena furthers the impossibility of discussing the **existence** of the bases on Australian soil and detours discussion into squabbles over 'joint control'. Apart from operating a 'more Australian than thou' brawl in 1963 (which Menzies won), the issue had the effect of further splitting the ALP, with Calwell and the right wing being cast as the main proponents of 'joint control', and leaving the left to munch on the complexities of arguing against the base being here at all. As a result the argument with which the ALP entered the 1963 election was based on an essentially **nationalist** rejoinder to Menzies' **gung ho**: namely, on the slight of not being recognised as an equal partner with the U.S. (thus the two flagpoles) in the anti-communist alliance. On the other side of the argument, sovereignty became a question of security, allowing the ALP's critics to characterise its demands as a breach in the alliance's defences, and, by implication, a default of national pride:

> To seek, as Labor does, joint control with the U.S. in operation [of North West Cape] would be to diminish the effectiveness of the base as a link with the U.S.'s defence chain.[21]

As a classic ruse, this strategy owes its power to historical precedent. To get 'host' countries in dire argument about who is more 'Australian' than who is at least an effective displacement of what is essentially a global class struggle; but more specifically, it enables a rhetorical slippage to occur whose main purpose is to lasso and corral the arguments of the left, alternately casting them as treason or, more effectively, as, 'in fact', the true historical intentions of the right. Thus Sir Francis Pym's characterisation of the Tory party in the U.K. in 1983 as 'the peace party', or Thatcher's of NATO as 'the major force for peace in the last 30 years' (both of which ventriloquise CND positions) or, indeed, Reagan's disingenuous 'zero option' proposals of 1983 — also a present from CND. It is also salutary (if scary) to witness the same divisive strategy being borne out in a recent pamphlet by E.P. Thompson, *The Defence of Britain*. Here, Thompson takes the bait by offering 'the choice between two Britains': on the one hand, the Britain of country lanes and the antique tranquillity that Thompson drives through on his way to a rally in Wales; on the other, the ugly one where the unsightly landscape is pockmarked by missile silos. To discriminate between the two, Thompson is forced to revive the spectre of Winston Churchill for comparison with Thatcher's un-British, gutlessness on the matter of the 'dual key' approach to the operation of U.S. bases in the U.K.:

> Churchill was gravely dissatisfied with [the U.S.-U.K. agreement] because it laid down conditions, not for 'joint decision', but for 'joint consultation'. And I have little doubt that if the real Winston Churchill were authorising the basing of a fearful new generation of foreign-owned weaponry upon our territory ... then he would very certainly have ordered a double key, and he would have worn their key on his watch-chain.[22]

The key term here (apart from the sycophantic reference to the watch-chain) is '**our** territory': the discursive register is indisputably nationalist, circumventing any possibility of construal in terms of class or capital. In an unfortunate way, the casting of anti-nuclear, anti-bases discourses in this mould is the triumph of the U.S. position. In Australia, part of the testimony to this victory is Des Ball's 1980 book *A Suitable Piece of Real Estate*, with its dedication 'for a sovereign Australia' — irrespective of what particular 'Australians' are involved, so long as they are **Australian**.

---

20. Rose, op. cit., p. 154.

21. Reid, A., 'Is This To Be Menzies' Biggest Gamble', *The Bulletin*, October 26, 1963.

22. Thompson, E.P., *The Defense of Britain*, END and CND, 1983, p. 18.

Bases, Depots and 'Sites'

Looking up the etymology of the word 'base' refers you to 'Lit. GK. *basis*, "stepping stone"'(*OED*). If the U.S. installations in Australia are to be studied as 'bases', then it seems important to extend the cultural and territorial usage of the word to include — further 'step' — the fact that the immobile land bases lead to a further 'stepping stone', the orbiting satellites themselves. Von Clausewitz' perception in 1827 was that 'base' is not a discrete notion but an abridgement of a wider concept: the 'base of operations', a **total system** rather than an isolated outpost. Even though 'separated in space and [though] they cannot be constituted into one whole' the concept of 'bases' is nevertheless 'an elegant piece of geometrical refinement [that is] merely a play of fancy, as it is founded on a series of substitutions which must all be made at the expense of truth'.[23]

There is also a local specificity about the notion of the 'base' in Australia that enters into and extends popular local mythologies about exploration, access to the interior, and the continent as a series of 'secret' places — depots, base-camps, 'sites'. The 'marked trees' of the Burke and Wills expeditions, with their imperative 'DIG', were invoked by Frank Clune in 1944 as a metaphor for sites of soldierly struggle and reading the land in extreme conditions. 'Staring at the ground like Robinson Crusoe,' Clune wrote, the explorers look for meaning in 'the solitary mark of a horse's hoof', in 'a history laid upon tree-trunks'.[24] Gold prospecting in isolated spots likewise aligns the discovery of mysteries with setting up camp and moving out in what Louis Marin calls 'the primitive gesture the secret makes [in] this setting-to-one side; sifting; sieving; the passage; the filter; discernment; distinction; the grain from the chaff; the nugget from the sand . . .'[25] (Shades of Pine Gap's rumoured role in scanning STD calls for suspicious 'key words'). In more recent times, The Flying Doctor, 'Flynn of the Inland' is found in Ion L. Idriess' 1948 account, organising the country into a quasi-military game-plan, operating from 'Base' to his 'Great Circle' of bases organised through 'Legionnaries'.[26] Flynn's notion of 'Circles', culminating in an overall 'Six Circles' plan, encompassing the continent from above, was a new mapping device to fire popular imagination:

One map led to another. He drew maps of present holding areas of the country, of the people, cattle, sheep, horses, farming, minerals . . .[27]

In each of these disparate examples, the 'base' holds a double relation (to the home-base and to the system that contains all the bases), but it is the system that is looked to by von Clausewitz for giving the base its 'meaning':

[As] all separate streams unite in great reservoirs, so much more may these be regarded as taking the place of the whole country, and so much more will the notion of the base fix itself upon these great depots . . . [But] this must never go so far that such a place becomes looked upon as constituting a base in itself alone.[28]

Von Clausewitz' advice is to downplay what a base is and to prevent the host country's attention from focussing on it — rather to assimilate the base to an overall 'presence' by the invader.

23. von Clausewitz, op. cit., p. 110.

24. Clune, F., *Dig: A Drama of Central Australia*, Angus and Robertson, 1944, p. 117.

25. Marin, L., 'Logics of the Secret', *Third Degree*, No. 2, 1985, p. 33.

26. Idriess, Ion L., *Flynn of the Inland*, Angus and Robertson.

27. ibid, p. 24.

28. von Clausewitz, op. cit., pp. 109-10.

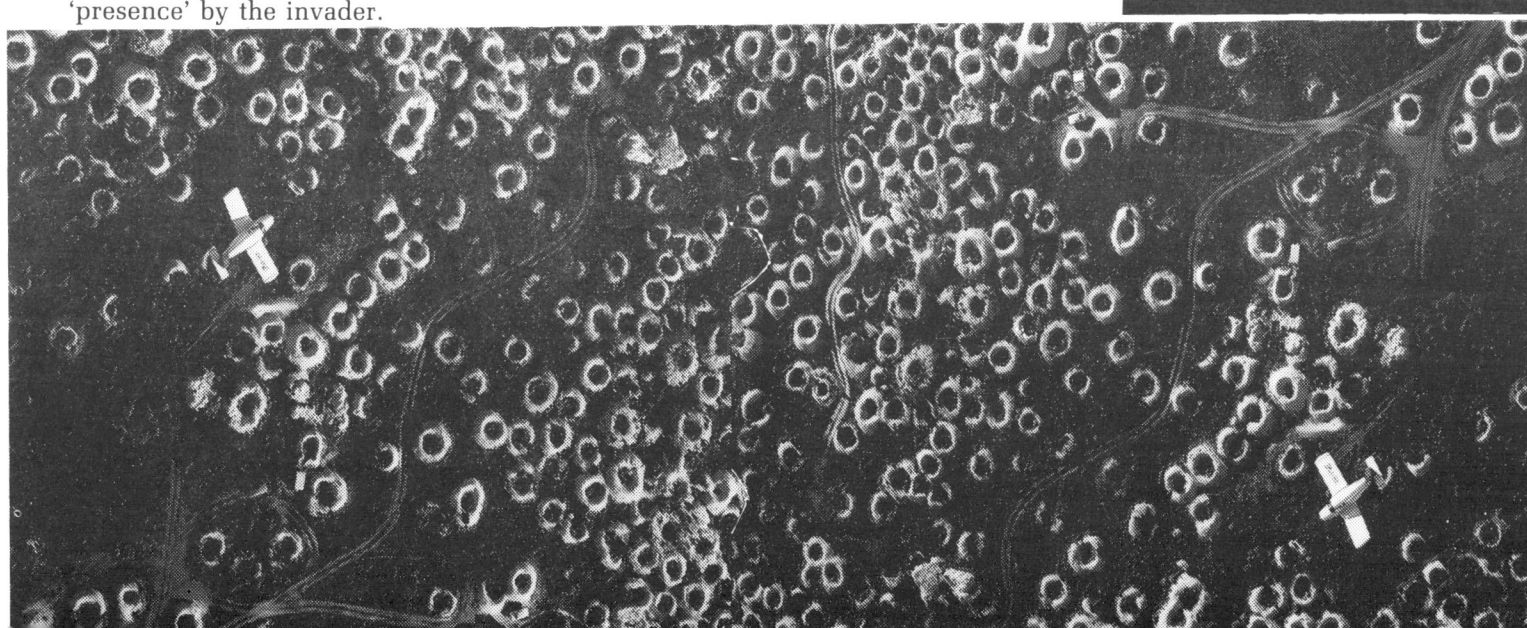

In the Pacific in the early 1930s, the problem arose in Australia in particular with regard to Japan's construction of naval bases in the Carolines, Truk, Ponape and Guam, in seeming violation of Japan's post-first world war mandate to the islands. To avoid incurring hostility from Japan, Australian and American suspicion chose to adopt as vague a reading of what 'base' meant as the Japanese themselves were doing. An American writer of the time wrote:

> To the general public, it might appear that a 'naval base' or a 'military base' are terms in themselves and require little explanation. To naval and military experts, however, they are quite otherwise. Explicit definitions in some phases of naval and military science are regarded as dangerous, since they may limit future action. It is more expedient to employ general terms lacking precise limitations.[29]

This interpretation was not lost on post-second world war American moves in the Pacific. When Singapore was being set up as a British base early in the 1930s, a controversy broke out over the position taken by one 'Commander J. M. Kenworthy, R.N., a member of the British House of Commons ... an opponent of the Singapore base project, who favours Sydney as the great Pacific base — on strategic grounds'. E. George Marks took the issue up in 1933 in a book called *Pacific Peril*,[30] and advocated for Australia a 'Palladium' concept (from 'the image of Pallas on which the safety of Troy was held to depend; a safeguard', *OED*) — based on Singapore. Singapore, while giving Australia a 'shield', Marks thought, would not be as vulnerable as Sydney. Furthermore, having the base in Singapore would elude Japanese interpretation of it as a base — such as would not be the case if Sydney were chosen.

A Founding Discourse: The Sixties

Paradoxically, the fall of Singapore in 1942 was cited by one of the 1960s commentators on U.S. bases in Australia as evidence that 'this throws the onus primarily and properly back on Australia'.[31] The early 1960s is notable in Australia for a move away from the populism of the 1950s (the purple prose in the yellow press surrounding Monte Bello, Maralinga, Radium Hill, Rum Jungle, etc) to the 'professional' armchair-strategist position exemplified by T. B. Millar, Hedley Bull and Ian Bellamy, as well as (in a more critical approach) A. L. Burns, Ian Turner, Robert Cooksey and Des Ball. In magazines such as *The Bulletin*, phrases like 'nuclear hostage', 'nuclear terrorism' and 'living in terror', became the perimeters inside of which 'argument' about the bases (position and response, *a la* TV) took place. As if to congratulate the readership on its grasp of the rhetoric of global arms strategy, successions of 'on the one hand but then on the other hand' discussions corresponding to current notions of 'liberal' debate filled the structured silence, in which, as the *Sydney Morning Herald* put it in an editorial in 1969: 'Government can hardly complain if citizens speculate'.[32]

Indeed, in the sense that armchair speculation became part of the codes of readership, it fulfilled the dual purpose of keeping up circulation and tying up the question of why the bases were here at all in interminable agonising about imminent deliverance into the hands of the USSR. Australia's **worst** enemy in this respect was, however, not the Soviets but knockers in Australia itself. A *Bulletin* article of 1963 with the salutary title 'How We Lost That Other Base'[33] recalled the fate of the first U.S. base on Australian territory, Manus Island. Set up in 1947 under Chifley, it cost the U.S. $100m to set up and, as a combined naval/air base with a harbour sheltering 600 ships, was the biggest in the world at the time. Unlike the bases set up in the 1960s, it had no taint of controversy over sovereignty or dual control connected with it: but by late 1947, the Americans had quit, and it became 'just the world's costliest junk-heap'.[34] The Americans' move to Guam represented the outcome of a controversy with H.V. Evatt over Australian-U.S. co-operation in all other bases in the area as 'uncommitted equals' under the U.N. By 1963, the U.S. was twice-shy when setting up North-West Cape, and questions of sovereignty took priority for anyone wishing to engage in opposition to the base. The 'exchange of letters' between the Minister for External Affairs, Garfield Barwick, and the U.S. Ambassador has the latter writing that 'consultation does not carry with it any degree of control over the situation or its use ... [It is] clearly understood that consultation connoted no more than consultation'.[35]

It is from this period in the early 1960s that the system of verbal and image-

29. Clyde, P.H., *Japan's Pacific Mandate*, Macmillan, 1935, p. 204.

30. Marks, E.G., *Pacific Peril*, Wynyard Book Arcade, 1933, p. 122.

31. Millar, T.B., *Australia's Defence*, p. 174.

32. *Sydney Morning Herald*, July 3, 1969.

33. Stanley, M., 'How We Lost That Other Base', *The Bulletin*, March 30, 1963.

34. ibid.

35. Millar, T.B., *Australia in Peace and War*, Appendix 9(b) (NW Cape Agreement), p. 476.

discourses on Australia started to be 'beamed back' to this country from the U.S. — even as Hollywood's version is 'beamed back' nowadays. The proliferation of journalistic 'scripts' on the bases in the 1960s took Australian-U.S. agreement as a *fait accompli*: 'co-production' on all matters except control.

As his justification for the bases, for example, T. B. Millar[36] offered the scenario of China or the USSR demanding concessions from the U.S. under threat of an attack on Australia. Millar's conjecture was that it would be highly unlikely if the bases were here and Australians were for them: the U.S. would protect their bases and, coincidentally, us too. In Alan Reid's opinion (see note 21), the bases were in Australia's self-interest since 'the bases would give the U.S. an added inducement to protect Australia'. A similar sort of blackmail could work with Indonesian designs on New Guinea, and North West Cape was invoked as being able to thwart these. A. L. Burns'[37] opinion was also that 'we certainly get a security return from America's position on New Guinea; and it now seems quite possible that America may wish us to become one of its nuclear allies'. Other writers, although less committed to the bases, were forced into the 'nuclear hostage' debate. Ian Turner wrote for *The Bulletin* in 1963 that Australia, with a population highly concentrated in cities, was 'particularly vulnerable to nuclear blackmail'.[38] Acceptance might provide the U.S., under these circumstances, with 'the incentive to defend Australia against local limited threat'. In another article in *The Bulletin*,[39] called 'Living with Terror', Michael Leifer saw the extension of this guardianship against being taken hostage as a 'balance of terror' with 'the development of invulnerable nuclear weapons systems on both sides of the cold war'.

This last phrase of Leifer's is a telling one, in the sense that it, along with others, still considers the 1960s situation to be continuous with the 1950s 'cold war'. In a similar vein, a *Current Affairs Bulletin* of 1964,[40] spoke of there being 'little pleasure to be derived from involvement in the cold war' in which 'grey areas of political and pseudo-military conflict' mean that choices are seldom made in black and white. References to the early 1960s as 'cold war' times still point to another aspect of the talk around the bases meant to mobilise support for them: the references are a flashback to a time when Australia had not wholly oriented toward the U.S. The replacement was above all useful for suggesting that without the bases, this orientation was not complete, and that without them, the U.S. might not bail Australia out of a 'hostage' situation. Would Australia, asked T. B. Millar, be 'expendable' to America without the bases? Even with them, thought Ian Turner, perhaps the U.S. would still not act, even if the bases themselves were attacked, leading to increased demand within Australia for acquisition of nuclear weaponry to protect itself, and the bases.[41] For Ian Bellamy, it was a matter of financial and political immaturity, since 'American financial investment in Australia alone is not enough surety that the U.S. will support Australia in all circumstances in which she might be reasonably expected to do so.'[42] Perhaps, Bellamy thought, 'the best course for Australia would be for the Americans to set up some real defence installations, such as a base for the maintenance of the Pacific Polaris fleet' (*a la* NATO). Millar's solution was a coming-of-age hypothesis: that, paradoxically given that joint control was denied, 'this station (North West Cape), once it is built, will mean that Australia ... is a producer of security as well as a consumer'.[43]

This is a discourse with its foundations laid in the 1960s, that has still to be confronted: it most notably and currently takes the form that (for instance, over uranium) it gives Australia international clout in international circles, or that having the bases here gives the Government muscle in the U.N. through its disarmament ambassador. Behind the ugly contradictions rampant here is a greater one — one that was foreshadowed by Whitlam's statement in 1974 that 'Australian personnel would commence moving into [Pine Gap] towards the end of the year'.[44] Further comment by Whitlam that 'the Australian Government takes the attitude that there should not be foreign bases, stations or installations in Australia' caused Peter King, writing in early 1975, to reflect that such talk 'would seem to foreclose the issue so far as Pine Gap is concerned — given that the Labor Government should still be in power in December 1975 when a year's notice to terminate the agreement could be given'.[45] At a similar juncture ten years later in 1985 (the agreement is renewable, or not, by decade), it is salutary to think of the circumstances of the Whitlam Government's fall: not when 'joint control' (whatever that is) was mentioned, but when the existence or closure of the bases was.

36. Millar, *Australia's Defence*, p. 172.

37. Burns, A.L., 'Labor and Defence', *Dissent*, Spring, 1963, p. 32.

38. Turner, I., 'The Exmouth Base (I): Opting Out', *The Bulletin*, March 30, 1963.

39. Leifer, M., 'Living With Terror', *The Bulletin*, March 30, 1963.

j40. *Current Affair Bulletin*, February 1964.

41. Turner, op. cit.

42. Bellamy, I., 'American Bases May Be Good For You', *The Bulletin*, November 22, 1969.

43. Millar, T.B., 'Australia and the American Alliance', *Pacific Affairs*, Vol. XXXVII, No. 2, Summer, 1964.

44. *Hansard*, April 3, 1974.

45. King, P., 'Credibility and Other Gaps: The Labor Government and The Bases', in R. O'Neill (ed.), *The Strategic Nuclear Balance, An Australian Perspective*, ANU, 1975, p. 121.

THINKING NEW THOUGHTS:
Australian Responses to the Question of Nuclear Armaments

Jocelyn Dunphy

In 1979 the mayors of Hiroshima and Nagasaki wrote in their Foreword to the volume: *Hiroshima and Nagasaki: the Physical, Medical and Social Effects of the Atomic Bombings:*

The currents of contemporary global politics ... are working against the aspirations of those who seek peace. Nuclear arms have become a mark of national power and pride and no-one seems to know how to stop the nuclear arms race.[1]

Their Foreword was written to introduce a 'comprehensive compilation of the findings that are so far scientifically confirmed'. Despite the empirical evidence and despite annual peace declarations issued by the two cities since the end of World War II, the contradictory aims described — the desire for peace and survival; involvement in national strivings for power — still make up the international dilemma. It is also Australia's dilemma and the dilemma of citizens who have to influence their government's choices. Information is widely diffused, yet the arms race goes on. What is the role of communication, action and thought in this situation? In their analysis, the two mayors quoted Einstein:

The release of atomic energy has so changed everything that our former ways of thinking have been rendered obsolete. We therefore face catastrophe unheard of in former times. If mankind is to survive, then we need a completely new way of thinking.

What new ways of thinking can we find at present in the nuclear paradox? In a talk on the ABC programme *Occam's Razor* in May 1985, Professor Bob Hunter of Sydney University spoke about the 'false logic' of the arms limitation agreements between the US and the Soviet Union. As an example, his text noted that what the 'Vladivostock' agreements of 1974 between the US and the USSR actually achieved was an *increase* in the numbers of weapons allowed, and an acceptance of this increase by public opinion. Taking issue with statements by John Howard which favoured Australia's participation in the MX missile program, he went on to inquire into the 'kinds of thinking' that are at work in present models of nuclear deterrence.

It is the theme of the 'kinds of thinking' involved in the nuclear debate that I want to follow up. In my first section, I shall outline the main positions, looking at Australia's particular place in the debate about peace. In the second part of my paper, I shall discuss the debate itself in terms of appeals to reason, the paradoxical terrain described by the mayors of Hiroshima and Nagasaki. This will lead to considering the notion of the 'nuclear state' and some aspects of social theory that are trying to cope with the interlocked models of reason and power. It will be within this worldwide problematic, rather than in terms of 'local colour', that I will ask how far Australian responses to the nuclear issue constitute what Einstein called 'new ways of thinking'

1. (Hutchinson, 1981).

1. Review of positions

Kosta Tsipis of MIT[2] recounts how the 'development, gradual understanding and eventual military application of the nuclear force' took 37 years from Becquerel's experiments with uranium in 1896 to the patent Szilard took out with the British Admiralty for a nuclear chain reaction in 1934. Ten years later, despite the moral doubts of Einstein and others over the Manhattan Project, the USA's bombing of Japan had a certain logic. Nuclear weapons offered 'an inexpensive way or wreaking destruction upon enemy territory without having to defeat enemy land armies'. The Allies held the nuclear secret. They knew that Germany had not developed the bomb. To display its force might create an advantage in bargaining with Stalin at the Potsdam negotiations. Roosevelt listened to the view of Niels Bohr that unless the US shared its mastery of the chain reaction with the USSR a nuclear race might result. Churchill's refusal, and the putting of Bohr under surveillance, only delayed the nuclear race until 1949, when the Soviet Union exploded its first atom bomb. 'From the quiet, disinterested research of Becquerel, the Curies, Rutherford and others', concludes Tsipsis, 'had emerged the most powerful physical force ever to threaten civilisation'.

Hunter's talk began with the issue touching Australia: our possible involvement in the MX project. When, referring to the dangers of the US change of option from deterrence armaments to 'first strike' weapons, he said, 'I believe we're talking here about the long term survival of life on this planet', he was speaking like Einstein and many others. I shall call this view the '**urgency argument**'. It is central to the nuclear debate.

Barry Pittock of the CSIRO writes in a recent article in *Search* (1985): 'I believe the internal logic of military development has led to a basic contradiction in which the very means developed to "protect" us is now the greatest threat to our survival. This requires that we go back and re-examine our basic assumptions'. The physician and activist Helen Caldicott compares the multiplication of nuclear weapons to 'macrobes, which are metastasising rapidly', and holds that activists, like a diagnosing oncologist, must scare the patient into a drastic change of lifestyle.[3] The New Zealand philosopher Peter Munz wonders whether the coming 'twilight' of humanist social science, foretold by some proponents of artificial intelligence, may not reveal itself instead as 'the light of dawn, even if it is only the dawn caused by the neutron bomb's final explosion'.[4]

This 'urgency argument', expressed by writers from different fields of research, was given political relevance by George Ball, US Secretary of State from 1961-66, who condemned President Reagan's proclamation of the SDI or Star Wars program as 'one of the most irresponsible acts by any head of state in modern times'.[5] Ball saw the SDI program as setting aside previous limitations to nuclear arms. He noted Reagan's preference for a 'technical fix' over arms-control negotiations; the President's desire to build 'overwhelming military power' and at the same time render such weapons 'impotent and obsolete', while remaining oblivious to the contradictions in his approach and forgetful of his obligations under NATO to consult his European allies. Ball concluded that should Reagan get the Star Wars project approved, arms control might no longer be possible, for we 'shall have passed beyond the point where verification is achievable'. In the ensuing escalation, 'the public will be so deceived by specious promises or confused by technological jargon that it will ignore the lessons of the past'. To pursue superior might rather than negotiation could thus be to risk 'catastrophic conflict' and 'enlarge man's

2. Kosta Tsipis: *Arsenal: Understanding Weapons in the Nuclear Age* (Simon and Schuster, 1983).

3. Helen Caldicott: 'This Beautiful Planet' in Herbert F. Vetter (ed.): *Speak Out Against the New Right* (Beacon, 1982).

4. Peter Munz: Review of Charles C. Lemert: *Sociology and the Twilight of Man*, in *Philosophy and the Social Sciences* 14.2 (1984, p. 406).

5. Quoted in Theodore Draper: 'Pie in the Sky' *New York Review of Books* XXXII.2 (14 February 1985).

ability to destroy civilisation'. Ball's hope that the public will not be deceived about the links between the SDI program and a nuclear disaster identifies the danger that lies in the choice of a military solution over negotiation. I shall call this identification the '*paradox model*'.

'Presumably no-one at all wants a nuclear war,' says John Wisdom.[6] The point of the paradox model is that the patience needed in negotiating, and in verifying that agreements are being kept is less attractive to major powers than a 'technical fix'. This dangerous position is explicitly justified when opponents of the nuclear race are labelled 'idealists'. An overview of this debate by Nagy[7] shows how the position of the 'idealists' goes back to Russell and Einstein, to those who saw the nuclear age as foreshadowing the need for radical political change, and called for a world government to eliminate war and control nuclear weapons. On the other side, 'realists' like Brodie early developed the concept of deterrence. This concept included the doctrines of 'flexible response' and 'limited nuclear war' now advanced by nuclear strategists to talk of logical concepts like 'pre-emptive retaliation'. Over the last 39 years this has been the rationale for the 50,000 warheads that now threaten to extinguish life on earth.

But it is not just that deterrence, retaliation or winnable nuclear wars are seen as more attractive projects than slow negotiation. In a recent study Theodore Draper has shown that the very process of negotiation is used as a manoeuvre by the major governments. In July 1982 for example Nitze and Kvitsinsky, in their 'walk in the woods' during the Geneva agreements, came up with a 'package deal' as opposed to the unsatisfactory numerical count used in weapons agreements up till then. However, their respective governments rejected this initiative, Moscow being the first to disown it. Again, it was recently revealed that in negotiations to reduce arms, the US used as bargaining chips the 20 year old Titan rockets, already obsolete and a burden to maintain. They are now being dismantled anyway, to make way for more sophisticated systems. Thus interest groups, whether political, financial or ideological, maintain the race and manipulate the processes of negotiation. The paradox consists in the choice of their short term gains over the urgent, but long term, goal of survival. Oppenheimer, scientific director of the Manhattan Project, held that the nuclear age would be seen as a phase in human history that was 'transitory, dangerous and degrading'. Nagy comments that perhaps there will be no-one there to say so.

6. John Wisdom: 'Types of Groups' *International Review of Psychoanalysis* (1985).

7. Anthony Nagy: 'How Can the World Survive Nuclear War?' *The Age* (March, 1985).

The paradox model implies that nuclear disaster could arise, not only from the stubborn pursuit of might by the superpowers, but from other quarters. Deng Tsiou Ping has lately spoken about China's need to develop her capacity if her neighbours continue to be a nuclear threat. India has spoken in the same way about Pakistan. Australia's main nuclear problem until recently has been the French testing of the *force de frappe* in the Pacific. Other nations could develop nuclear capacity. One of these could trigger the world wide conflagration. The Canadian Journal *Peace Research Review* points out that the main danger may well be an accidental triggering. It states: 'No thinking person wants a nuclear war. Yet day by day nuclear war plans are being made, and nuclear weapons are being held on alert in at least five major nations'.[8]

How does the paradox sustain itself? The 37 years needed to progress from Bequeral's study of luminescent crystals to the patent for a nuclear weapon were marked by a succession of scientific breakthroughs. In *The Command and Control of Nuclear Forces* the defence analyst Paul Bracken describes as 'the greatest single change in nuclear force' in the last 20 years, the shift in military communication from 'loose to tight coupling'. This is the so-called wiring between mechanisms of warning and response, which has now become so apprehensive and 'jumpy' as to need new backup systems. At the same time, other recent surveys of the US system of command, control and communications, known as 'C^3', show that the system is now so inadequate that for it to work at all policy must aim at a first strike rather than at deterrence or retaliation.[9] For the Yale historian Gregg Herken, refinements in improving the war machine, or in diplomatic strategy, don't amount to what Einstein would have called a 'completely new way of thinking'. Herken speaks of 'the momentum of technology' and denies that 'the subject of nuclear weapons is so technical and complex that it is best left up to the experts'.[10] Thus, rather than inventiveness on the part of the nuclear scientists, or the military or political advisers involved, we find a third model, what I shall call the '*dynamics model*' or '*momentum/inertia*'. The technology for nuclear weapons gains its momentum not from ideas that are new, in Einstein's sense, but from the inertia of already-thought ideas. Despite increased skills in all the fields associated with nuclear weapons, policy continues on the path undertaken.

Looking at this path, Herken analyses the 'exponential' growth of the power of destruction. Using recently declassified documents, he brings out the role of 'unexamined political assumptions', and of 'deeply held and often unstated beliefs'. The most striking is the belief of US officials in a 'preventive' or a 'winnable' war against the USSR. Even Eugene Rostow has described as 'paranoid' those who advocate a protracted war to destroy the Soviet Union. Herken's analysis of the abandoning of reason, and even of a 'psychiatric' element in so-called 'arms control', leads from descriptive models to an explicit statement on values. He quotes Rabi: 'There has been an atrophy of the imagination, a decline of the moral sense'. This move from an analysis of military tactics to the role of values links the urgency, paradox and momentum/inertia approaches to one that is specifically *ethical*.

8. Editorial, *Peace Research Reviews* IX.4 (1984).

9. Kosta Tsipis: 'It's Not Just the President Who Can Release Armageddon' *The Guardian* (23 June 1985).

10. Gregg Herken: *Counsels of War* (Knopf, 1985).

On the practical plane, if Rabi is right about a growing atrophy of imagination in the public, the ethical argument of activists must be able to capture attention. Given the way the momentum/inertia model functions, the onus of a change of direction must fall on protesters. Many professional groups make anti-nuclear activism a dimension of their work. They include SANA in Australia, Engineers for Nuclear Disarmament, Electronics for Peace, Psychoanalysts Against Nuclear War in Britain, peace movements and political parties. The Nuclear Control Institute aims to sensitize public opinion to the dangers of commercial profit from uranium, which can be easily used for bombs by terrorists. Movements like the Greens in northern Europe, or Greenpeace, go further and situate anti-nuclear ethics within a world ecological perspective. I shall return to this viewpoint.

How is an ethical model articulated? William H. Shaw expresses dissatisfaction with 'the narrow confines of games theory' familiar to the literature of international relations, and which Shaw identifies on the ethical level with the utilitarians. He looks for a moral theory which can 'integrate finely grained factual issues, or questions of probability, such as the chances of a nuclear accident'. How permissable is it to threaten what Paul Ramsey, Anthony Kenny or Douglas Lackey see as an immoral action, analogous to murder or at least kidnap? Shaw's essay casts doubt on clearcut condemnations of deterrence, yet admits 'the limits of a narrowly deontological perspective'. 'Of all the moral issues that face us today, nuclear policy is the one that, because of the complex factual issues and number of persons likely to be affected, most cries out to be handled in consequential terms'. On the analogy of the atrocities that have resulted when nations condemned war absolutely, only to be left without guidelines in the event, Shaw concludes that a total condemnation of deterrence could turn out badly.

To the extent that people find it dangerously unrealistic to cease deterrence and disarm unilaterally and yet are told that this is what morality dictates, they will in fact tend to ignore moral reasoning about nuclear matters altogether.[11]

Like the urgency argument, the ethical one is an appeal to **reason**. Yet the paradox and the momentum/inertia models show that in the nuclear race, reason is ignored, both in its common-sense role of recognising danger, and in its creative role of finding a new way of thinking. If we return to Herken's view that unstated beliefs and assumptions are the hidden basis of policy, we come to the fourth and perhaps the most important model, that of '*ideology*'. E. P. Thompson writes: 'The Peace movements cannot opt whether to be more "political" or not. They have challenged "the bomb" — and behind it they have found the full power of the state. If they are to reach "the bomb" they must now take on also a whole state-manipulated and media-endorsed ideology'.[12] For Salman Rushdie, the anti-nuclear campaign cannot be undertaken as a single-issue protest, as 'the bomb is the sharp end of the power structure which rules our lives'.[13] Rudolf Bahro[14] turns the model round the other way: '... the ecological crisis cannot be solved without putting an end to the arms race between East and West, without a new economic order between North and South, without social justice, human emancipation and so forth'. Thus a journey through the four models of positions on nuclear armaments — urgency, paradox, dynamics and ideology — reveals more than a simple military buildup, or a confrontation between nuclear states, as some activists put it. The rejection of reason by states is linked to a world order that brings together power, economics and ethics. To counteract inertia or unspoken assumptions involves going beyond any model which presents the nuclear crisis as a single issue.

2. Nuclear Armaments, Reason and Power

Bahro's situating of the nuclear issue at the leverage point of world order emphasises that, as he says elsewhere, 'the different political systems, with respect to the arms race, constitute a single system'. That system is the by-product of industrial progress:

When you look at the amount of raw materials that our society uses up; when you think of the steps we take to avoid the danger of losing our Middle East oil supplies; and when you look at the way in which the developing countries are placed on the treadmill of the arms race — then you can see how vital it is to go to the heart of the matter. Our protests in Europe against nuclear weapons have not the slightest effect on the Third World arms buildup — not the slightest effect. If a political movement is to have a chance of success, it must have an overall historical conception of its aim.

For Bahro the aim of the eco-peace movement is the 'liberation of consciousness'. This conception can be contrasted with the American Joel Kovel's analysis in *Against the State of Nuclear Terror*, another study of marxist inspiration.[15] Kovel focuses on the central role of the nuclear state and technocracy, 'the embodiment of scientific rationality in society', and calls for unilateral disarmament. Bahro's long-term aim, which extends the model of domination to the interlocked global system, appears more capable of remaining sensitive to the ethics of ambiguity called for by Shaw. In this his thinking resembles that of the later Russell.[16]

Essentially, the ideological model depends on our viewing those in power as rejecting reason. We have seen the use of terms like 'unspoken assumptions' or even the adjectives 'paranoid' or 'psychiatric'. The Freudian, William Brown, wrote in April 1939: 'From the standpoint of reason, war must ... be regarded as lunacy, and all who take part in it as lunatics'. Freud himself, in his letter to Einstein, *Why War?*, of 1932,[17] saw the arms race as a struggle of violence against humanism or *eros*. In *Humanism and Terror*, (1947), Merleau-Ponty spelt out the connection between violent social action and a rational program that remains unconscious of contradiction. His book made political sense of the Freudians' analysis of war in terms of unconscious factors. It also made ethical sense, for western idealist thinkers, of the marxist analysis of oppression and alienation. He wrote:

There is a mystification in liberalism. Judging from history and by everyday events, liberal ideas belong to a system of violence of which, as Marx said, they are the 'spiritual point d'honneur', the 'solemn complement and the general basis of consolation and justification' ... It is a powerful argument, in refusing to judge liberalism in terms of the ideas it espouses and inscribes in constitutions and in demanding that these ideas be compared with the prevailing relations between men in a liberal state; Marx is not simply speaking in the name of a debatable materialist philosophy — he is providing a formula for the concrete study of society which cannot be refuted by idealist arguments ... The value of a society is the value it places upon man's relation to man [sic]. It is

11. William H. Shaw: 'Nuclear Deterrence and Deontology' *Ethics* (January 1984).

12. *The Heavy Dancers* (Merlin, 1984).

13. 'Seeing Beyond the Bomb' *The Guardian* (21 April 1985).

14. *From Red to Green* (Verso, 1984).

15. (Pan Books, 1983).

16. See Linus Pauling: 'Would Civilisation Survive Nuclear War?' in R. Schoenman: *The Philosophy of Bertrand Russell* (Allen and Unwin, 1967).

17. In J. Rickman (ed): *Civilisation, War and Death* (Hogarth Press, 1939).

not just a question of knowing what the liberals have in mind but what in reality is done by the liberal state within and beyond its frontiers ... [18]

Bahro's position takes up the marxist analysis of violence at the point where domination has produced the nuclear crisis. His global model goes beyond single-issue views of nuclear protest or a conception of a power structure based simply on the nuclear state. Yet, though he insists on an overall historical conception, he offers no account of how, in history, society has abandoned reason. There is a problem in the ideological approach to nuclear debate, though this approach goes further than the others, and in its complex form makes sense of the nuclear crisis by 'going to the heart of the matter'. The problem is a practical one: does the approach via ideology leave us without a solution? Like Hunter, Ball and others who are urging a halt to the nuclear race, Bahro is appealing to reason and to public opinion. Yet the ideological model, in showing the neglect of reason by governments, suggests that the public cannot act, and that speech and reasoning are wasted. How can to write, recognizing unconscious forces (as Freud did), or even criticising 'lunacy' (as Brown did), still mean to call on reason within an international, industrial and nuclear society?

The issue of reason within modern western society was taken up by Horkheimer and Adorno in *Dialectic of Enlightenment*, and the concept of the Enlightenment provides a ground for the present discussion. The Enlightenment was the period which saw at once the Declaration of the Rights of Man, the American Revolution, and, stemming from that revolution's effect on Britain, the founding of Australia. Paul Connerton points out[19] how reason functioned at that time as a critique 'aiming to remove the political basis from beneath the absolutist state while ... obscuring the fact that this was taking place'. Reason achieved its historical aim in this period by veiling the identification of morals and politics. Habermas, Connerton points out, has shown how Enlightenment reason functioned through 'the existence of and the appeal to a critical public', and Marx's own strategy of attack on 18th and 19th century thought-categories relied on this same function of the public.

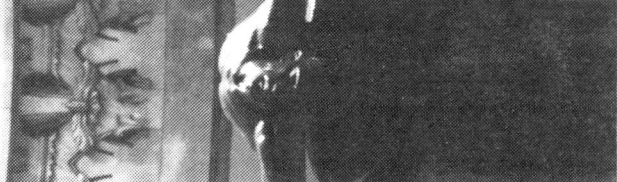

Via the notion of publicity, Connerton reviews the Frankfurt's School's attempt to rethink the marxian critique of power in society. Habermas sees enlightenment as 'discussion free from domination' yet the concepts he uses as a counterforce, such as emancipation or autonomy are historically rooted 'in the pre-revolutionary period of the 18th century Enlightenment'. Thus, to propose the 'test of justification through discourse' for 'the political system of state regulated capitalism [or] that of bureaucratic socialism' is to repeat the old 'bourgeois, pre-revolutionary abstraction' of the 'Judgement Seat of Reason'. After the 'radical solution' to the problem of autonomy was found in the late 18th century, reason no longer functioned as the critique of absolutism. Instead, it was integrated into the new bourgeois order, with parliaments, elections and a publicity which, today geared to affluence, inhibits a proletarian revolution. The Frankfurt School's notion of critique remains tied to 'the view of history as an all-embracing process in which a historical subject attains its essence, autonomy', yet while the work of the school as a whole has had as its driving motive the discussion of fascism, Connerton points out that Habermas was able to analyse the 'collapse of the liberal concept of publicity' without relating it to another collapse — that of 'the bourgeois world in the face of fascist terror'. Thus the Enlightenment view of history itself is exposed as a 'myth', yet one hard to replace.

18. English translation (Beacon, 1969).

19. Paul Connerton: *The Tragedy of the Enlightenment* (Cambridge University Press, 1978).

One understands why Bahro found Habermas to be in 'an historical impasse'. The belief that communication is the answer to domination through technology has not received any confirmation in history, and social theorists lack a clear model to express strong contrary evidence. Is it, as Connerton finds, that the Frankfurt School failed to 'locate their critical public', despite creative moves by Marcuse to gather a radical public from groups hitherto nonpolitical — Women's Liberation, Civil Rights, the anti-war campaign? Is it, as others have said, that critique of domination since the Enlightenment, despite Hegel's legacy of the Master and Slave, awaits developments that it has not received in the marxist reading? There remains too the pessimism of Freud, as found in his letter to Einstein. In *Why War?* Freud showed that despite this pessimism he did not despair of influencing public action.

3. Australian responses to the nuclear impasse

We can now consider Australian positions in terms of the world context. This includes the four models given above, the preference by governments for solutions of power rather than reason, and the structure of domination noted since the Enlightenment. In each case the main issue will be that of the relation between speech, or communication, and the public it seeks. I shall take three examples of Australia's response: the question of the use of nuclear arms; the mining and sale of uranium, with its use in armaments not made clear; the development of nuclear protest from grassroots influence to the status of political representation.

First, with regard to nuclear armaments, the MX issue, with which I started, touches the US-USSR polarity directly via Australia's membership of the formal alliance, ANZUS. Still on the level of public policy, Australia's confronting of France over the Pacific tests brings out the role of independent nuclear powers. 1985 has seen two signficant events. One was the refusal by the Lange government in New Zealand to accept U.S. nuclear vessels, and the twofold Australian response — not following New Zealand, but carrying out ANZUS-substitute exercises with the US. The other was the decision by the Minister for Defence to strengthen the Australian fleet with non-nuclear submarines as part of a lighter, more rapidly deployable defence force. One of the reasons given for this choice was Australia's lack of a backup nuclear industry.

Coming to the second example, many questions have been raised by the Australian mining industry's production of uranium, and sales of this uranium to foreign countries for peaceful purposes. These questions touch on international safeguards regarding eventual purchasers; the theft of uranium at different stages of the enrichment process, possibly leading to banditry or accident; the ecological consequences of nuclear waste; the Hawke government's claim that sales of uranium ultimately promote peace because they give Australia a voice in negotiations.

Thirdly, the difficult birth of a parliamentary Nuclear Disarmament Party and its choice not to risk contamination from other political forces are significant. We can ask in what way its members view other groups' 'unspoken assumptions', or recognize links between 'the economic order, human emancipation, social justice and the arms race'. We can ask too whether it reflects Merleau-Ponty's effort to acknowledge the truth in the critique of domination. The party's single-issue stance aims at grouping a larger public. Taking up Connerton's criterion of localising one's critical public we can put the further question: what does this aim tell us about the Party, or about particular qualities in the Australian public?

In order to relate these three examples, and the questions they raise, to the world context of the nuclear debate, we can look at how Australians perceive them. The anthology *Australian Defence Policy for the 1980s*, edited by Robert O'Neill and D. M. Horne,[20] offers contrasting views of ANZUS. Coral Bell shows its utility by pointing to the undefended spaces lying south of the USSR on the map, while Noel

20. (University of Queensland Press, 1982.)

Butlin takes the debate out of the US-USSR polarity by contrasting dependence on 'our great friends' with the notion of Australian sovereignty, and considers our role in the Pacific. His argument also claims to contribute to 'the preservation of peace and the survival of humanity'. However, his notion of national integrity does not include the problems we have noted, of power, violence or the historical loss of such integrity by others. The book has a conclusion by the historian Sir Keith Hancock, who quotes Lord Zuckerman: ' . . . one real danger of nuclear war is that we have ceased to understand what we are talking about . . . the possible elimination of the better part of the cultural history of our globe'. This culmination situates the book within both the urgency model and the global historical conception Bahro spoke of. Hancock's guides are Swift and Hobbes rather than Marx. His practical solutions are humanist in tone. They include a resumption of possession of the North West Cape Naval Communications installations when the agreement with the United States runs out; a national consensus on 'the issues of peace and war', and a move towards 'manpower and womanpower', rather than technological preoccupations, in our thinking about defence. If we return to the recent decisions by the Minister for Defence, it is clear that they coincide fairly well with Hancock's goal — a form of national independence which does not break with the United States; a stress on human deployability rather than on massive technology; a view of international relations which recognizes conflict but is not guided by the model of historical domination.

What do Australians say about the sale of Australia's uranium for peaceful use? It has been strongly contested by those citizens who believe all nuclear power is dangerous. Paul Levanthal of the Nuclear Control Institute, referring to danger from terrorists, said recently on ABC television that there is now more material available commercially than in the arsenals of the superpowers. Plutonium can be extracted from fuel burned in peaceful power stations. In order to make money the Australian government has given forward approval for sales. Logically this issue would not touch that of armaments except for the matter of controls. As these are and will remain inadequate, Australia's right to a voice among the international producers is bought at a price no-one knows at present.

Where does this choice fit in among the models of nuclear positions? Andrew Mack, joins his voice to that of the American John Kenneth Galbraith, to bring out what radical development theory has shown of investment in the Third World.[21] The poverty of poor countries results not from their inadequate institutions but from the exploitative dependency relationships which bind them to Western capitalist Metropoles. So one can ask: who buys Australian uranium? Who profits from the sale, and what model of the nuclear issue is expressed by the views of those who so profit? The Danish philosopher Peter Kemp has shown how it is possible to re-think 'the 19th century belief that, as technology advances, it will automatically solve its own problems and lead to universal human happiness'.[22] His fresh reading of Verne's 19th century science fiction lets us

... see, more clearly than Verne's ... contemporaries could ... that we are not foredoomed to be the slaves of so-called neutral and unavoidable Techne, we can choose, more or less, and we are responsible for our choices in scientific and technical matters.

Thus when we look finally at the political crystallisation of the nuclear disarmament movement, we can make sense of the difficulties the new party has experienced. Australian public opinion is divided between a conservative (or on its open and tolerant side, humanist) aspect, and a radical one, which is not reflected in power structures, even under a Labor government. The Nuclear Disarmament Party wishes to be a single-issue party, and to draw its following from the large group of those who support this single issue, but may disagree on questions that are specifically 'political'.

The force of my argument has been to show that if one follows through the argument models on nuclear agreements, then one concludes with the global one of ideology: unreasoning power-structures and domination. This includes the facts of historical exploitation, such as colonialism, which are still with us, and which we, while asserting our own integrity *vis a vis* our powerful allies, may well be practising

21. Andrew Mack: *Imperialism, Intervention and Development* (Croom Helm, 1979).

22. Peter Kemp: 'Death and the Machine: A Critique of Jules Vernian Reason' *Philosophy and Social Criticism* (1984).

towards lesser nations. I believe a so-called non-political or single-issue nuclear opposition, while it might answer the urgency argument, will not be able to cope with problems raised by the others: paradox, a dynamics of momentum/inertia, the ideological force of capitalist practice divorced from non-utilitarian morality. So, to succeed, such an opposition must rely on a hypothetical quality famous in Australian folklore: the often-expressed care for a fair go for others, a kind of vocalised 'quality of mercy'.

Just how real, or how reliable, is this quality? From Lawrence's *Kangaroo* to *Sunday Too Far Away*, published law reports, prison reports and inquiries into racism, evidence shows that the relation between communication and public opinion is here utilising a national myth. Freud's 'Why War?' stressed the element of instinctual violence. Historically, European Australians reached their country as people of the Enlightenment. We have read how Phillip desired a virtuous society, and communicated to the Aborigines that there would be the same punishment for crimes for everyone. King preferred to guide his colony by rewards, such as shorter terms, rather than by brutal treatment. Bligh strongly opposed, to his misfortune, the struggle for privilege of a would-be new landowning class. Yet the re-reading of Australian history, like the studies of the Enlightenment by European scholars,[23] shows how dark the other side of Enlightenment is. If we 'localise' the Australian critical public, we find first of all that it is a divided one: both conservative and radical. Our national myth is that of fair dealing. Can the new thoughts we aim to think be grounded in a trust that this myth will unite a divided public and solve complex problems that have global implications? I believe that appeal to public opinion here in Australia will have to go further, and aim at sensitizing a divided public to what Bahro called a 'general historical conception of aim'. Can this be done, given the 'unspoken assumptions and beliefs' arising from ideology? 'If mankind is to survive,' said Einstein, 'then we need a completely new way of thinking'. The challenge in Australia is to bring about a new understanding of society, transcending what Connerton described as the 'Enlightenment myth', transcending too the nineteenth century belief that 'technology will solve its own problems' and tackling the dark forces revealed by Hegel, Freud and our own history.

23. See Henry Reynolds: *The Other Side of the Frontier* (Penguin, 1982). See Jean Starobinsky: *Emblemes de la Raison* (Skira, 1975) and Peter Gay: *The Enlightenment* (Knopf, 1967). See also Greg Dening's anthropological study of Pacific history, *Islands and Beaches* (University of Melbourne Press, 1982).

CLOSE REMARKS
Placing Art and Theory

ON THE BEACH

NUMBER 9

OUT $4

Distributed by Manic Ex-poseur
P O Box 39, World Trade Centre,
Melbourne, Vic 3005

Produced in association with Artspace
11 Randle Street, Surry Hills, 2010

MEN WAR IN SYDNEY SUBURBS

Gavin Harris and Leigh Raymond

SEVEN DIE IN FATHERS' DAY MASSACRE
(A. 3 Sept)
THE TRAGEDY OF WHAT WAS JUST A FAMILY THING
(SMH 3 Sept)
PUB CARPARK BECOMES BATTLEFIELD ... SLAUGHTER IN THE SUBURBS (T. 3 Sept)
OUR DAD IS DEAD ... MORE STORIES, PICTURES p. 2,3,4,5
(M. 3 Sept)
VICTIM! BIKIE WAR: REVENGE FEAR ... MILPERRA MADNESS
(Sun 3 Sept)

1. Working On His Consciousness With the Odd Revelation

An invitation to be startled, to be tantalized, to be captured, to buy (or not), to look, to reveal, to be horrified, to be held in suspense until ... He put down the papers and opened a text:

In summary, the significations of newspaper news are governed by three interlocking codes and relations: relations of power between owners, advertisers, management, staff, readers, political institutions ...; semantic-linguistic codes in which significance is self-consciously articulated through the text's stylistic conventions, through time-honoured notions of newsworthiness ...; and a visual code that is built out of codes of framing, layout, typography, photography, graphics, pagination ...[1]

He could see it operating: the black reverse an omen of death; the gun that crossed the bike; a shocking, arresting grief; the collapse of *their* way of life. (Fig 1.)

Daily Mirror

News House,
2 Holt Street,
Surry Hills, 2010
G.P.O. Box 4245
Sydney, 2001
Telephone 288 3000

August 13, 1985

Mr Gavin Harris
2/115A Victoria Street
KINGS CROSS 2011

Dear Mr Harris

Thank you for your letter of July 22, 1985.

Permission is granted to reproduce page 3 of the Daily Mirror, September 3, 1984, in the August issue of Intervention conditional on the Daily Mirror not being portrayed in a derogatory manner and that the Daily Mirror is credited.

Yours faithfully

Roy Miller
Deputy Editor
DAILY MIRROR

Fig. 1.

He couldn't remember anything like it happening here; but it was something that could have been expected of them. Rifles, machetes, slaughter, carnage. A battled in their 'declared war'.[2] They've called Panania Milperra; and what happened a massacre (Goodman of Milperra, SMH 15 Sept). **THE MILPERRA MASSACRE**. He sat and was chilled by the severings, by the gratuitous deaths, by the death of an innocent, by the prospect of society falling into 'a new Dark Age with barbarians out to kill everyone' (Eyewitness 'Joe', A. 5 Sept).

Outside civilisation, outside commonsense, outside his commitment to the mortgage, to Katrina and Toby, to his career and decency . . . He was being told that it was totally un-Australian and Mad Max and tribalistic and American and lunatic and animal.[4] He was reading about the tattoos they wore like 'badges of bravado' and their black leather and their repulsive style and their rites and their arrogance (editorial, T. 4 Sept). 'Dirty, hairy and promiscuous' (editorial, T. 4 Sept), they treated their ol' ladies as 'sex objects in the most ancient sense' (Wilfred Jarvis, T. 4 Sept). And in the commuting slogs of those next months he could diet on the likelihood of Revenge, the prospect of ritualistic and bizarre funerals, bedside vigils, grieving and orphaned families, police mobilisations and heroic dawn raids, definitive explanations, protracted and sensational court hearings, record-breaking statistics, incarcerations, suicide, arson, harassment by neighbours . . .[5] And when journalists could find nothing else they beat up such human(e) interest stories as: **BIKIE ARRESTED AFTER HE WEDS SWEETHEART** (Dream Day Shattered, M. 24 Sept).

'Newspapers select, associate and exaggerate "undesirable" characteristics to stereotype marginalised groups in negative ways. These groups are used to label the entire group and its putative members. For example, they might typify an isolated and pariah group as outside culture, animals, barbarously violent, physically repulsive, and stupid. This process of stereotyping serves several discursive functions. Firstly, it reinforces the marginalisation of groups and individuals by identifying them *only* through a narrow and pejorative set of characteristics. And secondly, because the newspaper assumes that its reader will share its reasonable speaking position (the instantly recognisable "real" and "true" judgements that it provides) it seeks to foreclose any alternative analysis.'[3]

48 WAR/MASCULINITY

'The day out that became a tragedy' (M. 3 Sept).

'Hordes of bikies stormed into the car park brandishing shotguns and baseball bats. Stunned patrons dived for cover in the hotel as volley after volley was fired' (T. 3 Sept).

and/or

'The Comancheros, Bandidos and Gypsy Jokers roared into the carpark and started to brawl, at first trading punches and then wielding baseball bats and chains. Fifteen more machines arrived, racing past the sales tables and through the crowds. Some of the bikies had shotguns and rifles strapped to them . . . an alley cleared between the two gangs, who started shooting at each other . . .' (A. 3 Sept).

and/or

'. . . I'd seen a bloke pick up a shotgun and put it next to a bike . . . He picked it up again and suddenly bikies were all around him trying to grab the gun as he held it in the air. Then the gun discharged and all hell broke loose.' (Miss Y, an unidentified witness quoted in T., 3 Sept).

and/or

'I told my blokes to stay on their bikes and I walked across to one of the Comancheros. He had a pump action shot gun which he pressed into my guts. I looked at him for a second and told him to put the gun away and we would fight man-to-man. I shoved the gun away and down and it went off and then it all started' (Unidentified Bandido spokesperson, M. 3 Sept).

How brave and manly they were to pick a public holiday area full of holiday-makers to enact their gun feud. A father will have lost his daughter on Father's Day. A mother and her family will grieve. The loss cannot be replaced.' (SMH 12 Sept).

And on these trips he could read comparisons between them and the 'tribal warriors and the superpowers who have engaged in so many "braver" battles for supremacy' (SH 9 Dec); between their battles and World War II (T. 4 Sept) and the St Valentine's Day Massacre (M. 5 Sept). And later, when the commital hearings had begun, between these and the Nuremberg trials and Kafkaesque bureaucracies (A. 22 Oct). Some of the accounts had been structured like Hollywood narratives; others acknowledged their debt to different media models . . . *Mad Max, The Trial, Two Tribes go to War*.[6]

They were making these suburban events into a paradigm of Universal Tragedy, Peace and War, the Enemy within (barbarous and violent killings and their ramifications); into a realisation of horrifying and sexual pleasures (*Mad Max* and so many westerns he'd seen); into a mix of moral indignation, sympathy and admiration; into fabulous entertainment; into an anticipation of what might come. Our land was being threatened by a dystopic future. Their discourses were inscribing a possibility upon us now. Variety, familiarity, irrationality . . . contradictions, irresolutions — they lured us in 30 cents instalments, with the promise of the next day's Truths.

He understood that a barbecue and motorcycle parts market had been set up on Father's Day, Sunday 2 September at the Viking Tavern Carpark. And then, whatever happened, happened.

He compiled an inventory of the carnage. There had been about 25 men 'out to kill' (Mr X, T. 3 Sept): shooting their heavy gauge rifles, their shotguns; swinging their baseball bats, their rubber truncheons, their metal pipes, their machetes and bicycle chains . . . The papers were telling him that six people, including innocent Leanne Walters, had died from gunshot wounds. It seemed that 3 Comancheros had fallen together: 'one had a shotgun blast in the neck, one to the chest and another to the head. They were all shot at close range' (SMH 3 Sept). As well, one bikie had been stabbed in the heart. *The Sydney Morning Herald* reported that more than 20 others had been injured (3 Sept). One casualty had his arm hacked off with a machete (SMH 3 Sept); another had an eye torn out; yet another had his kneecap 'explode in a mass of red' (Mr X, T. 3 Sept). 'Jock' Ross, the Comancheros' President copped 40 shotgun pellets in the head and neck.

Leanne Walters, 14 year old kid, casualty of dishonourable masculinity, 'normal fun-loving daughter' (M. Sept), passively vulnerable and selflessly active, she was the little girl, the raffle-ticket seller who 'copped it in the chin' (SMH 3 Sept). Her hitherto obscure life had been sought out and recorded only because she had fallen in her collision with (the bikies') power. Her body became the site of other (textual) powers; her life a set of significations: attractive innocence/femininity; repeated bad luck; disease; willpower; survival; violent and purposeless death. She was suddenly being cast casually into popular memory. (Fig 2.)

2. Revving Up

So reading the news and his mass comm. texts he slowly assembled ideas for a class essay. His consciousness registered images and dream residues; the sensuality of leather, sweat and petrol; surfacing memories of the sound, the sight of a phalanx of them roaring along Sarsparilla Street; real, hard men. And one night, as Katrina had waited for the lights to change, that sallowing highway light had bathed their disciplined black convoy. And then ... Toby sprawled in front of the TV, Katrina bringing in the Chicken Marengo; his wine became oil and the bird on the casserole dish stretched its wings to fly through fire. The table throbbed ...

He knew they would be sitting there. Day after day.

Now in the rows, in the cages, in the courts. Now in the 'cattle trucks' that sped them — imprisoned, from prison through peak hour traffic — to prison. To hear the logic of lawyers. Evidence. Day after day.

What kinds of men were they? Heroes or what? What had they felt? What had it done to them? Had they changed? When would they have been observed enough? He wanted to speak about it to someone. That might have made it clear, perhaps less painful.

'She shouted to her friend: "Look out he's got a gun". Seconds later bystanders saw her blown five metres, her face distorted and blood pouring from a wound. A bystander said, "It was horrible — the girl's head was covered in blood — there was nothing left of her face. She was hit so hard by the blast her jaw seemed to have blown off!" Witnesses said several bikies stalked around the scene of the shootings with guns in both hands as police tried to restore order. One man said: "It was as if they were acting within the law. After the girl was shot, another bikie carrying a gun casually went to a car, got some beer and passed it to his mates ..."

'(A Sydney couple) said that what had been a face a few split seconds before was splattered over the t-shirt of a young man standing next to her' (A. 3 Sept).

'The motorcycle, originally conceived as a means of transportation, has become an object of dreams and fantasies. It is represented as the embodiment of freedom and individuality; it is an object which transmits fear and adventure; it is a thing which makes us children again; it is an escape and a respite from civilisation; and it is the medium through which individuals can achieve self-transcendence and rebirth. Contemporary Americans' insecurities and troubles also find their outlet in the motorcycle. It is no coincidence that much advertising content and media themes stress the virility, the vitality, the strength, the self confidence, and the individuality that one can achieve on a motorcycle. For those who have been dulled and dominated by instrumentalised occupations and mindless urban routines, the motorcycle provides a modern odyssey, a means of shoring up oneself in the face of it all, and an object for transforming one's identity. It is a tranquiliser, an equaliser, and more. It is a machine that can be used to express innumerable cultural emotions and impulses.'[7]

'But in the fifties, the lower class male who had never known the indignities of commuter trains and backyard barbecues still seemed to be the last repository of defiant masculinity. Hollywood introduced a new breed of nihilistic, overtly sexual male rebels, who were either rejects from the middle class (James Dean in *Rebel Without A Cause*) or terrorists emerging from an invisible underclass (Marlon Brando in *The Wild One*).'[8]

'Locke suggested that fraternity is formed not by birth but by election, by contract; Plato's fraternity based on the division of labour excludes the family; Durkheim's organic solidarity is the opposite of kinship. This brotherhood is not made inside the family, nor by the father; it is not born of the flesh, but of the spirit; it is not natural but artificial.

Rousseau would say it is based on will; in the vocabulary of Freud's *Totem and Taboo*, it is totemic brotherhood.'9

Reckless (1984); *The Outsiders* (1982); *Mad Max II* (1980); *The Warriors* (1979); *Mad Max I* (1979); *Stone* (1974); *Easy Rider* (1969); *Bikeboy* (1967); *Leather Boys* (1964); *Lawrence of Arabia* (1962); *Rebel Without A Cause* (1955); *The Wild One* (1954).

Smalltown party-girl: What are you rebelling against?
Johnny: What've ya got?10

'The truth is that *The Wild One* — despite an admittedly fictional treatment — was an inspired piece of film journalism. Instead of institutionalising common knowledge, in the style of *Time*, it told a story that was only beginning to happen and which was inevitably influenced by the film. It gave the outlaws a lasting, romance-glazed image of themselves, a coherent reflection that only a very few had been able to find in a mirror, and it quickly became the bike rider's answer to *The Sun Also Rises*. ... They saw themselves as modern Robin Hoods ... virile, inarticulate brutes whose good instincts got warped somewhere in the struggle for self-expression and who spent the rest of their violent lives seeking revenge on a world that done them wrong when they were young and defenceless.'11

But he could only sit in the night, alone, staring at papers and books and clicking the cap of his engraved Parker.

... 'Oh God', he thought as he handed it in.

A = *Australian*; M = *The Daily Mirror*; NT = *The National Times*; S = *The Sun*; SH = *Sun Herald*; SMH = *Sydney Morning Herald*; ST = *Sunday Telegraph*; T = *Telegraph*.

All citations without a year at the end refer to the period Sept — Dec 1984.

1. P.M. Tristess, *From Foucault to Flaneurs*, Feral Press, Parramatta, 1989, p. 111.

2. *The Sydney Morning Herald* 9 Nov, paraphrasing the Crown Prosecutor at the Committal Hearings, wrote: 'The leaders of two rival bikie gangs, the Comancheros and the Bandidos, declared war on each other during a phone call three weeks before the Viking Tavern massacres, a court was told yesterday'.

3. Tristess, *Foucault*, p. 77. See also T.E. Perkins, 'Rethinking Stereotypes', *Ideology and Cultural Production*, ed. Michele Barrett et al, Croom Helm, London, 1979.

4. Editorial *The Australian* 5 Sept; *The Australian* 3 Sept; *Sun Herald* 9 Sept; *Financial Review* 4 Sept; *Financial Review* 4 Sept; *Telegraph* 4 Sept.

5. *Telegraph* 5 Sept; *Telegraph* 6 Sept; *Telegraph* 3 Sept; *Mirror* 3 Sept; *Sun* 7 Sept, *Sun* 25 Sept; *Financial Review* 4 Sept; *Sydney Morning Herald* 13 Nov; *Sun Herald* 9 Dec; *Telegraph* 18 Jan 1985; *Telegraph* 29 April 1985; *Sydney Morning Herald* 32 May 1985; *Sydney Morning Herald* 8 June 1985.

6. *The Australian* 3 Sept; *Australian* 22 Oct; *Sun Herald* 9 Sept.

7. John Alt, 'Popular Culture and Mass Consumption: the Motorcycle as Cultural Commodity', *Journal of Popular Culture*, 15:4, Spring, pp. 134-135.

8. Barbara Ehrenreich, *The Hearts of Men: American Dreams and the Flight from Commitment*, Pluto Press, London, 1983, p. 57.

9. Norman O. Brown, *Love's Body*, Vintage Books, Random House, New York, 1966, pp. 9-10.

10. *The Wild One* (1954).

11. Hunter S. Thompson, *Hell's Angels: the strange and terrible saga of the outlaw motorcycle gangs*, Ballantine Books, New York, 1969, pp. 89-90.

AFTER MILPERRA ... WHERE DOES THE ROAD LEAD?[1]

It was about the mid sixties. Hunter S. Thompson had been riding alongside the Angels for a while and making notes. That was until Hunter S. and the Angels fell out. But he wrote his book anyway and when it got published the Angels didn't seem to mind too much.[2] Meanwhile, here in Australia, 'Jock' Ross set up his gang.

He called them the Comancheros. He might have got the name from a Californian gang that was around then. Hunter S. mentioned them a bit in his book.[3] And maybe the American gang pinched their name from the Comanches because they fought back when their territory got invaded by the cowboys. But there's another version of how they got the name. In *The Australian* an FBI agent said that Jock might have got the idea from a '61 John Wayne movie, (A. 8 September). It was even called *Comancheros*. The Duke was a Texas Ranger who tried to stop a bunch of outlaws (The Comancheros) from selling rifles and booze to the Comanches.[4]

Anyway Jock became president of the Comancheros and got to being called 'supreme commander' and 'sole voice of authority' (PE:[5] 9 Jan '85). Then seventeen years later they split up. That was in the middle of '83 (A. 8 Sept).[6]

The papers were pretty vague about what happened next. The two clubs seemed to get on okay for a while. But then 3 Comancheros got beaten up when they went to a Bandidos' pub. (SMH 13 Nov).[7] This is why Jock rang 'Snoddy' Spencer. He was the leader of the Bandidos. All this happened round about 9 August '84. These two leaders laid down battle rules. These ground rules said 'no approaches or assaults to be made at the houses of any gang members or in public places' (SMH 4 Sept).[8] After this Snoddy told his men 'something has to be done about Ross and the Comancheros permanently besides bashing them' (PE: SMH 14 Nov). The men had a vote and they decided to go to war. The vote was 14 to 12 or 16 to 14 (PE: SMH 20 Nov). Then they burned the old Comanchero colours (PE: SMH 14 Nov).

Later on they started accusing each other of what have been called 'assaults and approaches'.[9] Bandidos' lawyer, Murphy, reckoned the Bandidos went to the cops five times over 3 months. This was *The Telegraph's* story (T. 13 Sept).[10] *The Herald* said it was at least fifteen times in 3 weeks. (SMH 4 Sept.)[11] But the Wentworthville cops claimed they didn't have any records of any of this and headquarters couldn't say if any of the other stations had got any of these complaints (SMH 4 Sept). An anonymous Bandido had said that someone shot at one of their houses (SMH 4 Sept). Bandido's lawyer, Murphy, said Snoddy was shot at four different times (A. 22 Sept).[12] And according to that Bandido turned crown witness, Bernard Podgorski, some Comancheros beat up Bongo Snake and stacked his 185k Harley on top of him (PE: SMH 8 Jan '85).

Of course the Comancheros had their own version. They told the cops that Bandidos had gotten into their places and beaten them up (ST 9 Sept).[13] Whoever was in the wrong (if anyone was), on that Father's Day morning, some Bandidos rode past a Comanchero's place. Crown Prosecutor Viney, in presenting his case for the Crown, told the court that the gangs felt this was 'a public taunt' (SMH 13 Nov). He said that was why the Comancheros decided to go to the Viking Tavern. They knew that if the Bandidos were there they'd have a fight (Crown Prosecutor Viney to the court, paraphrased SMH 13 Nov). And according to Podgorski, who was giving evidence for the Crown, the Bandidos went because they were told the Comancheros weren't there and because Snoddy said 'we would go ... to show other clubs anyway because we are at war and we will show our colours anywhere and we are not afraid to do so' (PE: M. 19 Nov). *The Herald* report was nearly the same and also had, 'He said if they are there we would go ahead as planned' (PE: SMH 20 Nov). The rest is history.

WAR/MASCULINITY 51

1. The title of my essay comes from the end of *Aussie Biker Culture* (Sydney, Kevin Weldon and Associates). This magazine was on the stands by early October '84. It got a write up in the *Sun Herald* (14 Oct).

2. Hunter S. Thompson, *Hell's Angels: the strange and terrible saga of the outlaw motorcycle gangs* (Ballantine, 1967).

3. Thompson, *Hell's Angels*, mentions the U.S. Comancheros on pages 14, 100 and 129. Today's FBI doesn't mention them so they might have gone underground or died out between now and then.

4. I haven't seen this movie but different TV movie guide books say it's pretty good. *Halliwells' Movie Guide* says it's an 'easy-going cheerfully violent western with lively rough-house sequences'.

5. PE: Podgorski's Evidence in court. Bernard Podgorski was a Bandido who became a Crown Witness at the committal hearings of the Bandidos and Comancheros. Podgorski had a lot to say about what happened during the six weeks that he gave evidence for the crown.

6. There's a few versions of when they split up. Some sources suggested it was before Snoddy etc. went to America (M. 3 Sept, SMH 3 Sept). Others say it was after they got back (A. 8 Sept, T. 8 Sept).

7. Crown Prosecutor Viney told the court that this happened. Paraphrase of *Herald* account.

8. The statements about contact between Jock and Snoddy and the events that happened after this are a paraphrase of Sgt. Wood, police prosecutor, to Fairfield Court, following arrests connected with the events.

9. Sgt. Wood, police prosecutor, to Fairfield Court. See n. 8.

10. Bandidos' lawyer, Murphy, to the Court, paraphrased in the *Tele*.

11. An anonymous Bandido quoted in the *Herald*.

12. Bandidos' lawyer, Murphy to the court.

13. A 'detective' 'working out of Bass Hill police station', quoted in the *Sunday Telegraph*.

The papers could have attempted to figure out why it happened. But instead they preferred to utilize the technique for conveying information which they commonly adopt for tragedies like the famous Mt Panorama riots and football hooliganism. This information is conveyed in terms of shock stories with gory spreads without attempting to give a detailed analysis of the particular tragedy. Only some points of view get aired. People get a go if they've got status and/or some recognised expertise — politicians, wowsers, psychiatrists — and the like. Or because they have aired the view of the 'man in the street'. Yet if these types can get to speak, other types can get misquoted and misrepresented. The bikies, for instance, definitely felt that they had been misunderstood. In fact at some stage or other both gangs have got so pissed off with journos that they have stopped co-operating with them. The Bandidos did this at the beginning and the Comancheros ended up doing it too (re Comancheros SMH 8 June '85). And, come to think of it, you could also make a list of the sorts of people who didn't get a go at all. This list would have in it radicals, feminists, illiterates, ratbags, the bikies' wellwishers and the like. And you've got to remember too that people like professors and lawyers tend to get their go in other places like journals. So when you realise that the papers can censor who speaks, how they speak and what they can say, you can see that they're capable of reworking what happens.

Nevertheless a few types did try to explain it. First, there were the bikies. Then there were the politicians, the editors and the so-called experts. Of course, they began by saying how unbelievably shocking it was. Yet when they went on they usually gave only one or two reasons. You can divide these explainers into two groups. The first sort was the people who took part in it. As well as the Bandidos and the Comancheros there were their mates and the cops. And, soon enough, the FBI got into the act. All these people pointed to only one or two events. Then they went on to claim that these events caused it all. Yet, as we'll see later, some of them felt that these events were just the tip of the iceberg.

The other lot got onto their favourite hobby horses straight away. These ones made out that what happened was indicative of some social problem or other. Then as soon as they told us what this problem was they told us how to cure it. It was usually something pretty predictable — like drugs, or something trendy — like video porn, or useless — like peace armies and new gun laws. You could just about figure out who they'd be. As well as the newspaper editors there was Premier Wran, Police Minister Anderson, Opposition Leader Greiner, a smattering of the types who write into the papers, Festival of Light mouth Fred Nile, that bikie priest from Melbourne called John Smith, a psychologist and, last but not least, the RSL. It's worth having a look at all these explanations to see what they amount to. But before I do this I must pause for a moment to explain my sources. In attempting to make sense of all this I had to work my way through a host of multifarious explanations that I gleaned from literally hundreds of news items. To make matters worse, these items had been written to meet the demands of newspaper deadlines. Perhaps this is why they often tended to be unsystematically organised, incoherent, all over the place. Anyway, I want to examine some of the conditions that helped to make the massacre possible.

First, there were those who were actually involved in the whole series of events. Taking them one by one and starting with the Comancheros. Jock was in hospital so two of the others spoke for the Comancheros instead of him. Acting leader JJ claimed that drugs had been responsible for the breakup (SMH 3 Sept). And Jock's own wife Vanessa, also pushed this drug line. When *The Sunday Telegraph* journos asked her, she said 'Jock was filthy on drugs . . . He's kicked plenty of people out of the Comancheros over the years because of them'. She made out that the Comancheros were pretty decent. She said that they nearly all had good straight jobs. Vanessa reckoned that the gang's drug dealers wanted to keep Jock as national president. This was because he was 'so well respected'. She said, 'That way they could do their drug deals and keep their image — but Jock wouldn't have any part of it' (SMH 9 Sept).

Within a week, the Bandidos were made out to be international speed runners. The FBI said that, back in '83, some of our local bikies (the ones who became the main

Australian Bandidos) visited the American Bandidos who lived at Corpus Christi in Texas. The Bureau claimed that the two gangs had 'partied' together. It also claimed that these American bikies lived off speed and coke dealing. They needed a chemical called P2P to make speed. This chemical is illegal in the U.S. but legal here. When the Aussie bikers got home from O.S. they fell out with Jock. That's when they set up their own club — The Bandidos (A. 8 Sept). They called it this because their new leader Snoddy said 'they wanted to be allied with the club that stood for bikies and brotherhood and the Bandidos did that' (**Aussie Biker Culture** [ABC] p. 34). Vanessa had more or less the same angle on it. She said Jock walked out of a meeting because of drugs and that he took 7 members with him. She said, '. . . seeing what the FBI is saying about drugs and the Bandidos, it all makes sense' (ST 9 Sept).

Needless to say the Bandidos had another explanation for what happened. Their version became big news when Podgorski was in the witness box for 6 weeks giving evidence. But even at the very beginning an anonymous Bandido was making out that the Comancheros had 'insane ideas'. They wanted to 'conquer the bike scene' and try 'to make an army out of the motorcycle club' (SMH 4 Sept). This claim was also made by a one-off mag. It called itself *Aussie Biker Culture* and it appeared on the stands not long after all this happened. This mag made out that it was about serious journalism. But it was really pushing the Bandido's line. It had chapters on the Angels, the Rebels and the Bandidos and other pieces on bikes, lifestyle and tats. It ended up with a photo essay called 'The Massacre That Was Milperra'. Then the very last picture was of a bikie riding the open road and underneath it said 'After Milperra . . . where does the road lead?' Then the next two pages were real black. You got the idea that even if you can never know what the bikies' future holds it's likely to be crook anyway. All this made the Bandidos sound just like all the other outlaw gangs around. In fact the pictures helped to show us that they even looked pretty much the same as the others. But the Comancheros didn't even get a look in. These 'serious' journos got a lot of mileage out of someone they called 'a part time enthusiast who had ridden with the Bandidos and knew the club well'. This so-called enthusiast also claimed that the Comancheros were 'turning into a commando unit'. He said that they were climbing over barbed wire and learning guerilla tactics. This is why the Bandidos split (ABC p.33).[14]

And later on, when Podgorski was giving his evidence he said that Jock was 'more into military ideas than motorcycling' (PE: S 22 Nov). Podgorski reckoned that the Bandidos thought that Jock was a bit of a joke. This was because he called himself 'supreme commander' and set up a Comanchero strike force like the SAS. He also posted armed sentries round their camp sites. But, according to Podgorski, Jock wasn't the big man that he pretended to be. Jock was supposed to have made up stories about his military past. Podgorski said he began to see through it all when he found out Jock had only ever been 'a corporal in the engineers' (PE: S 22 Nov; PE: T. 10 Jan).

Podgorski gave some examples of their jokes against Jock and the other Comancheros. When Jock declared war the Bandidos had this joke that the Comancheros would try to attack the Bandidos' Birchgrove clubhouse 'by a submarine via the harbour' (T. 10 Jan '85). Podgorski also said that whereas the Bandidos lived for their bikes, the Comancheros were more into cars (PE: S 22 Nov; PE: SMH 23 Nov). He claimed that the Bandidos only ever saw one Comanchero riding a bike in the six months before Milperra. He identified this Comanchero as Jock. Podgorski told the court that he got a real laugh out of this 'because the man normally never rode motorcycles' (T. 9 Jan). Of course, one of the Comancheros' lawyers said all these allegations were based on hearsay and on Podgorski's 'personal dislike of the man' (T. 10 Jan).

Let's go back to that Father's Day. As soon as it happened, the cops put 50 men onto the case. This was to clean up the mess at the Tavern. They also had to guard the bikies in hospital and to question people and make arrests. But they weren't saying what caused it all. They might have thought an early explanation might backfire on them later. Or it could be that the press hadn't asked them — or hadn't printed it. But the cops did say that the gangs had been having a blue for a while.[15] All that

14. Incidentally he also said that none of the Bandidos were into heroin. He said, 'They've got this unwritten law that anyone caught using heroin faces instant dismissal. They reckon that's what destroys a club first. There's no hiding some of them smoke marijuana, hell, everybody smokes marijuana it seems to me' (ABC p. 34). But saying this doesn't necessarily mean they couldn't have been into other drugs. Or that he'd know, for that matter.

15. At about the same time the cops kept saying it was a really tough case. No one was talking. I don't know why exactly. The eyewitnesses could have been scared. But as well as this the bikies have a code of honour that says you can't grass on mates (T. 4 Sept).

Anderson would say was it had 'to do with the complex issue of ill feeling between the two gangs' (SMH 5 Sept). And they held back some information from the press. When they gave out the Comancheros' rules they took out No. 5. We found out later that it said, 'Any member found taking or dealing in drugs will be instantly dismissed' (NT 7 Sept).

By the Tuesday the cops reckoned that it might have been sparked by a really big drug rip-off and/or a 'long simmering' dispute over pub drinking territories (SMH 5 Sept). This was when their boss, Commissioner Avery, went off on a completely different tack. He began by saying that the police had done a good job. Then he said people should feel safe enough not to have to carry arms or to feel they had the right to. Only cops had the right to carry guns. This was because they were the ones who were supposed to be enforcing the law. He said that if everyone started carrying guns then 'we'd be back in Neanderthal days — not civilisation' (M. 5 Sept). He was really saying that it was up to the Force to maintain civilisation. Then he said, 'Vengeance is mine saith the Lord'. I couldn't figure what this was supposed to mean. It could have meant that the bikies weren't to avenge what happened but to leave things up to God. But I got the idea that he was making out that the cops knew what God wanted and were keeping it all under control. Yet another meaning could have been that the government deals in justice (and leaves God to do the avenging). Whatever the case we were supposed to feel pretty lucky that the cops had come along quick smart and saved Sydney from falling back into Neanderthal times.

Also when he said Neanderthal times he was pushing the bikies outside civilisation. And it implied that we wouldn't want to be like them. This was to keep us in line. But on the face of it, a sizeable part of the bikies' lives was typical of your average suburban Aussie bloke. They had videos and Hills Hoists and at least one of them (Jock) had a pool. Also their ladies and kids were pretty supportive after Milperra. So while his men were trying to figure it out and were doing the spade work, Avery was doing his job. This was to make out that his men were doing a great job and how necessary they all were. When you think about it the FBI was doing the same sort of self-justification snow job. This was when they were claiming that all their spying on bikies would help control international drug running.

Now we can get on with that other main group of explainers. These were the ones that hopped onto their hobby horses. Newspaper editorials are notorious for this kind of attitude. Corruption in the ALP and tax rip-offs are examples of this. And so when it came to Milperra, they whipped themselves up into a lather of indignation. You could see that froth flying in *The Telegraph*. The bikies were 'animals who have come to the end of the road' (T. 4 Sept). Meanwhile *The Australian* was ashamed.

This is not the way Australia works ... if we are to ensure that Australia remains a fair and peaceful land, swift firm action must be taken to bring within the strictures of the law those whom we have until now allowed to live outside it. (A. 3 Sept.)

The Sun said more or less the same thing. Except it also said that since the 'bikie fanatics' couldn't keep their violence to themselves then the cops should be allowed to keep a much closer eye on them in future, (S. 3 Sept).

Basically, they were saying that Milperra was caused by slack laws or slack cops. They were saying that we needed to tighten up the laws or make new ones and put the screws on the cops for not doing their jobs properly. If we did this everything would be OK again.

The Financial Review said that lots of bikies broke the laws that said they had to wear helmets. Because they got away with this they thought they could break any law they wanted to. Gun laws especially needed tightening up. But there were other reasons as well. In the 50s cheap wheels became pretty common. Another reason was today's unemployment. This had something to do with social problems like drug dealing and car stealing. Some so-called sectional interests keep up high rates of unemployment. These interests were also to blame. But then the editorial made a big leap. It started to guilt trip its own readership. The editorial finished up saying, 'If you want to know who caused the violence on Sunday and you have a job — just look in the mirror' (FR 4 Sept).

What this seemed to mean was that you could blame the economy for Milperra. The economy had made bikes so cheap anyone could get one. Then because the economy happens to be going through a rough patch the gangs got dangerous. If the economy was good they'd be law-abiding and have decent jobs. They wouldn't have to get money in other ways. But nobody knew what to do about it. This was because too many selfish people had too much at stake to try and change things. This is a pretty funny concoction of pop sociology and economics. It mixes up economic factors and social problems and violence without really saying how they relate. It's like it was clutching at the same tired old straws to help it explain this first-time-ever event. But once it had set off on this track it came up with some pretty pessimistic conclusions. Namely that society could never change because of the sectional interests. Things are so bad that even if people with jobs should be made to feel guilty that's the full extent of what can be done about it.

Wran and his mates' line was that the government must make us feel safe in our beds. At the beginning Wran was pretty vague. He said that his government would deal with the lawbreakers 'accordingly' (A. 3 Sept). Then he said he'd get tough on louts and hooligans. He promised new gun laws and new consorting laws. There would also be a new law to stop louts giving lip to motorists. *The Telegraph* decorated him with the headline 'Wran Outguns Bandit Bikies' (T. 10 Sept). Wran's Police Minister Anderson backed him up. Anderson's story was that their new gun laws would mean there'd be fewer murders and armed hold ups. *The Herald* thought this was pretty good. Then it remembered that Wran made these same promises six years ago (SMH 4 Sept). Of course, Opposition Leader Greiner went in to bat for the Libs. He also said that Wran's boys had been going on about new gun laws and the like three times before. Greiner said nothing ever came of it. He wanted all firearm offenders locked up. But then Anderson got his own back. He reminded Greiner that the Libs had been anti-tougher on gun laws before the last election (SMH 4 Sept).

So what we got was the usual point scoring session that passes for political debate in this country. Everything about this round was typical. The government thought it had to have a say. So that we'd know that it was doing something. Then the Opposition thought it had to make its presence felt and run the government down. What both sides were really saying was 'leave it up to us'. Of course, this would mean new laws and fewer freedoms in order for them to get on with it.

Needless to say some people could see through these political machinations and the newspapers' tough talk. One such bloke wrote to *The Herald* to say that these changes in the law only dealt with the symptoms of the problem. He went on to say that the real problem was 'apparently . . . inherent' in 'human nature'. He reckoned that Milperra was all about lethal competition and that this sort of thinking could lead to the extinction of our species. For him the Milperra Massacre was just the same conflict as in 'Ulster' and as confrontation between 'the West and Russia' (SMH 12 Sept).

Where do you start with this? You can't just say there's some basic human nature without explaining what you mean by this and providing some argument that it's not socially induced. Also, you can't jump from this little incident to the big ones like global confrontation. There are too many factors you'd have to consider. You could make a case for our tendency to think 'either/or' where 'either' is all the positive things and 'or' is all the bad things. But you've also got to analyse specific historical, cultural and philosophical factors for each case, which just wasn't done.

Other people were worried about where the violence came from. Terry Walsh wasn't going to be guilt tripped by that *Financial Review* editorial. He said that the employed hadn't pushed the unemployed up against the wall. He reckoned we all got off on 'defiance and lawlessness'. This was because we were the heirs of a 'brutal culture'. This culture was the Vikings, Teutons and Celts who celebrated 'the orgy of death as a way of purging treachery'. He claimed we were the same. He said, 'It's a long bloody road from Valhalla to the OK Corral but it's on TV every night and it's not surprising that it appears outside a pub in NSW once in a while' (FR 25 Sept).

I don't want to go into this one in much detail. 'Defiance and lawlessness' suggests that all laws are equally moral for all people and that breaking a little one — like jaywalking and fare evasion is the same as breaking a big one — like murder and tax evasion, and that we only ever do it for a lark. Then you've got to remember that the Vikings, Teutons and Celts were very different sorts of cultures. Besides, only some of us have got that sort of blood.

Finally, he has a pretty bleak world view when he shrugs his shoulders and says you've got to expect seven deaths every now and again because of westerns.

Clean morals campaigner the Rev. Fred Nile MLC said the same thing as Terry Walsh. Only he blamed what happened on what he called a society brutalised by an out-of-contact porn-and-violence video industry. He reckoned that videos are 'desensitising people' and make them get fact and fantasy mixed up. He said, 'It was only when . . . [the bikies] . . . were hit with bullets themselves that they realised that . . . [the violence] . . . was real.'[16] Bikie priest John Smith went along with this. *The Telegraph* put him in because he was the bloke who traded his dog collar for a leather jacket and his parish Holden for a Harley. Having it both ways if you ask me. Anyway this Smith claimed that Milperra was the product of 20 years of growing madness. The sort of madness you got on TV and in pop video clips. Some Wahroonga lady called (Mrs) Denise Burden gave the nod to this view (SMH 12 Sept).

I don't think much of this sort of explanation. First off, you'll notice that none of them say how video-porn and the TV etc., actually caused Milperra. They seem to think violence is only one thing. They never stop to think that violence changes over time and in different situations and has different purposes and powers and so on. They don't see the difference between genocide, rape, self-defence, roo shooting and gunning down your ex-mates. Also, I can't figure out what pop video clips have got to do with it. This one's a bit off the planet. These sorts of people always pick on the latest thing. Even if clips are really common they can't have had a proper look at them. Most clips aren't violent in any sense of the word. I will admit that the most frequent form of violence in them is sexist. But the Fred Niles of this world would have an uphill battle proving that watching these porn and *Countdown* videos is a direct cause of incidents such as Milperra.

There are a couple of other sorts of explanations to go. A *Telegraph* journo asked a psychologist called Wilfred Jarvis what he thought about it all. She picked Jarvis because he had just written some stuff about bikies. This Jarvis really had his finger on the pulse of the mind of society. For Jarvis, society is breaking up. More and more alienated and aggressive groups are getting around. Real families are splitting up like atoms on 3 Mile Island. People who can't find status or decent employment any more turned to 'emerging groups' which say 'we love you, you can identify with us and take on our folk customs and feel real satisfaction'. Jarvis called these groups 'pseudo-families'. People identified with them because there weren't enough real families around anymore. This made Australia 'a society in a state of unprecedented revolution' and that's why there's going to be more 'interesting and quite threatening things' like what happened at Milperra (T. 4 Sept).

But what does Jarvis base all this on? He starts off by thinking that the family is the basic social unit. Then he reckons that everyone would want to belong to one. And then that, if you did belong to one, you wouldn't want to have anything to do with what he calls alienated groups. But what about the five Campbell Brothers? They had wives and kids (lots of them). Jock Ross and JJ were family men too. Jarvis seems to think that everyone wants and gets the same things out of 'the family'. Like the Fred Niles of this world, when they think there's only one sort of violence, Jarvis seems to think there's only one sort of family. Only one sort of gang too, for that matter. The way they quoted him in *The Telegraph* he doesn't distinguish between all the

---

16. This was reported in *The Manning River Times* (5 Sept) because Nile was in Taree to speak to a Call to Australia Party rally prior to the '84 federal election. Nile's party describes itself as 'a political coalition of Christian citizens and action groups united in their desire to build a better Australia'. I included it here because it was photocopied and posted out in their September media release.

different sorts of things different sorts of people want and get from different sorts of families and gangs. And, while I'm at it, what proof's he got that society is breaking down? Where's his evidence? But I suppose if you've got a fixed idea about what society is, inevitably you're bound to think that it's breaking down.

This brings me to the RSL. They were having a talkfest in Melbourne so they were probably all fired up to make public statements. It could also have been because they might have been getting flack because one of the bikies was military and others of them had been in the armed services — one of them had even guarded the Royals at the Palace. The RSL spokesperson said that military experience wouldn't have caused what happened. Then they went off on their hobby horse. This was that we needed a community service corps so young people could get a sense of self and national pride (M. 6 Sept). But the RSL didn't seem to understand that they were offering the sort of goody-two-shoes stuff that the bikies had probably never wanted in the first place. After all, they called themselves outlaws and got off on being 1%ers.[17]

In this rundown from the bikies to the RSL I've tried to show that none of these so-called explanations can really help us to figure out why Milperra happened. These 'explanations' might look like a good account of the causes but they aren't really. But it should be noted, in defence of the journos, that they may feel that explaining things is not really part of their job any more. Maybe it never was.

But even if they had taken the trouble to embark upon an in-depth analysis of the causes they'd pretty quickly have found themselves at sea. This is because when someone says something causes something else he or she is making out that there's a direct connection between the cause and the event. But a better way of looking at it could be that when someone starts talking about the conditions that make something **possible** he or she is talking about a whole range of things that are connected and which, although they don't directly cause the event, are necessary for it to happen in the way it does at the time that it does. This second way of looking at things isn't the be all and end all. It has problems because the idea is so open-ended. Almost anything could be dredged up as a condition of possibility for any event. However the idea allows us a more useful explanation of things that affect events and that are necessary for them to happen than do simple causal explanations.

Considering this, there are a few really important things to take into account when you look at Milperra. Among these I would number:
1. Sydney's suburban sprawl — why some suburbs became posh and others became Housing Commission. You could see bikie gangs as efforts of some men to try to move about and impress themselves in the sorts of public places like streets etc. that men claim. So the sprawl provided a space for them to make out who they were and who they wanted to be, and to say things about themselves (like the Comanchero rules).
2. Public transport, cars and bikes. A bike isn't about getting around in the sprawl. Maybe these two wheels came to mean speed, manoeuvrability, control, risk, escape, freedom, being tough. It's no wonder that both gangs came out with lines like 'we'll cut up [the victims'] ... bikes and bury their bodies on top of them ... They'd like to know they went with their machines still under them' (M. 4 Sept). This gives you some idea of how they felt about them.
3. Bond group — both groups got reported as saying how important their 'brotherhood' was. Snoddy 'makes no secret of the fact that he feels everyone of the 37 members is his brother' (ABC p.34) and someone else said 'I never make friends with outsiders' (ABC p.60). These men knew who their mátes were and their rules also reflected what they felt they should do for each other.

Besides these there are a lot of other conditions, like speed, freedoms, how easy it is to get hold of weapons, etc. But perhaps the most seriously neglected of these in terms of study is ... men: what (Aussie) men are like; what they think about themselves and what kids and ladies think about them; how men think and feel about

17. The bikies were pretty anti society. As I've already said, the local Bandidos thought the American lot were OK because they were into bikes and brotherhood. The Yanks had a line that the FBI claimed went something like this: 'A one percenter is the one out of a hundred of us who has given up on society. And the politicians' one-way law. This is why we look repulsive. We are saying we don't want to be like you or look like you ... We are outlaws and members will follow the outlaws' way or get out. All members are your brothers and your family' (A. 8 Sept).

other men, about men's social structures and social spheres. Having a look at men would help us understand events like Milperra. It would help us understand why it was almost entirely men (and not ladies) who were apparently involved; why these and other bikies get off on bikes, violence, aggro, being tough and being in gangs; how the papers represent these sorts of goings on.

A lot of things influence the way men are. One writer has said that family, work, class and leisure help shape men.[18] But I reckon things like ethnicity, sexuality (normal, homo, fetishists), age, feelings about things like technology, death, mateship, ladies, time, speed and space are important too. Another writer said that in our society there is a culturally dominant form of masculinity. This is the aggro, capable of violence and toughness form.[19] It's one that's anti-homo, anti-fem, sexually normal, into putting down ladies etc. But I reckon this has got probs because as I said before there's lots of different types and capacities for violence etc. If you don't say exactly which one you're talking about then it's a bit hard to know which one you mean. Also in our society, some of these capacities for violence are considered OK and don't rate a mention, others get the thumbs down. The papers' responses to the bikies are an example of a really big thumbs down to a particular kind of violence. All of them gave you the idea that the bikies had gone too far but they cashed in on it as well.

One of the really big problems in this area is that very little study has been done. So, in a way, before you can make claims about there being a culturally dominant form of masculinity you need a whole lot of evidence to show that it is the culturally dominant form, and how it is the dominant one. So you can see that though a couple of writers have got the ball rolling vis a vis masculinity study, a lot more work needs to be done before we can say what the whole process might look like.

Overall, I've tried to show that the papers' way of explaining how Milperra came about is a bit simple and crook. There are other ways of looking at it which might help us understand things a bit better. And I've tried to suggest what they might be, very briefly. So for me, this is where the road has led after Milperra.

B + + (You could do much better than this)

Steve — Though your essay, at times, bristles with interesting ideas and you communicate in a simple, direct and straightforward way, I think your style is too colloquial for the complex issues it attempts to convey. It's a pity you didn't have the space to go into more detail in the last part of your essay which contains some of your most suggestive ideas. Perhaps you could take up these ideas in another way. (Come and see me.)

R.D.

18. Andrew Tolson, *The Limits of Masculinity* (Tavistock London 1977).

19. This writer is Bob Connell who has written a number of essays which look at the issue. See for example, *Which Way is Up? Essays on Class, Sex and Culture* (George Allen and Unwin, Sydney 1983); Connell, D.J. Ashendon, S. Kessler, G.W. Dowsett *Making the Difference* (George Allen and Unwin, Sydney 1982); Connell, S. Kessler, D. Ashenden, G. Dowsett *Ockers and Disco-maniacs* (Inner City Education Centre, Sydney 1982); Connell, Tim Carrigan, John Lee *Hard and Heavy Phenomena* (unpublished paper); 'Men, Masculinity and Violence', *Challenge*, no 73, Feb 1985.

subscribers

Next **INTERVENTION** Publication contains articles from:
Meaghan Morris, Liz Gross, Luce Irigaray, Brigitte Carcenac, Gayatri Spivak, Stephen Knight, Frazer Ward, Noel Sanders, and others.

Papers/IMAGES are also called for **FLESH**, a publication on/around/through a BODY OF IDEAS - to be published early in 1986.
Subscription Rates (per 3 issues)

   individuals-$20.00; institutions-$40.00;
   overseas -$A25.00 & $A45.00 respectively.

All new subscribers will receive their choice of one (1) back issue, free.

Intervention Publications :   PO BOX 395, Leichardt, Sydney, Australia. 2040

WAR: MACHINING MALE DESIRE

Adam Farrar

Introduction

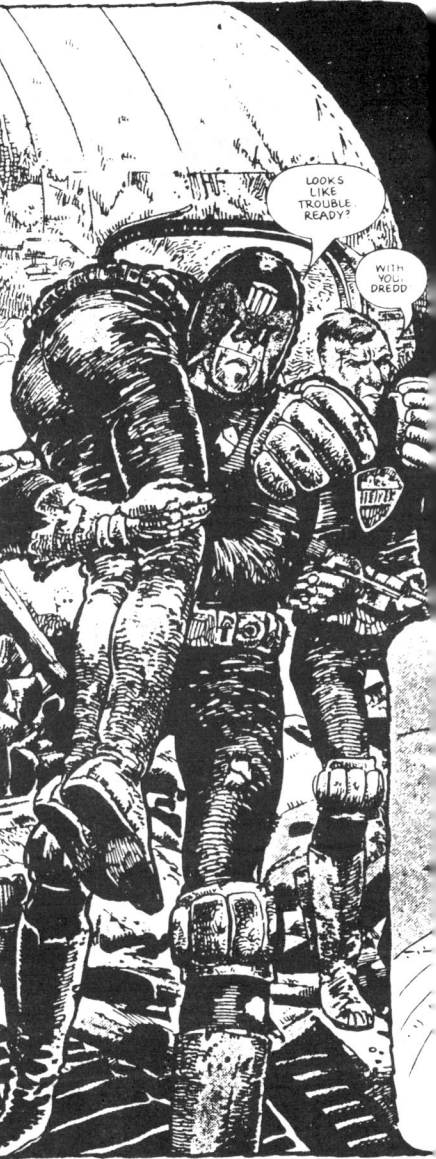

The observation that there is a special connection between men and warfare is a commonplace. Recently this commonplace has been given political teeth with the development of a critique of 'masculinist' values, practices and cultures. There are, it is claimed, a wide range of practices which are not only in the interest of men — securing patriarchal relations of power — but which also function in the construction and maintenance of male identity. These practices with their associated values and systems of belief constitute a hegemonic culture of masculinity, from under whose sedimentations a feminine culture is only now being excavated. As the desperate and intractable situation produced by society's military obsession has forced many people to look for new political strategies, women's actions have offered such a new hope. A corollary of these activities is the focus on war as a male problem. War, on such accounts, is a paradigm of masculinist practices because its pre-eminent valuation of violence and destruction resonates throughout other male relationships: relationships to other cultures, to the environment and, particularly, to women. If the 'masculinism' of war is the explanation for its intractability, then we must follow this path to its conclusion, wherever that may be.

At the same time, some caution should be observed. First, it is clear that masculinity will only be part of the explanation of war. The political economy of war — of the whole military, industrial, security complex — is throwing new light on the black and the twilight-zones of the economy. War has been recognised as playing a central role in capitalism for a long time. However, an explanation of war will never be adequate until it can account for the male domination of war: and similarly, no account of men will be complete unless it can explain why men fight wars.

This raises another problem. Recent discussions of sexual difference[1] have shown how difficult it is to pose the question 'what's male (or female) about ... subjectivity, actions, institutions, society, the history of thought?' Although a battery of notions have been tried — gender, masculinity, masculinism and patriarchy — none of them have very successfully captured the theoretical vantage point demanded by the question. None of them have allowed us to see what's at stake for men in the extraordinarily wide range of activities which detailed work has shown to be specifically and stubbornly 'men's activities'. So far, most of these categories have led us into a circle when we ask the crucial question: 'what's at stake for men?' Descriptive notions like 'masculinity' or the literal sense of 'patriarchy' simply refer us back to the purely contingent and historically specific fact that men do adopt certain 'roles' or positions of 'authority'. The less descriptive notions of 'masculinism' or the political use of 'patriarchy' refer us to a dominant culture of men marked out by 'values' such as violence, aggression, universalisation, or the oppression of women. None of these would fully explain what's at stake, even if the explication of the roles or values were richer or more convincing.

1. H. Eisenstein and A. Jardine (eds.): *The Future of Difference* (Boston, G.K. Hall & Co., 1980); M. Gatens: 'A Critique of the Sex Gender Distinction', in J. Allen and P. Patton (eds.) *Beyond Marxism?: Interventions after Marx* (Intervention Publications, Sydney 1983); or H. Eisenstein: *Contemporary Feminist Thought* (Unwin, Sydney 1984).

In this paper I want to develop an account of 'male desire' which I think overcomes this problem. In particular I will argue that certain central, legitimating, aspects of the much wider military, industrial, security complex, are crucially concerned with a radical transformation of the form of desire into what is paradigmatically male desire. Unfortunately, 'desire' is something of a buzz word today, used in a confusing variety of ways. My use is adapted from Deleuze.[2] What I mean will become clear later, but so that the term doesn't hang in the air, I will say here that 'desire' means the active process of assembling the world of events, its objects and subjects, on the plane of 'immanent intensity'. A particular advantage which I hope will emerge from this approach is an explanation of what is at stake in both the extraordinary participation of men in modern combatant armies and in the technological and strategic production of destructive terror which is replacing them. But first I want to draw attention to how slight our examination of the relation between war and masculinity has been to date, and to some of the more obvious traps which surround the formula 'war is masculine'. So far, there has been no systematic attempt to show how masculinism explains the social production and maintenance of the institution of warfare or the initiation and conduct of actual wars. Rather one finds a number of interesting but tangential topics explored.

Suggestions

Considerable work has been done, notably by Susan Brownmiller,[3] to show how the conduct of war is invariably fought on two fronts: one against enemy soldiers, the other against all women subjected to the combat. What has been established is a direct link between warfare and male sexuality, particularly rape. This is born out by the explicitly sexual references and representations which permeate combat training. However, there are a number of explanations which would account for these observations without making warfare dependent on masculinity. For example, a more general connection between death and sex, or violence and male sexuality has often been argued.[4] Again, the plausible explanation that rape is the further subjugation of the vanquished by violation of its sexual property, shows warring societies to be patriarchal but does not show war to be masculine.

In a similar way, many of the institutions associated with war can be shown to be particularly masculine. The RSL, ANZAC Day reunions, films such as *Gallipoli*, all rely on practices and values central to male bonding, and perhaps more importantly, father-son initiation. But this shows us nothing about warfare itself. Rather, we learn that in a male dominated society in which warfare is conducted by men, the representation of war exploits this male activity to perform the important function of bonding men. This suggests that there is considerable male investment in the maintenance of warfare, but not that war is a necessarily masculine activity.

Another very suggestive explanation is implicit in Brian Easlea's work, particularly his latest book *Fathering the Unthinkable*.[5] This is (and here I am extrapolating from what Easlea says) to explain war by reference to its technology, which is essentially masculine. Easlea's account contains two main theses. One is that all societies have exhibited a variant of an Oedipal dynamic in which the male child's identification with his mother and the feminine is subsequently replaced by induction into the male world. The central feature of this male world is participation in 'men's magic' which is a substitute for (and envy of) women's procreative power. I will return to this thesis later. The second of Easlea's claims is that with the Scientific Revolution 'man's magic' was replaced with a much more potent technology/knowledge. In what might be seen as an historical Oedipal transition, Mother Nature was replaced by a nature ripe for penetration who would reveal all her inner secrets to a sufficiently forceful suitor. Easlea claims this language, these metaphors and the explicit identification of this new knowledge as masculine,[6] imparts a specific logic and impetus to a science whose inevitable outcome is today's nightmare military technology.

2. Cf. P. Patton: 'Notes for a Glossary' *I & C: Power and Desire* No. 8 (1981).

3. S. Brownmiller: *Against Our Will* (Penguin 1973), Ch. 3.

4. For a discussion of the wider role of violence within social discourse see M. Foucault (ed.): 'Tales of Murder', in *I, Pierre Riviere* (Penguin 1978).

5. Easlea: *Fathering the Unthinkable: Masculinity, Scientists and the Nuclear Arms Race* (Pluto, London 1983); cf. also his *Science and Sexual Oppression: Patriarchy's Confrontation with Women and Nature* (Weidenfeld Nicholson, 1981).

6. For another account of the masculinity of the new rationality of the Enlightenment, see G. Lloyd: 'The Man of Reason' *Metaphilosophy* 10 (1979); also *Radical Philosophy*, 34 (1983) Women, Gender & Philosophy issue.

This account is suggestive in two directions. First, by shifting the burden of the account to the forms of knowledge and the material technologies which mediate social practices, the connection between war and masculinity is removed from the unsatisfactory arena of roles (the 'brave soldier') or dispositions towards violence. Second, it has the potential to account for the masculinist practices which result from masculine knowledges. In particular, it locates the exploitative and destructive character of these practices in a contradiction inherent in the basic model of male 'creativity' which is conceived in terms of rape and violence.

Unfortunately the account is nothing more than suggestive. Easlea does nothing more than show that these metaphors (rape, male birth and so on) are used as justification, particularly when the interests of problem-solving contradict the external interests which prompted the investigation. He examines at length the contradictory motives of those scientists involved in the Manhattan Project who

... spoke of their fears of atomic weapons in the possession of the Nazi government as being ... the principal reason why they attempted to initiate the Manhattan Project ... However, so much more mysterious becomes the fact that the Los Alamos scientists intensified their efforts after the surrender of Nazi Germany.[7]

According to Easlea some of the explanation lies in the birth metaphors used by the participants: 'His eyes were aglow. He had seen a miracle. It was a turning point in history; the birth of a new era'[8]; or in another case, 'the first cry of a new born world'[9] as their bombs, christened 'Fat boy' or 'Fat man', were successfully delivered.[10] But such metaphors, once again, only show that the means of **representing** significant practices in a male dominated culture are constructed in terms which are significant to men. They don't show that the practices so represented are necessarily masculine. Easlea suggests that such 'men's magic' is a condition of the construction of a separate male identity, but a good deal more needs to be said before such 'men's magic' can be shown to underpin modern military practices.

Finally we have a range of literary or anecdotal accounts of the particular pleasure or even love which attends men's experiences of war. Last year *The Australian* republished an article from *Esquire*[11] in which an author who has '... seen enough of war to know that I never want to fight again, and would do anything in my power to stop my son from fighting', asks 'why ... do my thoughts turn back to a war I didn't believe in and never wanted to fight? Why do I miss it?' He answers: 'I miss it because I loved it.' War lends experiences great intensity. It eliminates most of the background decisions, simplifying everything, existing only in the moment. Comradeship and trust are matters of basic survival not utopian dreams, and are constantly reinforced by the ever present utter loneliness of death. In all these ways it is an enactment of 'mythic' oppositions. To quote again: 'It is, for men, at some terrible level the closest thing to what childbirth is for women: the initiation into the power of life and death'.

No doubt all this is true. It explains why, as a bonding process, war is tremendously successful. But even this is only masculine insofar as bonding is sexually segregated and it is contingently the case that men fight wars. However, there is a hint in the article of the significance of the **technology** of 'men's magic', a point which is implicit but undeveloped in Easlea. Describing the power of indirect action that accompanies a finger on the trigger of a bazooka or M16, the author goes on:

It's like the magic sword, a grunt's Excalibur: all you do is move that finger so imperceptibly, just a wish flashing across your mind like a shadow, and poof! In a blast of sound and energy and light a truck or a house or even people disappear.

There is no doubt that there is something special about this sort of power, a fascination with the fact that the effect is so disproportionate to the act of wielding it. This is an effect which is missing from other technological marvels like television, ISD telephone calls and so on, but is experienced in part even in the smallest slingshot. While there is no reason to suggest that this a peculiarly male experience, it is plausible to suggest that since it is the **only** such avenue of magical power available to men, it has thereby a special and jealously guarded significance. In

7. Easlea, op. cit., p. 83.

8. ibid, p. 88.

9. ibid, p. 96.

10. ibid, p. 95.

11. William Broyles Jr: 'Why Men Love War' reprinted from *Esquire* in the Weekend Australian, November 17-18, 1984.

saying this I am gesturing at Easlea's view that 'men's magic' is a substitute for women's procreative power. That notion (womb envy) is I believe, too literal to be of much use, but it does direct our attention to the significance of such moments of intense experience which I will look at more closely later on. The most we can plausibly draw from this is an understanding of why the horrors of warfare didn't eliminate it as a social practice almost at the outset; it does not explain the occurrence of war.

What do we mean by 'war'?

At this point we should try to get clear just what it is that men have a stake in: what do we mean when we talk about war? I think it is fairly clear that we can't easily talk about war *per se*: an inter-tribal cattle raid, a medieval crusade and modern nuclear war are incommensurable. Even in the case of contemporary 'military' phenomena the range is much too broad. Certainly not all of these events are significantly male. Nonetheless it is very tempting to talk of some central case without which none of the other phenomena would carry the meaning 'military', and this central case is combat. I think our intuition about what constitutes combat is clear, but at the same time, 'combat' is only described by the formal (and perhaps circular) requirement of being that which is counted as the central case of military activities, and then extrapolated, through 'family resemblances', with various phenomena in different cultures. Again, even in our own times, the 'combat' involved in a 'terrorist' war, a guerrilla war, a conventional war and a nuclear war are all very differently constituted. Nonetheless, one of the central themes in these 'family resemblances' will be the male investment in these activities.

Clearly the political function of war is not, as it is invariably represented, that of a final sanction in dealings between nations or groups. That account restricts 'war' to events or periods of actual combat, but combat is only one moment of military activity. Rather than being a sanction, combat is much better conceived of as the legitimating instance — the warrant of the validity — of a much wider net of social interactions. It seems to me that it is historically compelling to describe these interactions as functioning to construct, or at least constrain, the forms of political authority within a nation or group. At the same time they do so in ways which are functional for the dominant forms of social power and organisation within that group or nation — dreamtime totems, shamanistic magic, kinship structures, religion, economy and so on. The kind of political agents so determined may often be quite equivocal. The present relation between the military, intelligence networks, networks of alliances, political blocs, individual states, governments and economic interests is clearly equivocal in a way that the coincidence of feudal authority and military interests was not.

The first point is that combat must be seen as only a legitimating instance of a complex social interrelationship. Secondly, this military substructure is one of the essential factors in constructing the historically changing forms of social collectivity. In saying this I am arguing against any attempt to reduce war/military activity to an effect of either a political authority, or the economy, or male power. Rather, the social meaning of the institutions and forms of social power referred to is legitimated by the symbolic force of those acts which are paradigmatically acts of war. And again it is important to remember how completely these paradigmatic acts of war can change. It must be doubted that the indescribable devastation of a nuclear explosion would be recognised as an act of war by those societies for whom 'war' means the fleeting bravado of an inter-tribal cattle raid. What is startlingly constant is that the agents of these acts are men or male institutions.

When we look for the male connection with war we need not expect to explain the whole social investment in military relations. What is male about war in the broadest sense is its legitimating moment, the warrant for the intelligibility of the wider network of acts and institutions. The warrant of combat is only redeemed when the intelligibility or legitimacy of other areas is in danger. In the rest of this paper I want to look at what male investment in those moments is.

Combatants and Non-Combatants

Warfare is not simply conducted between warring participants, it is also conducted against non-combatants. Whatever else we say about war as the violence of men towards men, it is also necessarily violence of men against all other non-combatants, particularly women. While almost all representation of war is solely concerned with the nature of combat, the actual character of agency in war is also crucially determined by the character of the relation to immediate non-combatants. This point should be distinguished from the obvious claim that the outcome of war permits the victor to exert control over the vanquished group; it changes the legitimate authority. Instead, the point is that the norms of individual relations are set aside. Expropriation, murder, enslavement, rape are not outmoded aspects of war, nor are they accidental excesses, nor are they simply the prerogative of the victor. They are the necessary outcome of the changed forms of legitimation which operate between combatants and non-combatants. War is not just a relation between regimes, or between combatants, but between the activity of war and the lives of the civilian population caught up in it.

This is an essential feature of the phenomenology of war; of the kind of agency constituted in war. It is also a precondition for many of the social functions of warfare in different societies and periods: exogamy, forced labour, colonial exploitation, the production of new markets and so on. Of course the particular relation to the civilian population has varied in different societies and historical periods. In some cases the civilian population has been the direct object of contention: the capture of wives, the enslavement of a labour force. In other cases

it has been more abstractly constituted as warfare focused on the capture of markets or the demand for subsequent reconstruction. But to focus on the paradigm of combat as a relation between soldiers, or even between weapons systems, is to miss a vital feature of the legitimating instance of war. An extraordinary change in the norms of behaviour towards, indeed in the very perception of, other social agents and day to day social life, must take place.

It is here that the part played by science/technology in constituting the phenomena of war is most important. The history of war seems, even more than the history of productive labour, to exhibit a decline in the direct workforce accompanied by a technological increase in productive (destructive) power. War may never have been a cottage industry, but it has certainly been a tribal one involving almost all males. The division of labour which led to a standing army decreased direct participation except in extreme cases. There seems to be some reason to believe that the mass slaughter of combatants exhibited in WWI (brought about by technical improvements) was something of a watershed in the use of combatant forces. Their use is much more marginal now, both to the main theatres of world power conflict and to the central strategic aim of modern war (to destroy the enemy civilian infrastructure). This focuses our attention, as did Easlea, on the way in which the scientific technical military complexes are constructed as masculine.

One reason for stressing this point is that it is within this relation that one of the fundamental changes in modern total war has taken place. The non-combatant victim of total war has been moved to the front of the stage while the combatants have become less and less signficant. And like the challenge to the Medieval witch-hunts which began when increasing numbers of men became caught up in its violence, so total war has produced an unprecedented challenge to its own legitimacy.

A second reason is that insufficient attention is paid to the extraordinary process which is a precondition for most major periods of modern conflict: the double **transformation** of civil society into, on one hand, soldiers and, on the other, a newly vulnerable form of civil life. Among the few analyses of the reorganisation of civil society in the context of war is the discussion by marxist feminists of the wartime use of women as a source of productive labour. This was the basis for later analyses of women's economic position as a reserve army of labour. However, the reserve army theory has itself been largely discarded in favour of a more complex analysis of the ways in which 'work' is socially constituted around dichotomies such as public/private, paid/unpaid, productive/consumptive and so on.[12] Just as it is difficult to explicate the non-paid work and activity of women in traditional marxist categories, the same is true of wartime civilian activity, and for the same reasons. Once again we are looking at a sexually segmented form of social activity, and categories which don't make this fundamental will be inadequate. Modern warfare is predicated on a massive and rapid re-allocation of social agency along sexual lines. Any analysis of warfare which doesn't pay particular attention to how the site of male activity is relocated from production to soldiering will provide a very partial picture indeed.

12. A. Game and R. Pringle: 'Production and Consumption: Public vs Private' in Dorothy H. Broom (ed.), *Unfinished Business*, (Allen & Unwin, Sydney 1984) p. 65, and Game and Pringle *Gender at Work* (George Allen & Unwin, Sydney 1983).

13. Eg. the gradual transition from the early entry of the patriarchal family unit to a male operated 'masculinised' machine to today's 'family wage'. See E. Zaretsky: *Capitalism, the Family and Personal Life* (Pluto Press, London 1976).

If we are to understand warfare then, we must also understand why men participate. But while the social mechanisms, the social pressures and the ideology by which this is effected are extensive, the fundamental condition that men set on their entry to a form of social activity is that it be **constituted as male**.[13] To refer to an area as 'male' is not just a description of its sexual composition or of an expressed unwillingness to break down its sexually segregated character. Rather, it is to refer to the way in which that area is constituted so as to sustain the social constitution of masculinity itself. This may not be unique to war. Other things being equal, most men would not choose to work as miners, for example. But we miss a central feature of such work if we simply focus on the economic necessity or even the traditions and defence of working class communities which played such an important role in the British miners' strike, and ignore the investment in masculinity which lies at the heart of such work.

In the case of war, the constitution of the activity as male is more important. Firstly, because some of the most frightening features of modern war exhibit a form of rationality which a number of commentators have argued is specifically male.[14] This rationality has become linked to war through the modern development of military technology and strategy. It includes the tendency to globalise destructive capacity, the tendency (against all expressed intentions) to increase rather than to decrease coercion as a medium of social and international 'rationality', and the increasing tendency to introduce a symbolic dimension such as 'strategic balances' and 'kill ratios'. The second reason for stressing the prior sexual constitution of the activities which men and society take up in times of war is that the process is actually the converse of the more familiar shifts in the sexual division of paid work. At these times, men enter an area of work previously filled by women, with associated low pay and economic or professional marginalisation. The entry of men then legitimates the area of work and consequently rates of pay increase. In times of war, men enter en masse a form of activity which at other times would simply not exist, under conditions which most would normally consider intolerable and which only promise to get worse.

We cannot simply explain this entry either by the ideology of nationalism or coercion. Certainly coercion plays a significant role as the history of conscription, shanghaiing and military sanctions (particularly against desertion) bears witness. It seems that violence and coercion generally play a major role when young men are initiated into male practices and values. The main thing we must notice, however, is the extraordinary value placed on war by future and past participants. Fathers continue to send their sons to war despite their own experiences. Various national or class traditions (such as the only partly mythical 'Australian digger') strongly resist the coercive forms of authority in the army precisely to fight more effectively. The Esquire article quoted earlier is eloqent testimony to the ambivalence accompanying the exposure to war. Coercion may play a vital role in coping with that ambivalence, but once the balance is tipped, many, probably most, men are not unwilling to fill the role. In the same way, the appeal of nationalism undoubtedly plays an important role. Its relative absence was clearly one of the reasons for the unpopularity of the Vietnam war. Finally, its highly abstract nature for most of the 'free world' (the U.S. excepted) must be one more reason why the war posturing of the superpowers has trouble finding supporters.

To be a member of a social collectivity, be it a clan or a bourgeois state, one must be an appropriate social subject. And it is clear that the imperative of nationalism, insofar as it entails a commitment to soldiering, refers only to male subjects. Nationalism, while just as compelling, has quite a different meaning to women. So if we are to understand the effects of nationalism or the strategies of coercion, we must first understand how they are functional for masculinity. Otherwise they will not help us to understand the radical redistribution in social activity, particularly the shift in the constitution of 'men's work'.

The Solipsist Male

While the transformation of civilian males into combatants is in need of explication, perhaps we can come at it from another angle. If, as I argued earlier, combat is not the aim, or the outcome, or the logical conclusion of the various much wider politico-military interactions between societies, but rather the redemption of the warrant of legitimacy for a complex variety of social agencies, then it must at all times be legitimate **in its own right**. It is therefore tempting to suggest that this legitimacy is provided by its being in an almost unique way a **male** activity.

In some societies this was self-evident. To be male was to be involved in the activities of combat. It is much less obvious in our own case. Certainly the representation of war — in games, in cinemas, in RSL clubs, in reunions — is almost always concerned with male bonding. This is significant, but such instances of male bonding are not sufficiently widespread to be more than a minor part of the constitution of men today. We must identify what is significant about combat for men. A number of

14. Easlea (op. cit.); see also L. Birke et al (eds.): *Alice Through the Microscope: The Power of Science Over Women's Lives* (Virago 1980); E. Fox Keller: 'Feminism and Science' *Signs* 7 (1982); cf. also Ch. 10 *Contemporary Feminist Thought*.

observations made so far seem relevant. Combat involves a *gestalt* shift in which one's relation to people and things changes utterly. All the norms and mores which determined our attitude to others are changed. If we are to avoid the view that without the humanising constraint of civilisation the natural beast emerges, we must ask what underpins this new life form. After all, considerable work is required to effect this *gestalt* shift.

To answer this we must return to that remarkable description of the power of weapons quoted earlier:

... All you do is move that finger so imperceptibly, just a wish flashing across your mind like a shadow, and poof! In a blast of sound and energy and light a truck or a house or even people disappear.

What this illustrates is the replacement of the norms of intersubjectivity, of communicative action, by a direct relationship between wish and manifestation. Most action is structured around the norms of intersubjectivity, which are primarily communicative.[15] Even in aesthetic or productive acts, the intelligibility of one's own action or product depends on effecting a meshing of mutual intelligibility. Most social activity involves the construction of an understanding which is mutually intelligible. Such understanding is not fixed but is constantly in play and can be constantly undermined by stubborn misunderstanding, by changing the rules of the game, by broken promises, by coercion ... in short, by the diverse **flows of power** which underpin all social action. The other side of this coin is the intensity which pulls some actions, moments or interactions into the foreground for one pregnant moment or another. I am inclined to think that the notion of *jouissance*, for which we have no English equivalent, best captures this phenomenon. *Jouissance* is not just 'pleasure' which is centred around physiological sensation, but rather a cross between the physical content of **pleasure and intensity**. Deleuze talks of 'intensity' in explicating the notion of desire. We might say for Deleuze, that desire consists in the assemblage of events on the plane of immanent intensity.[16] The phenomenology of alienation consists in precisely the absence of *jouissance* or intensity in those situations where the humanly necessary presupposition of intersubjectivity is systematically precluded. *Jouissance* then, seems to be the measure of our understandings (the plane on which we 'machine' our intelligible world) within the constant flow of intersubjectivity, of communication, of symbolic action.

Now, as I remarked earlier, one of the main features of the phenomenology of war is the unique intensity of experience. War experience is exactly the converse of alienation. In war, the elimination of all the norms of intersubjectivity produces, not alienation, but the most intense *jouissance*. The machining of events on the plane of intensity (to use the Deleuzian image), the form of desire, is utterly transformed. Power no longer consists in the capacity to redeem the warrants of communicative intersubjectivity. It consists in the ability of the spear, the sword, the gun, napalm, the bomb etc. to manifest 'in a blast of sound and energy and light' (or in another time, in the blood of a severed limb or a disembowelled body), the merest 'wish flashing across your mind like a shadow'.

15. Jurgen Habermas, *Communication and the Evolution of Society* (Heinemann, London 1979).

16. This is my own formulation drawn from Paul Patton's explication in 'Notes for a Glossary', op. cit.

There are two aspects to this. First, it is the world of solipsism, or narcissism. It is not the world in which this or that subject acts. Rather, in that instant of power, the world is **identical** with the agent of the power, of the wish and the gun. We can see how this literally cashes out Easlea's notion of 'men's magic'. Magic, after all, is also the manifestation of a wish, not through the mediation of labour or social practices, but through the mediation of either an object of power and/or, much more importantly, a word or formula. This leads directly into the second point: while the example we are referring to is an example of an individual combatant's intense narrowing of focus, the phenomenon is most acutely manifested in the non-combatant world of super science and nuclear technology.

To illustrate the advantage of the scientific/technological version of the *jouissance of combat*, we must consider the fragility of the soldier's experience. Like orgasm, while there may be a moment of universal power, it is one which immediately collapses into the everyday world of fear and negotiation. It may be reproduced with the next bullet or bomb, but it constantly teeters on the brink. In another sense too, it is fragile. Its intensity and *jouissance* depend in large part on the moment of **magical transformation** where the independence of people and things is sucked away and frozen in an instant of solipsism. In effect, the power of that moment, its intensity, is equivalent to the power of those intersubjective negotiations or practical barriers which have been circumvented. But this means that the *jouissance* is limited, not just by the impermanence of the frozen moment, but also by the particularity of the play of power transformed.

The solipsism of nuclear weapons technology has no such fragility. It fixes the whole material and social world in frozen abstraction. As Easlea showed, the scientists working on the first nuclear weapons were transformed by the belief that their work not only comprehended, but made manifest the ultimate secret of reality in the explosion of each nuclear bomb. Scientific rationality has, in any case, been shown to hold the solipsist view that the collective scientific knowledge, thought, wish, is literally identical with fundamental reality.[17] But the epistemological open-endedness of this notion of fundamental reality provides military technology with an ongoing research project (whose continuous promise makes the fleeting fragility of moments of individual combat seem ludicrous): namely, to harness more and more fundamental forces for more and more total destruction.

Easlea argues that military technology is masculine. The significance of his emphasis on military technology is that it suggests that combat, the legitimating instance of society's military function, is a specific case of the male construction of technological rationality. We may see other examples of it. Video wargames present a fairly clear and insufficiently examined case: some of the images involved, such as those of *Custer's Last Stand*, a video game which involved the rape and murder of Indians, seem more than just suggestive. Aspects of computer culture, such as 'hackers', exclusively male computer virtuosos who live in an isolated and solipsist world bounded by all the possible ramifications of their computer networks, deserve more attention.[18] The virtual transformation of modern nuclear war into a computer wargame is another obvious link.

However, Easlea's account rests on the notion of a 'distortion' of scientific or technological rationality produced and reproduced by the psycho-social anxieties of each of its male practitioners. The distortion is the result of such rationality being conceived as the male transcendence of the feminine relationship to nature (particularly procreation), a conception which is overdetermined by the metaphorical extension of a male sexuality at work on the feminine body of nature. But while these metaphors are poignant and pervade the self-representation of male practices, they are an insufficient basis to explain the pervasiveness of the practices of warfare and science. Instead, we must turn to an account which considers our construction and experience of the world, which will locate the specific *jouissance* of combat and military technology, of pure war and pure science. That is, an account of desire; and specifically **male** desire.

17. The most explicit statement of this attitude I have seen was made by Darryl Reanney (who is science director of Gene Link Ltd.) in his article 'Gut Feelings — new thoughts on origins' in the *Age Monthly Review*, April 1984.

18. S. Turkel: *The Second Self: Computers and the Human Spirit* (Granada 1984).

Male Desire

The term 'desire' provides the most effective way to talk about what is male about masculinist practices; in this case, war. Warfare is crucially concerned with a radical transformation in the form of desire. While male subjectivity[19] should be understood as something variously, often conflictingly, constituted in a multiplicity of possible situations and interactions and discourses,[20] nevertheless, there is a 'hard core' of masculine subjectivity. The possibility of constituting or invoking this is what I call 'male desire'. Combat, I would argue, is significant precisely in that it is one of the few and most sustained occasions in which the **male subject** is predominantly the subject of **male desire**. Here, he is very much a 'centred' subject. Since this desire turns out to be solipsistic, the subject is so centred that it in fact vanishes, since there is no dualism of subject and object.

The use of desire avoids the essentialist problems associated with, firstly, Freud's reduction of the desire-like notion of a 'wish' to the notion of 'drive', or 'instinct', or the repressed unconscious of our conscious intentions;[21] and secondly, Lacan's notion of desire as the impetus produced by the lack between (or incommensurability of) a need for satisfaction and a linguistically compassable demand.[22] Instead, the present use of 'desire' focuses our attention on the ways in which events, discourses, understanding, objects, subjects — the shifting ingredients of a life world — are assembled so as to provide significance or *jouissance* with different kinds of intensity. This allows us to see why masculinity can be so elusive and why it certainly cannot be captured in 'roles'. It is not an essence, an attitude, or an undifferentiated kind of subject, but rather a **potential** way of assembling the world which can at any time be invoked or retreated from. We can only really capture 'masculinity' in those few moments of unalloyed male desire — pornography, rape, science and ... war.

One of the effects of the development in the last few years of what Hester Eisenstein[23] calls a woman-centred perspective in feminist theory was a restatement of the problem of how the sexes are differentiated. Rather than asking how women are the 'other', are different from the male norm, the problem became how do men become differentiated particularly from the original maternal model. Particularly in the U.S. this question has been asked, by people like Nancy Chodorow, in terms of a theory of object-relations.[24] At the same time, as Easlea also argued, a good deal of sociological and anthropological work has demonstrated the way that such differentiation usually requires the vigorous intervention of other men and even then continues to exhibit insecurity. Generally speaking, such accounts rely fairly heavily on the unsatisfactory model of a more or less clearly described identity, self or subjecthood. Similarly they often rely on the notion of roles or forms of behaviour appropriate to such an identity. And it is certainly inadequate to explain complex social, political, economic relationships, from patriarchal authority to practices such as warfare, in terms of individual psychology and insecurity.

By talking about forms of desire, the important points raised by these accounts can be dealt with more adequately. The model of the early development of a self-image through 'identification' with the mother is a rather clumsy and unsatisfactory one. If instead we focus on the urgent problem posed by the infant's need to gain control over the plane of 'satisfaction' or 'intensity' it is clear that it will be launched into a regime of desire which is partly co-extensive with the mother's desire. It is machined around the contours of the mother's physical presence and absence. This is not reducible to 'identification', but rather is an evolving symmetry of desire.[25] While for the child the flows of intensity are always dependent, thereby impelling the child towards the progressive construction of worlds offering greater control, the plane of intensity must always be construed as immanently accessible. More than that, the very dependency (particularly if the mother/infant relationship is particularly close) means that it must be construed as mutually intelligible, almost co-extensive. This means that there is not, as Lacan would have it, a total gap

---

19. The notion of subjectivity here is not one of a unitary ego or even a constant social subjectivity such as 'worker' or even 'man'. The subjectivity of any biological individual is constantly in play.

20. I am using 'discourse' in a very broad sense which would include eg., philosophical discourse, legal discourse, the plastic discourse of painting, and so on.

21. I am referring to Deleuze's objection that psychoanalysis produces a constrained unconscious in order to teach us 'Lack, Culture and the Law; that is to say the reduction and abolition of desire'. See 'Four Propositions on Psychoanalysis' in P. Foss and M. Morris (eds.): *Language, Sexuality and Subversion* (Feral Publications, Sydney 1978).

22. Lacan is the specific target of Deleuze's criticisms (cf. n.20).

23. H. Eisenstein: op. cit.

24. N. Chodorow: 'Gender, Relation and Difference' in *The Future of Difference*.

25. This evolving desire — the machining of the world on the place of immanent intensity — although differently described, is precisely what both Freud and Lacan spell out in such painstaking detail; particularly the account of the development of the distinction between self and the outside world in 'Instincts and Their Vissisitudes' in Freud: Standard Ed., vol. 14, and Lacan's account in 'The Mirror Stage as Formative of the I', in *Ecrits*.

between the pre-linguistic child which cannot name its needs, and the post-linguistic child whose demands are constrained by the prior consitution of what is linguistically intelligible. That account limits the plane of intensity to discrete but inarticulable needs. But this creates its own apparent paradox by begging the question of whether intensity depends on signification. For Lacan this question begging means that his attention is focused on how the male's Oedipal dilemma is solved by his entry into the real of the symbolic: i.e. language. For Lacan, desire's role is a part of the unconscious and pre-history of this real.

However, with a more Deleuzian account, there are much more fluid possibilities. The child's gradual accession to more various and more potent forms of subjectivity, including the position of subject of language, may well include those in which the experience of *jouissance* or intensity is not experienced as inter-subjectively co-extensive. Nonetheless such co-extensiveness is from time to time recaptured (even by men) in empathy, in some moments of sensuality, in moments when we are acutely aware of another person's attention, in some communal religious and aesthetic experiences, and probably (this time not by men) in mother/child relationships. In most cases, however, it is replaced by less immediate forms of mutuality. The shared norms of intersubjectivity which underly linguistic communication are probably the most common.

Nonetheless, Lacan and Freud and the anthropological studies Easlea draws on point to something signficant. That is, that in addition to, and forming a radical break with the gradual accession to forms of agency and their correlative life worlds, male children are inducted into male desire. There are a range of accounts of the mechanisms of such induction. Freud's account of the Oedipal dynamic is one, although it is clear that even insofar as we accept all its details, it is a very historically and culturally specific account. The more communal forms of male initiation, in their turn, seem to rely on a more specific rejection of an earlier childish (feminine) taint. Easlea and others argue that this depends on a fairly explicit rejection of and jealousy towards women's childbearing capacities. These are replaced by 'men's magic' which continues today, having evolved during the Scientific Revolution into technological knowledge/science. Whatever its plausibility as an anthropological account of some societies, this is certainly not an adequate general account. While science/technology may have some analogies or even some functional similarities to the secrets of male initiation, they simply do not play the same role in inducting men into male desire. Childbirth envy plays a role in primitive initiation ceremonies, and it may have some physical significance to many men, but there are simply no grounds for believing that it universally underpins male desire.

Nonetheless we can say something about the form of male desire and its effects. As Freud and Lacan make clear, what underlies all male interdiction, however it is effected, is a promise. Or rather, the form of a promise, since any attempt to specify the promise will prove partial and highly particular. A promise is an act (paradigmatically a speech act) whose 'truth' conditions, whose warrants, are deferred. I doubt that any actual promise, any such speech act, ever has much to do with induction into male desire, despite the way Freud talks. But such talk is intelligible because deferral lies at the heart of male desire.[26]

On our account, 'desire' is the machining of the worlds in which we have access to an immanent plane of intensity. Deferral means that while the objects (or signs) of the *jouissance* are constantly before one, the subjecthood, the condition of access to its intensity, is always deferred.[27] These objects acquire an intense signification which impels their obsessive circulation in discourse and image and action. In some areas of male desire, the condition of access to their *jouissance* may be actual accession to the position of the Subject of a given discourse,[28] but in most cases it is probably more *ad hoc*, diffuse, or fleeting. One of the best examples is the objectification of male sexual desire in pornography. In pornography there is a momentary halt called to deferral, to the elusive circulation of desire, as the viewer enters into a kind of proxy subjecthood via the narrator, or more importantly today via the authorising position of the camera. Actually this is oversimplified. The

26. This notion of deferral involves two debts. The first is simply to notice some resemblance to the Derridian notion of the deferral of meaning within the circulation of a discourse. My present account owes a lot to discussions with Phil Barker.

27. I am using 'subject' and 'object' as familiar and convenient, but not necessarily exclusive ways of referring to the ways the items of a life world are divided up.

28. Accession to the position of 'master' or 'professor' is a good case. Barker has discussed this in some detail in discussing philosophical biography and autobiography.

viewer in fact enters a relation with an actual subject — the actual author or cameraman — whose absence permits the viewer to assume the authorised position. But this is hardly a very secure position. The very tenuousness and artificiality of the subjecthood demands an obsessive repetition of the pornographic image if the *jouissance* is to be recaptured. The same is true of male sexuality itself. As men struggle to become the subjects of the circumstances and representation of sexual intensity, they attempt to overcome the elusiveness of that constantly deferred position as the subject in sexual desire. In all cases, male desire means that within the lifeworlds of this peculiarly male subjecthood, these worlds are only suffused with intensity when the circulation of desire is momentarily frozen.

Perhaps there's a formal character of such a freeze, of these moments of entry into the subjecthood of male desire such as pornography, rape, combat and scientific rationality? One of its main features is its narcissism. The elusive circulation of desire is halted by simultaneously occupying the position of both subject and object; that is, the object of one's pleasure, *jouissance*, the source of intensity, is oneself as the subject of events, of power, of desires. It seems to me that this is exactly what we observed as the source of the intensity of modern combat. It is tempting to suggest that this may also explain the peculiar birth and creation metaphors of the quasi-combat of nuclear weapons technology drawn out by Easlea. It could also lead us to ask how certain images, discourses or technologies mediate the 'machining' of such subjects of male desire.

Does this account fall foul of the requirement that war or any social activity should not be explained as a set of psychological dispositions or attitudes? I don't think so. This attention to male desire is in no way intended to explain war. The varied social function of war remains to be elaborated. It does, however, tell us something vital about one of its legitimating instances — combat — and possibly something about its newly developing legitimating instances such as weapons technology and strategic balances: namely, how entry into their worlds is entry into a world machined around male desire. On this framework we might be able to go on to the laborious task of filling out the changes in forms of authority, institutions, social values which facilitate the periodical entry of men to such a world of male desire in times of war, and perhaps the historical transition we seem to be undergoing towards an epoch of technological total war.

STRUCTURES OF IDENTITY: GENDER AND NATIONALISM

Ross Poole

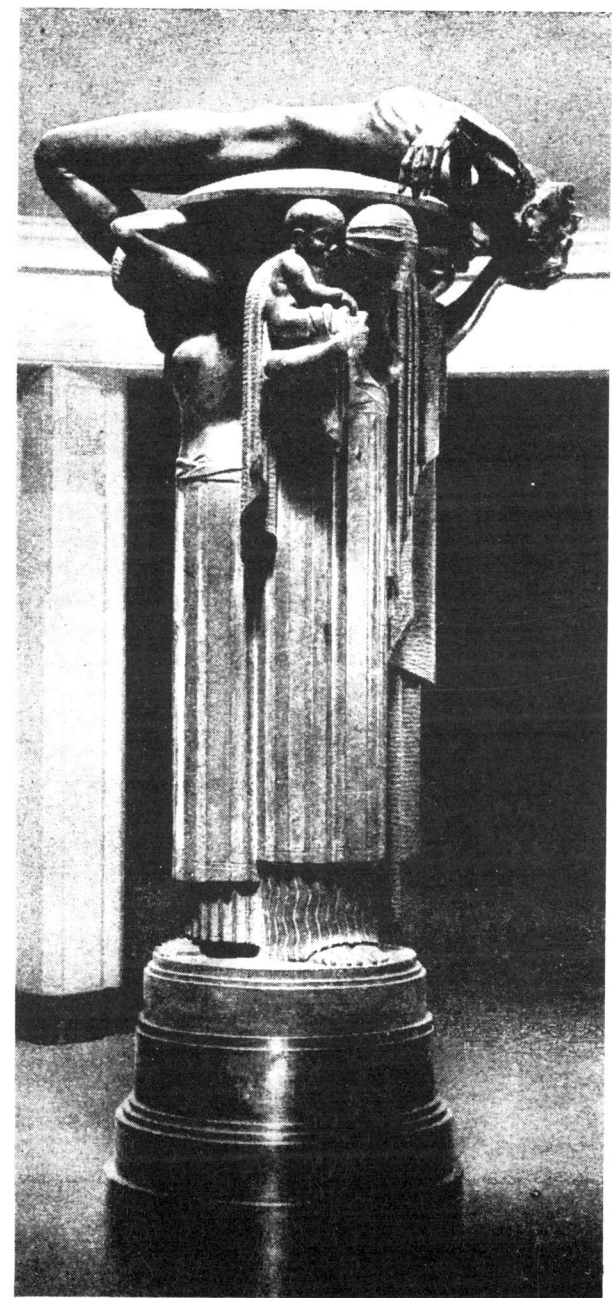

No more arresting emblems of the modern culture of nationalism exist than cenotaphs and tombs of Unknown Soldiers. The public ceremonial reverence accorded these monuments precisely because they are deliberately empty or no one knows who lies inside them, has no true precedents in earlier times ...

The cultural significance of such monuments becomes even clearer if one tries to imagine, say, a Tomb of the Unknown Marxist or a cenotaph for fallen Liberals. Is a sense of absurdity avoidable? The reason is that neither Marxism nor Liberalism are much concerned with death and immortality.

  Benedict Anderson: *Imagined Communities*

Recent feminist peace initiatives have focused attention on a number of questions concerning the relationship between masculinity and war, and between both of these and nationalism. In this paper, I pursue some of these questions. I display various figures of masculine and feminine identity as these are constructed in certain discourses about modern society, and I relate these figures to a conception of national identity.

The argument is a relatively limited one. There are many structures which enter into the constitution of masculinity and femininity and I treat only two or three of these. Hence, there is a certain incompleteness to the discussion. However, what emerges — at least in terms of the constructions displayed here — is that there is no unique relationship between masculinity and nationalism; and, indeed that nationalism makes use of both masculine and feminine elements in its construction. I will also suggest that to the extent that there is a special association between masculinity, nationalism and war, it is an indirect one, mediated by a more direct and significant association between masculinity and death.

One

One of the most pervasive structures of modern life is the market. This is a form of economic life in which the products of human labour, and the capacity to labour itself, take the form of commodities which exchange against each other at a rate determined in the first instance by aggregative forces of supply and demand, at least insofar as these find representation within the market. Both to its bourgeois celebrants and its Marxist critics it is the pervasiveness of market relations which is, perhaps above all else, definitive of modernity.

The market — the sphere of commodity exchange — requires and produces a quite specific form of individuality — an 'abstract individuality' which conceives of itself as existing independently of specific material and personal relationships. Those who participate in the activities of production and exchange and in the human interactions encompassed by market relations must conceive these as available but also as replaceable means to conceptually different ends. The market requires, for example, a form of property that is alienable at will; hence a relation to specific property holdings cannot be thought of as essential to the identity of the property owner. Effective participation in the market requires that an individual be able to move from one sphere of activity (work) to another, in response to market pressures. Hence the individual cannot conceive of a particular kind of work as essential to his identity. Finally, the market requires that the individual conceive others, not as objects of non-transferable emotion (love, hatred), but in terms of a measured assessment of how they contribute to the fulfilment of his purposes. Within the sphere of market relations, individuals must conceive of themselves as having an identity and purposes which are distinct from — and abstract with respect to — specific possessions, activities and individuals. This allows for the operation of a certain concept of rationality (instrumental reason) in which the sole task of reason is that of evaluating various means (possessions, activities, individuals) in terms of the efficiency of their contribution to given ends.

It has been remarked often enough that the abstract individual protagonist of market relations (who has always existed more happily in liberal political and economic discourse than in real life) is male. This is so, not just because it has been mostly men who have figured in market transactions, but because these structures have come to constitute one form of masculine identity. To be a masculine subject is, at least in part, to have an identity independent of specific possessions and activities, to be capable of a degree of impersonality in one's relations with others and — perhaps above all — to aspire to the norms of instrumental reason. It is paradigmatically masculine identity which is constructed through the 'isolation effect' of commodity exchange.

Market relations do not comprise a self-sufficient domain of social existence. If the market is to reproduce itself there must be a social mechanism through which immature human individuals are provided with the nurture, care and social identity necessary for them eventually to participate in market relations. But these activities are different in kind from those involved in the market, and presuppose a distinct form of individuality. The activities of reproduction involve commitments to particular individuals and relationships, where these are not conceived of as replaceable means to distinct ends. Thus, the identity of the individuals is not constructed in abstraction from certain activities and individuals; rather it is constituted by those activities and by relationships to those individuals. As against the atomised individualityy constructed through the market, the kind of individuality appropriate to the sphere of reproduction, i.e. of domesticity, defines itself in terms of specific activities and individuals. Since there is an intrinsic connection between this mode of individuality, its activities and its goals, there is little scope here for the operation of the concept of instrumental reason which assumes their separability.

The sphere of reproduction, i.e. of domesticity and family life, constitutes itself as a private realm set off against the public domain comprised by market activity. It is also the sphere in which feminine identity is constructed. Again, this is not simply because it has been mostly women who perform the relevant activities, but rather because these structures inform the conception of what it is to be a woman. Thus, femininity involves a form of identity constructed out of relationships with specific others (husbands, children), and certain activities (caring, nurturing) concerning those others. It is not directly subject to the isolation effect of commodity exchange. Since it has little place for the operation of the dominant market conception of reason, it is constructed as devoid of reason and its activity as expressive and emotional, rather than calculated and rational.

We should not assume too simple a bifurcation of male and female identity in terms of the public/private distinction. Male identity is constructed in both spheres. Men must represent their families and provide for their needs in market activity. The instrumentality and contingency which infects their relationship to activities and individuals within the market does not affect their relationship to those they represent. Thus, their abstract individuality is tempered by their identity as 'breadwinner', and this role is not an instrumental one, but is essential to their identity. On the other hand, they must also represent the public world of work, order and rationality within the family. Indeed, unless these principles were represented within the private sphere, it could not function to reproduce, not just the physical individuals, but the structure of individuality required by public life. It is thus the woman who must embody in her existence the principles of family life and the practices of nurturing and commitment that it requires. In this way, the duality between public and private finds expression within the structure of private life.

Men and women, as thus constituted, are subject to quite different conceptions of morality.[1] The function of public morality is to constrain the behaviour of those whose bonds are the essentially impersonal ones of commodity exchange. It defines the relevant rights of property and contract, and imposes norms of impartiality and justice. It imposes itself on the individual as the external force of law or the internal force of duty. Private morality, on the other hand, concerns the intimate and the particular; and it imposes special responsibilities to specific others. Those subject to this morality are unlikely to be moved by obligations to impersonal others or by a concern for universal right. Hence, the alleged lack of a sense of justice in women, which has worried moral theorists from Rousseau to Freud. Public morality marks out constraints on available lines of behaviour; infringement results in punishment or guilt. But private morality defines certain activities as constitutive of one's identity; hence, failure to perform the required tasks involves a real threat to that identity.

Public (masculine) and private (feminine) moralities are different in content and form, and are often opposed to each other. Despite this opposition, however, each presupposes the other. Hence neither can claim a self-sufficient moral status on its own.[2]

1. For a fascinating empirical account of the different conceptions of morality among men and women, see Carol Gilligan: *In a Different Voice* Cambridge, Mass. & London: Harvard University Press, 1982).

2. For a further account of the above, see Ross Poole: 'Morality, Masculinity and the Market', *Radical Philosophy* 39 (Spring 1985), pp. 16-23.

Two

There is a second dimension in which the market is parasitic on another sphere of social existence. Market activity, consisting of voluntary acts of production and exchange, presupposes an institutional framework of property and contract. This consists, on the one hand, of the administrative and coercive apparatuses of the state, and on the other, of a widespread propensity to respect the property of others and to keep to one's contractual agreements (the external and internal components of public morality mentioned above). The market is, in a certain limited sense, a sphere of freedom; but it presupposes a realm of necessity.[3] Which is to say that it requires both the coercive power of the state and also corresponding internal constraints on individual behaviour.

The contrast between these two spheres may be drawn in terms of the different conceptions of individuality involved. The identity of the market individual is abstract with respect to specific activities and hence specific obligations which may be incurred in market transactions. Abstract individuality is just that form of individuality which is free of obligations except those which are voluntarily entered into. However, the obligations embodied in the state and the norms of individual behaviour necessary to sustain the market are not matters of voluntary choice, but are necessarily incumbent upon the individual. Thus, they must be supposed to be part of the identity of those individuals subject to them.

The difference between this conception of individuality and the abstract individuality of the market emerges when we consider the content of the obligations embodied in the state. For the state exists, *inter alia*, as the coercive apparatus necessary to protect the market from internal recalcitrance and external threat. It must have, therefore, the moral capacity to punish its citizens and the right to require of them that they sacrifice themselves — their property, even their lives — on its behalf. The content of the obligations involved goes beyond anything that might voluntarily be assumed (except as the result of massive miscalculation) by a market individual. The state embodies the power of death; and death is, from the perspective of that individual, both the ultimate sacrifice of self-interest and the ultimate irrationality.[4]

Sacrifice of self-interest at the behest of the state is not just a residual power to be exercised *in extremis*. A society made up of individuals whose interrelations were based solely on the calculations of instrumental reason would lack the social cohesion necessary to maintain itself in existence. Market behaviour must be constrained by dispositions, e.g. to respect the property and person of others, which restrict the operation of rational self-interest. Hence, the residual power of the state over life and death is best conceived of as an extreme form of the more muted and undramatic sacrifice of self-interest required in day to day market existence.[5] Still, the extreme form is important: it shows in a stark and exemplary way what state power is about. Prisons and wars may not constitute the major business of the state; but that the state have the capacity to punish its citizens and call upon them to die on its behalf is essential to its existence.

In order to make sense of the obligations involved here, the state must present itself as embodying a deeper community which underlies the market — a *gemeinschaft* underlying the *gesellschaft*. That is to say, it must define a form of identity which subsumes the abstract individuality of the market. This form of identity will have four characteristics: first it must not be a matter of choice for the individual, but must pre-exist and pre-structure the choices that he and (as we shall see) she makes. It may appear as part of the pre-social order of things, as 'natural' as one's sex, or it may be recognised as socially and politically constructed. But it must be inescapable. Second, it must define goals which are worth sacrificing one's particular self-interest for. Or, to put this another way, it must provide for a kind of self-fulfilment to which the aims of market individuality are subordinate. Thus, and third, it must provide a conception of self which transcends that of market

---

3. To put it Durkheim's way: the sphere of the contractual rests on the basis of the non-contractual. See *The Division of Labour in Society* (N.Y.: The Free Press, 1964), espec. Ch. 7.

4. See Hegel: *The Philosophy of Right* (Oxford: Clarendon Press, 1965), pp. 209-210.

5. Cf. ibid, p. 164.

individuality, a self which has its being as part of a wider and more encompassing set of relationships. Fourth, the self is defined as a member of a community with others who share that deeper identity.

Three

Historically, the community which has provided this identity has been the nation. Standardly, though not universally, the nation has been constructed on the bases of a common territory (the 'ground', in a literal sense, of national identity) and a posited sameness of culture and cultural heritage. Sometimes these ingredients have been supposed to have an existence in a common blood, race or ethnic grouping. Nationalism, the sense of belonging to a nation, has found its political expression in the nation state; and to find such expression has been a central aspiration of incipient nationalisms. Conversely, and in the present context more significantly, the modern state has found its principal of legitimacy in the claim that it is the political embodiment of this more primordial community.

To many theorists of modernity, nationalism is an essentially atavistic phenomenon, constructed out of cultural relationships which the spread of the market would eventually destroy.[6] There are two strands to this argument. The first is the tendency for networks of exchange relations to extend across national boundaries, and thus to create an international economic order. This is important, but will not be discussed in detail here. Until recently, this tendency has expressed itself more in terms of national rivalry than internationalism. The second is that the form of identity constructed through market relations is incompatible with that required by nationalism — and must eventually destroy it. But, paradoxically, not only does market individuality require this deeper form of identity, but the modern world, of which the market is such a central feature, has been especially congenial to the emergence of nationalism. Nationalism is historically almost co-extensive with the emergence of market societies (though it is not, of course, unique to them). While nationalism has made use of pre-modern cultural artefacts, and has often claimed a pre-modern (sometimes primeval) genealogy, it is a quintessentially modern phenomenon. It is, therefore, in the modern world that we should pursue its aetiology.

In the relatively limited context of this paper, the form in which this question arises is whether the two forms of social life displayed so far, and their associated forms of identity, provide the conceptual resources necessary to construct a figure of national identity. It would not be too surprising if they did not. The models deployed here are highly schematic ones, and they abstract from many features of social life which would need to be taken into account in order to generate an adequate concept of nationalism. Still, I will suggest that the models do provide two of the major resources necessary, if not to construct, at least to comprehend a concept of nationalism.

In the first place, the market imposes a certain social homogeneity on the sphere of public life. While market relations tend to create large scale inequalities, and in their capitalist form (i.e. where there is a labour market) they presuppose them, they also create a form of identity, that of abstract individuality, which is common to all participants in the market. This identity is expressed in the politico-legal framework as the equality of free juridical subjects (property owners, contract makers).[7] Despite separation and competition, there is a sense in which market individuals can recognise each other as sharing a common identity. The market also imposes mobility: horizontal, as its members move from one sphere of activity to another in response to market fluctuations, and vertical, as fortunes are made and lost. It requires a common conceptual currency in terms of which exchanges are conducted, and it assumes a common (instrumental) rationality. Thus, the market militates against the existence of a number of culturally isolated and heterogeneous communities, which have been characteristic of most other social forms. It provides, if not the basis, at least the social space for the emergence of a common national culture.[8]

6. This was certainly Marx's view; see, e.g. *The Communist Manifesto* (in Marx & Engels, *Collected Works*, vol. 6 [London: Lawrence & Wishart, 1976], p. 488): 'In place of the old local and seclusion and self-sufficiency, we have intercourse in every direction, universal interdependence of nations. And as in material, so also in intellectual production the intellectual creations of individual nations become common property. National one-sidedness and narrow-mindedness become more and more impossible, and from the numerous national and local literatures, there arises a world literature.'

7. See Evgeny B. Pashukanis *Law and Marxism: A General Theory* (first published 1924; English translation London: Ink Links, 1978), espec. Ch. 4.

8. These points are well made in Ernest Gellner: *Nation and Nationalism* (Oxford: Blackwell, 1983), Ch. 3. However, Gellner explains these phenomena in terms of the demands of industrialism, not the market.

The other major resource required for the construction of a concept of national identity is provided by the sphere of domesticity. The nation is constructed through a re-location of relations and identities constituted within the private realm. The nation is — something like — the family inscribed in the social space created by the market.

It is a familiar feature of the rhetoric of nationalism that it invokes the language of the family and kin relationships. One's country is 'home'; it is androgynously one's 'father-' and 'motherland', and the ties of nation are often presented in terms of 'blood', 'inheritance' and the like.[9] In part, this is a matter of relocating the considerable psychic investment one has in one's family in a wider and more encompassing set of relationships. The emotions and needs which are extruded from the sphere of commodity exchange by the operation of impersonal and rational self-interest, are not merely contained within the private realm, but focused on and suffused through the nation. But what makes this possible is the construction of a new form of identity on a model analogous to those constructed in and through the family.

The main feature of national identity, as of that form of identity constructed in the private sphere, is that it is constructed, not through separation (the 'isolation effect' of the market) but in terms of relationships with others. Thus, the aspirations of a specific individual come to be inextricably bound up with the well-being of others. An action which from the point of view of the self-directed individual constructed in the market would be a pointless piece of altruism, becomes a mode of individual self-fulfilment. To have the identity in question (that of family or nation) is to be subject to certain kinds of emotion (e.g. shame, pride) which are provoked by actions, not necessarily of oneself, but of others who share that identity. Certain kinds of activity, e.g. the nurturing or supportive behaviour required to support the family, or the patriotic deed required by one's country, are conceived of, not merely as instrumentally effective in achieving certain ends (and certainly not one's self-directed ends) but as expressive of one's identity and necessary to sustain it.

National identity is a way of conceiving oneself (though, of course, not the only way). As such it provides a source of pleasures, pains, desires and frustrations which are not available in other modes of self-conception. To assume or discover that identity is to recognise the nation as its basis. Here, the parallel with the family is something more than a mere analogy. Just as the family is the source of one's physical existence and of a certain kind of social existence, so too one's country is the source of another kind of social existence. And just to the extent that this mode of social existence

9. See Benedict Anderson: *Imagined Communities* (London: Verso, 1983), p. 131.

enters into one's conception of what one is, then to that extent the nation is the (androgynous) parent of what one is, and one's fellow nationals constitute one's kin.

There are two significant agencies through which this form of community is constructed. The first is provided by the state itself. It is a familiar point that the market requires an effective administrative and coercive apparatus, but also tends to undermine the beliefs and relationships which traditionally legitimise that authority.[10] Hence, the modern state has had the task of constructing its own form of legitimacy. The exigencies of a market economy have provided it with the means to do thus: control over education and (thus) culture.[11] Nationalism has been brought into play to provide the content. A number of cultural artefacts have been employed in this task, but if the above argument is correct, the conceptual and psychic resources have been provided through the relocation and enlargement of that form of identity associated with the family.

The second agency arises through the structures of individuality constructed through the market and the family. Take the market individual first. For such an individual other persons and relations will then only have signficance to the extent that they mediate between the individual and his ends. The locus of what is meaningful is essentially self-referential. But the task of providing one's own meaning is a daunting one; and is constantly threatened both by the demands of ordinary living and, more signficantly, by the actuality of mortality. Death can only be experienced by such an individual as a rude invalidation of what his life is about. It is not just the end of meaning; it also renders what was meaningful, meaningless. To a limited extent, the structure of domesticity presupposed by market relations provides a framework of purposes which go beyond the individual existence of the market individual. However, a more universal and satisfying transcendance is provided if the individual can find an identity within a more global framework of relationships. Within that framework, particular strivings have a signficance that they cannot have within the market or even the family. More significantly they define — indeed, give birth to — a kind of identity which promises an existence beyond that allowed by human biology. The nation may not be immortal, but it presents itself as such, and this is the promise that it makes to its members.

Femininity, insofar as this is constructed through the family, is already relational, and therefore exists in a framework of meaning beyond that of the individual. To that extent, the attraction of nationalism as a form of identity will be weaker. Nevertheless the domestic web of meaning is a limited and parochial one, existing within a wider network but excluded from it. Just to the extent that the nation embodies the relational and feminine in a more universal context, it will provide its compensation and gratifications for this form of individuality too. However, as we shall see in a moment, there are significant differences in the ways in which femininity and masculinity are incorporated within forms of national identity.

Four

War is only one of the many activities undertaken by the modern state. Nevertheless, it is essential to the functioning of the state that it have the moral capacity to wage wars, so the business of war takes on a unique significance. Modern nationalisms have largely been forged through wars; but even — perhaps especially — where this has not been the case, the commemoration of war has had a central role amongst the rituals of nationalism. While patriotism may be demonstrated in any number of ways, it has been service in war which has constituted its exemplary form.

The waging of war involves employing the means of violence in the attempt to kill as many as possible of the citizens of an enemy state, to destroy its resources and in any way possible to diminish its capacity to fight.[12] However, the rituals of nationalism do not emphasise the activities of inflicting violence, destruction and killing. What is emphasised is the aspect of suffering and death. War is important for national identity, not so much because individuals have shown that they are prepared to kill for their nation, though this does demonstrate that the moral force of nationalism overrides that of conventional morality; but because men — and

10. See, for example, Joseph Schumpeter: *Capitalism, Socialism and Democracy* (London: George Allen & Unwin, 1943; reprinted 1976), pp. 134-139.

11. Cf. Gellner: *Nations and Nationalism*, p. 34.

12. Cf. von Clausewitz: *On War* (Abridged edition, Harmondsworth: Penguin, 1982), p. 101: 'War is an act of violence intended to compel our opponent to fulfil our will.'

sometimes women — have been prepared to suffer and die on behalf of their nation. This constitutes the nation — and the state, which claims to be the political embodiment of the nation — as having a value beyond that of the goods to which individuals ordinarily devote themselves. In this way, and perhaps only in this way, does the nation show itself to be worthy of existing.

For the individual the sacrifice of particular individuality in war demonstrates the achievement of a more encompassing form of identity. It shows that the aspirations which have moved the individual to act (to suffer, to die) are not those of the particular individual who represents his household in the market, but those of an individual who has identified his own existence with that of the nation. These aspirations are, at least symbolically, common to all those who share this deeper identity. In nationalism, as in religion, the voluntary act of self-sacrifice establishes an identity which transcends that of the individual who suffers death. Facing death is the paradoxical proof of immortality. It is the achievement of a locus of meaning sought by, but denied to the forms of individuality constructed in the family and the market.

The ways in which masculinity and femininity are constituted within nationalism are significantly different. Up to a point, the relationship between men and their nation replicates that between the market individual and his family. The male identity as potential soldier is as inescapable as that of breadwinner, and the nation becomes the family to be protected and fought for in a wider world by its male representatives. But the ways in which the activities of the soldier are discursively constructed are quite different from market activity. Not only does the activity of war involve destruction of property and risk of life, but it also requires a kind of commitment to one's fellows far beyond anything conceivable within the market. In the commemorations of war, what is celebrated is not so much the acts of murder and destruction, but the mutual caring, comradeship and readiness for selfless sacrifice amongst those who fought. What is forged in the ritual commemoration of war is a kind of identity, exemplary for nationalism, which transcends the isolation and separation characteristic of market existence. War is not so much the construction of a new and virulent form of masculinity, as the recovery for masculine identity of that relational form of identity constructed within the family. It is, in this sense, the return of the feminine.

Insofar as the nation, in whose interests men fight and die, becomes the family, its members — those 'at home' — become wives, mothers and children. Those who fight and die do so, not just as citizens or even as men, but as husbands, fathers and sons. What is involved here is a universalisation of the domestic. Each soldier is father/husband/son to every woman. Each woman is mother/wife/daughter to each soldier.[13] It is as thus constituted that women enjoy the fruits of victory, suffer the agonies of defeat, and experience the anxieties and pains of loss and bereavement. Women do enter into national identity, at least insofar as this receives exemplary expression in the representation of war; and the form of identity they are provided does transcend the limits of the domestic and the particular. However, it does so not by transforming, but by generalising their domestic identity.

Five

13. Thus, Hegel: *Phenomenology of Spirit* (Oxford: Clarendon Press, 1977), p. 274. 'In the ethical household, it is not a question of *this* particular husband, *this* particular child, but simply of husband and children generally; the relationships of women are based, not on feeling, but on the universal.'

Particular nationalisms and national identities make essential use of cultural artefacts and traditions which are much more local and specific than anything captured in the abstract models articulated here. Thus, while the account provided so far is intended to have resonances with, for example, the way in which Australian national identity was consecrated through the sacrifice of Australian troops in the First World War in futile battles on the other side of the earth, it could only be part of an adequate explanation of how the ANZAC symbols worked. To provide a fuller explanation, we would need to take into account a range of elements quite specific to Australian history and culture. These would include, at least, the circumstances of federation ('states' rights'); Australia's disturbingly ambivalent relation to England (significantly the 'mother country'), as well as the various polarities between city and country involved in the construction of the 'digger'. Nevertheless, a major part of the significance of the Gallipoli landing was that it showed that Australia signified something worth dying for. Indeed, through this battle Australia became something worth dying for; and this established that being 'Australian' constituted an identity which transcended that of the particular self-directed and mortal individual. these features are not culturally specific ones, but are universally characteristic of modern nationalisms.

While the market, the family and the nation are complementary — indeed symbiotic — spheres of social existence, they exist in uneasy relationships with each other. In particular, the pervasiveness of market relations tends to undermine the structures of family and nation. Thus, the reality of the modern family (single parents, working wives, unemployed husbands) bears little resemblance to the conceptual models displayed here. The capitalist market produces and reproduces divisiveness, poverty, marginality and demoralisation, all of which consort badly with the rhetoric of nationalism. But the very threat to these structures, and to the forms of identity they sustain, generates its own counterpressures. The family and the nation are 'illusory communities';[14] they do not correspond in any simple way to actual social reality, but they do correspond to widespread and deep-seated needs and desires, and — like other illusions — tend to construct their own reality. In the case of nationalism, the fact that men and women have died on behalf of their nation is taken to show that the nation must exist and be worth dying for. Given this, individual men and women are provided with an identity, and thus with a range of aspirations, hopes and fears, pleasures and pains beyond anything provided through the more mundane aspects of their existence. The nation provides its members with a framework of significance denied to them in the actualities of commodity exchange and family life. In the last instance it promises — what no other sphere of social life can provide — immortality. Hence, the rhetoric of nationalism, which both appeals to and constructs that form of identity,[15] has a force which stands in almost inverse relationship to its empirical adequacy.

The figures of masculinity and femininity used in this account are highly abstract. At best, they indicate some of the structures through which gender identities are constituted, and thus pick out only some aspects of our actual experience of ourselves and others as masculine and feminine subjects. Almost certainly, other aspects will also be involved in the construction of national identity and the relationship between nationalism and war. Still, some tentative conclusions can be reached in terms of the analysis attempted here. First, it is a mistake to think of the nation as constituting a specifically male domain; it is constructed around both masculine and feminine identities. Indeed, it provides for masculinity a certain kind of recuperation of the relational and feminine aspects of social existence excluded from the sphere of commodity exchange. Further, it seems that the primary importance of war in relationship to the nation is, not so much as an outlet for primeval (male) destructiveness, but rather to provide an arena for self-sacrifice. What nationalism provides for the individual is a certain kind of transcendence of his or her particular existence. It thus provides a significance to individual existence which is otherwise lacking. Self-sacrifice is (at least for those individuals who survive) the proof of this larger significance.

14. Not quite 'imagined communition' in Benedict Anderson's sense. Anderson uses this term to cover 'all communities larger than primordial villages of face to face contact (and perhaps even these)',*Imagined Communities*, p. 15. It would be nice, however, to have a terminology which allowed for the possibility that some non 'face to face' communities might be less 'imagined' than others. For the provenance of the term 'illusory community', see Marx: *On the Jewish Question* in Marx & Engels *Collected Works*, vol. 3 (London: Lawrence & Wishart, 1975), p. 154: 'In the state ... [man] is the imaginary member of an illusory sovereignty, is deprived of his real individual life and endowed with an unreal universality.' See also Marx & Engels: *The German Ideology* in *Collected Works* vol. 5 (London: Lawrence & Wishart, 1976), pp. 46-48.

15. In the olden days, I might have said 'interpellates individuals as (certain kinds of) subjects'. See Louis Althusser: 'Ideology and Ideological State Apparatuses' in *Lenin and Philosophy and other essays* (London: NLB, 1971).

WORKING CLASS BOYS AND 'CRIME'
THEORISING THE CLASS/GENDER MIX

Chris Cunneen

The following paper attempts to draw the links between masculinity and class as they combine in the process of criminalisation. An analysis of this process shows a distinct differentiation between genders. However, almost without exception, postwar research on 'delinquency' assumed the 'delinquent' to be male. Feminist theory has been responsible for demonstrating these supposedly universalist theories to be in fact gender blind. For an accurate picture of the way in which working class youth are criminalised through the state apparatuses an analysis which is gender specific is important. There is a huge variety in explanations for 'delinquency'. In the first part of this paper, theories which have attempted a 'sex difference' explanation are examined. In the latter section I have tried to demonstrate the manner in which class and gender are constituted **together** in the process of 'crime'.

Theories that attempted to discuss 'male delinquency' in terms of 'masculinity' usually did so from a point that assumed patriarchal relations to be 'natural'. Invariably the responsibility for masculine criminality among juveniles was placed squarely on the shoulders of the mother. The ideology of motherhood was used in a variety of ways. Either the mother was overly protective and therefore the young male had to prove his 'masculinity' through rebellion and 'delinquent' acts, or the mother was overly neglectful of 'her' child's behaviour. These theories were richly embroidered with psychological jargon. The mantle of scientific neutrality, however, barely disguised the reality of unequal relationships.

During the 1950s the popular theories of John Bowlby attributed the cause of male 'delinquency' to maternal deprivation.[1] Those placed in positions of authority over the family structure were trained by the state to look for signs of a 'neglectful' mother. Take, for instance, an article in *Health Bulletin* (1953) entitled 'Delinquency and its Contributing Factors'. Its author, Arthur W. Meadows, explained to Infant Welfare Sisters the general conditions associated with delinquency: 'The parents of delinquents are often lacking in intelligence and education, and it has been estimated that 10% of them are dependent [on the state]'.[2] Notice the automatic

1. Bowlby, J. *Maternal Care and Mental Health*, World Health Federation, Geneva, 1952.

2. Meadows, A.W., 'Delinquency and Its Contributing Factors', *Health Bulletin*, No. 110, 1953, Victorian Department of Health.

equation between the need for welfare and biological inferiority. The father of the delinquent was 68% likely to be an unskilled or semi-skilled worker. The mother was often employed outside the home. Meadows described the home life as 'unsettled', excessively 'quarrelsome'. The family moved a lot, generally obtaining rentals in deteriorated areas.[3] There was no thought here that Meadows was describing, in fact, the economic conditions of significant sections of the Australian working class in the early 1950s. The adolescent male delinquent was easily identifiable, according to Meadows, because of specific physical and cultural habits: he was 'defiant of authority', had a 'history of difficult behaviour', was 'invariably maladjusted', a truant, poor at his work and attracted more than usual by tobacco, film shows and games of chance. The 'delinquent' was the antithesis of the 'model' student and the 'model' apprentice. These family and individual characteristics enabled the social worker, the teacher or, in this instance, the community nurse to identify the (potential) delinquent.

However, the cause of the behaviour was located in problems of mothering. According to Bowlby this type of delinquent behaviour could only be understood as a form of compensation for maternal deprivation. Other pseudo-scientific works supported this with empirical evidence. For instance the works of Healy and Bronner were cited as further proof of the awesome need for correct mothering. The Healy and Bronner study of 100 delinquents and 100 non-delinquent brothers and sisters 'proved' that it was rejection in early childhood that led to the delinquent behaviour. Delinquents scored higher on a scale of 'unwantedness' which included the following categories: unwanted child; abortion attempted; much worried pregnancy; very sickly pregnancy; premature birth; difficult delivery; very early bottle fed; very late breast fed; very difficult weaning; cross, fussy babyhood; difficult sphincter training; severe head injury; etc. etc. Further 'idiosyncrasies' found in the delinquent population included masturbation, nail-biting and thumb-sucking. The answer to delinquency was surprisingly simple: better mothering. All the images which accompanied Meadow's text depicted women as mothers with plump, cuddly, happy children.[4]

Influential studies during the late 1940s and 1950s also looked at male delinquency as a demonstration of problems in masculine identity and status. Certain male adolescents were seen to display delinquent behaviour because of anxiety over their 'maleness'. This explanation conveniently accounted for male 'aggressiveness' and 'exaggerated masculine posturing' that supposedly characterised much 'delinquency'. According to this tradition, the anxiety over masculinity was a result of female-centred families. Male delinquency was a 'protest' against maternal domination.[5] Talcott Parsons argued that among the 'lower class' and 'Negro families' boys gravitated towards the mother as the central object of identification because of the occupational instability and familial transience of the father. The mother became the emotionally significant adult.[6] Adolescent boys turned towards 'compulsive masculinity' as a result of uncertainties over their own identification. Other theorists followed similar paths. Miller gives the best summary of this position:

The genesis of the intense concern over 'toughness' in lower-class culture is probably related to the fact that a significant proportion of lower class males are reared in a predominantly female household and lack a consistently present male figure with whom to identify ... Since women serve as a primary object of identification during the pre-adolescent years, the almost obsessive lower-class concern with masculinity probably resembles a type of compulsive reaction-formation.[7]

3. ibid., p. 5.

4. ibid.

5. Greenberg, D., 'Delinquency And The Age Structure of Society', *Contemporary Crises*, 1, 1977, pp. 189-223.

6. Parsons, T., 'Certain Primary Sources And Problems Of Aggression in the Social Structure of the Western World', *Psychiatry*, 10, 1947, pp. 167-181. Parsons, T., *Essays in Sociological Theory*, Glencoe, Free Press, 1954.

7. Miller, W.B., 'Lower Class Culture as a Generating Milieu Of Gang Delinquency', *Journal of Social Issues*, 14, 3, 1958, p. 9.

Albert Cohen disagreed with this position and thought what Parsons was describing was more attributable to the middle-class family than to the working class. Cohen maintained that 'lower-class delinquency' among males was a reaction to failure in schools run along middle-class standards.[8] The exact behaviour that Parsons, Cohen and Miller defined as male delinquent needs further examination. Parsons saw the problem as principally 'aggressive behaviour', Cohen identified it as 'malicious, non-utilitarian, negativistic, hedonistic behaviour', and Miller talked about 'tough, aggressive, irresponsible acts amongst lower-class boys'.[9] All theorists viewed the behaviour as irrational and without any instrumental purpose. Thus there was a combination of two points of ideology fundamental for capitalism and patriarchy. Working class male resistance is irrational, it is simply a sign of overly exaggerated masculinity which is caused by inappropriate family relations in the first place, in particular a family structure that is mother-dominated. According to Parsons this was exacerbated by a 'strong tendency to instability of marriage' among the 'lower-class'. The point is simple: aggression in working class males is irrational, and it is a woman's fault.

Thus 'mothering' became of particular importance in any explanation of masculine delinquency. Incorrect proportions of it, or an upset in the balance of the 'natural' nuclear family was held to have dire effects, particularly on working class males. (However, I do not wish to suggest that in fact there is no connection between the acquiring of 'masculinity' and the role of 'mothering', nor that certain types of male behaviour criminalised by the state demonstrate the contradictory demands of capitalism and patriarchy.)

Other theorists who attempted to explain male adolescent 'delinquency' in behaviourist terms did so through variations of role theory. The transition to male adulthood could introduce problems of anxiety. This was suggested by David Matza in *Delinquency and Drift*. 'Masculine anxiety' was reduced with the attainment of 'successful' adulthood. Bloch and Niederhoffer[10] interpreted certain forms of 'delinquency' such as drinking, sexual experimentation, and stealing cars as responses to age status problems. Adolescents were encouraged to aspire to adult behaviour but denied the prerogatives of adulthood. The problem with these theories was that they failed to elaborate any coherent analysis of class and gender.

Starting from a similar theoretical point as Parsons concerning the importance of 'primary identification', Nancy Chodorow in *The Reproduction of Mothering* traced the development of a psychic structure in women which compelled them to 'mother'. Explicit in Chodorow's accqunt was a theory of masculinity. Superficially at least, it appeared similar to Parsons and Miller's account of 'compulsive masculinity' among 'lower class' males. According to Chodorow the formation of male gender identity was difficult. Because primary parenting was carried out by women, the process of 'individuation-separation' for boys involved conflict. Boys had to develop as 'not-females', therefore any qualities taken to be female had to be repressed and what was considered feminine devalued. The personality characteristics created in men

... reproduced both an ideology and a psychodynamic of male superiority and submission to the requirements of production. It prepared men for participation in a male dominant family and society, for their lesser emotional participation in family life, and their participation in the capitalist world of work.[11]

The crucial difference between Chodorow's and earlier accounts of masculinity such as Parsons' was that Chodorow was attempting to draw the lines of a theory of masculinity in relation to the construction of fenimity. For Parsons the problems of compulsive masculinity were the problems of one class and one race — not surprisingly the 'lowest'. For Chodorow the problem was the construction of gender. She offered a more sophisticated explanation than a simplistic role model by demonstrating that the constitution of gender was involved in personality structures. If primary parenting were changed then the psychic structures demanding satisfaction through power, domination or mothering would also be altered. However a central problem with Chodorow is the failure to demonstrate the simultaneous construction of class.

8. Cohen, A., *Delinquent Boys. The Culture Of The Gang*, Glencoe, Free Press, 1955.

9. For further discussion, see Cloward, R.A., Ohlin, L.E., *Delinquency And Opportunity*, New York, Free Press, 1960, p. 51.

10. Greenberg, op. cit., p. 193.

11. Chodorow, N., *The Reproduction Of Mothering*, University of California Press, Berkerley, 1978, p. 180.

In Britain several writers have attempted to analyse working class, adolescent male behaviour in a manner which allows the dynamics of working class culture and the struggle of resistance to be understood. Of fundamental importance in this tradition is the view that such behaviour is 'rational' and 'purposeful'. Willis in *Learning To Labour* indicates that exaggerated masculinity was the 'lads' response to an oppressive situation.[12] Corrigan in *Schooling the Smash Street Kids*, demonstrates the resistance to schooling by many of the boys.[13] Both Corrigan and Willis show that there is not simply one 'masculinity' defined by aggressive behaviour. There are the 'lads' and the 'ear oles', those who are too scared to misbehave and those who instrumentally study for a particular job. Connell, et al in *Making The Difference* also demonstrate that there are competing 'masculinities' in their study of Australian school kids.[14] Humphries' historical study *Hooligans Or Rebels?* shows that 'larking about' and resistance to the imposition of compulsory schooling through persistent rule-breaking and opposition to authority were characteristics of working class youth culture which were viewed as delinquent.[15]

Explanations of the gender/class dynamics of the working class males referred to as the 'lads' is still problematic. Willis draws most clearly the correspondence between the culture and the relations of production found on the factory floor. Other writers have pointed to the nature of life for the dispossessed youth of the working class. Robbins and Cohen in *Knuckle Sandwich*[16] describe the 'deranged mood' of violence, the 'We Hate Humans' futility of a 'masculinity' gone mad. Williams, Murphy and Dunnings' study of soccer hooliganism, *Hooligans Abroad*, lays the blame for trouble on the 'lower working class'.[17] They refer to the 'lads' whose macho style is demonstrated by 'gambling, exploitative forms of sex, street smartness, heavy drinking'. Yet explanations seem to stop at description. The violent masculine style of football hooliganism is attributed to the open violence of life on council housing estates. These relationships 'are both to some extent caused by, and reciprocally play a part in maintaining, the poverty of the lower working class'.[18] There is a reluctance to push the explanation further. The problem is that some forms of resistance and aggression may not be gender specific: both males and females will fight against oppressive situations. However, many of the particular practices described are specifically masculine. They cannot be accounted for in terms of class while ignoring the construction of gender. The above authors either consciously or unconsciously equate youth with male adolescence.

Seabrook in several books draws out some of the linkages between prolonged unemployment, social decay and various forms of working class masculinity.[19] He does not shy away from the problems of racism and sexism which often give form to the anger of working class boys, and points out that the talk of adolescent males is full of brutality, racism, domination and sexism. What he suggests is that we should understand that they are talking in metaphors, images and feelings defined by an ideology that has commodified all relationships. For Seabrook the over-riding problem is that all capitalism has to offer the working class young is a sense of functionlessness and purposelessness. The social development of youth has become a function of market relationships. The only (self) expression of youth is within the pre-selected choices of the marketplace. There is no purposeful work for young people. Their role is pure consumption, but with an insufficiency of means. Seabrook's view is pessimistic. He sees that 'gratuitous violence' or the British riots of 1981 as a reaction to a sense of despair, a blind lashing out that suggests a growing political impotence within the working class rather than a resistance to capitalist values. While Seabrook demonstrates the importance of market relationships, he does not see that those relationships are gender-ordered.

12. Willis, P.E., *Learning To Labour*, Saxon, Westmead, 1979.

13. Corrigan, P., *Schooling The Smash Street Kids*, MacMillan, London, 1979.

14. Connell, R.W., et.al., *Making The Difference*, Allen and Unwin, Sydney, 1982.

15. Humphries, S., *Hooligans Or Rebels?*, Blackwell, Oxford, 1981.

16. Robbins, D., Cohen, P., *Knuckle Sandwich*, Penguin, 1978.

17. Williams, J., Dunning, E., Murphy, P., *Hooligans Abroad*, Routledge and Kegan Paul, London, 1984.

18. ibid., p. 13.

19. Seabrook, J., *Unemployment*, Quartet, London, 1982. Seabrook, J., *Working Class Childhood*, Gollancz, London, 1982.

In the last section of this paper I would like to concentrate on the crime par excellence of young working class males: car theft and associated motor vehicle offences. The discussion needs to be prefaced by two remarks. Firstly most juvenile crime is instrumentally rational. Secondly it is unemployed or lowly paid youth who commit most crimes. Greenberg cites studies in England, U.S.A., Taiwan, Holland, Israel and Argentina as presenting a uniform picture of the class based nature of young people's crime, and showing that crime is instrumentally related to the leisure activities of youth.[20] It is of the utmost importance to perceive the rationality and intelligibility involved in the crimes of youth. This applies equally to females as to males. As Pearson points out in an article on the history of working class 'crime', what appears mindless and senseless usually reflects the logic of ruling class definitions. The owners of capital always confer supreme rationality on their own actions.[21]

The most recent figures for juvenile crime in N.S.W. cover the year ending June 1983.[22] In that period 4,880 girls and 30,749 boys had offences or complaints laid against them. Only 3% of offences/complaints were not proceeded with or did not come before the court. It is signficant that the greatest proportion of offences for both males and females were break, enter and steal and other property offences: 53% of females and 42% males fell into this category.[23] Thus in actual offences committed there is a large proportion which are not gender specific. However the court reaction to the crimes is gender specific. Girls are far more likely to be incarcerated for their sexuality through the use of 'welfare' legislation.[24] Further there is a very large proportion of male crime which relates to motor vehicles. Over 36% of all complaints against teenage males in N.S.W. were for motor vehicle theft and other related motor vehicle offences. It is a highly gender specific crime which effectively criminalises thousands of young males. It is not only male youth who steal cars but it is likely that it will be young males who are caught. The police clear-up rate for motor vehicle theft is very low. Only about 10% of reported thefts result in any charges being laid. However 80% of people caught stealing vehicles are between the ages of 12 and 20, 56% are 15 to 18 year olds.[25]

20. Greenberg, op. cit.

21. Pearson, G., 'Goths and Vandals — Crime in History', *Contemporary Crises*, 2, April 1978, pp. 119-39.

22. Y.A.C.S., *Annual Report*, 1983.

23. ibid., pp. 75-78.

24. Miller, L., 'Runaway Girls: Uncontrollable or Unsupported', Marrickville Legal Centre, Sydney. Cunneen C., 'State, Capitalism and Youth', Cottle, D., *Capital Essays*, Sydney, 1983.

25. N.S.W. Bureau of Crime Statistics and Research, *Motor Vehicle Theft in N.S.W.*, Statistical Bulletin 10, October 1980.

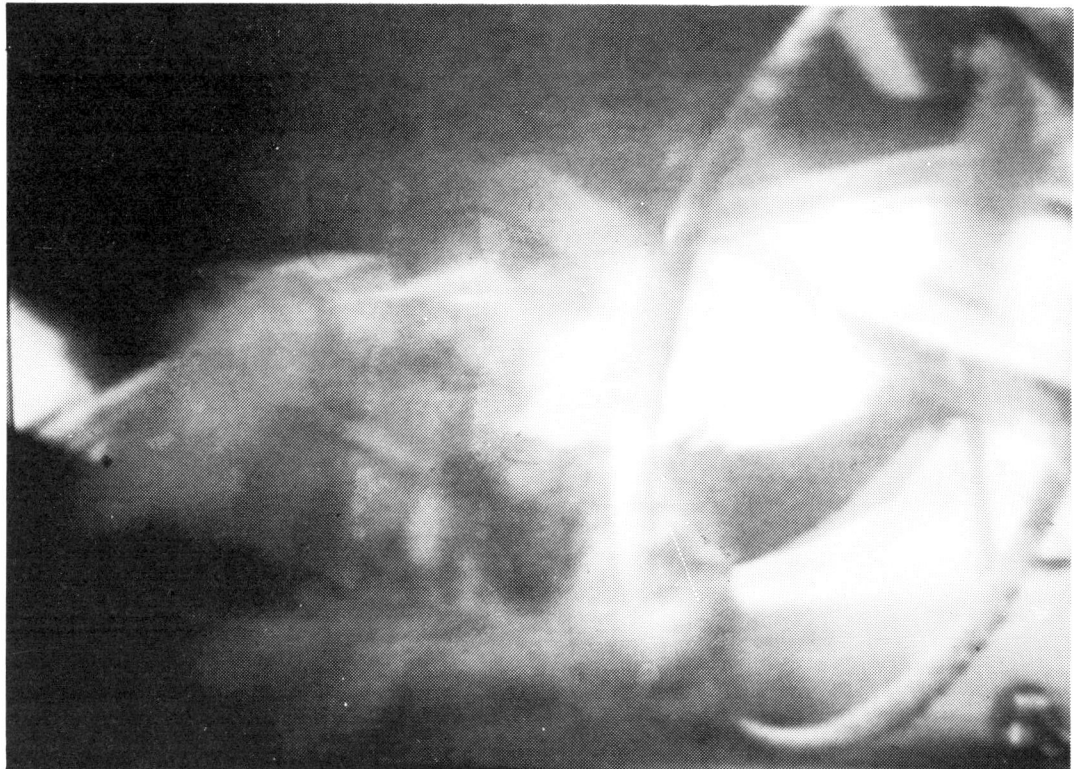

Thus it becomes necessary to analyse the manner in which cars and motorbikes come to fulfill such an important role in the structuring of class and gender among working class males. The relationship of males to cars involves a particular practice which defines masculinity, while class relations are integral to that practice. Class and gender are involved simultaneously in the process of structuring the relationship. The male relationship to the car or motorbike is one of power. Power over objects, power over the 'world', power over women. Several feminist writers have drawn the links between masculinity and male power. Game and Pringle in *Gender At Work* comment on the symbolism of the computer as the phallus:

The computer is the ultimate in machines, the giant phallus. Men see it as an extension of the social power they are allocated through possession of a penis. Indeed they see it as an extension of the penis ... Simultaneously, they regard women as toys and as objects to have power over.[26]

Machines, like the penis, are seen as supremely powerful. Technological domination and sexual domination go hand in hand. Dinnerstein also links technological control and forms of rationality to masculinity. The desire to turn the world into a machine, the worship of automation is part of the 'male realm'.[27] While I would want to replace Dinnerstein's 'spirit of maleness' with concrete historical practices of masculinity, her point is important. There is a necessity in seeing the ways cars and motorbikes are symbolic objects of masculine power. Advertisers have long recognised the links between fantasy, masculinity, domination and 'success' under capitalism. Motorbikes and cars have been associated with women and racehorses: 'Long Legged and Easy to Live With' (Moto Guzzi); 'Mounting Excitement' (Kawasaki).[28] Probably the most obvious is the naked woman stretched over the long extended forks of the motorbike. Here the images of machine and penis, with the fantasies of domination, exploitation and power, are complete. Women are treated as objects of desire while men are desiring subjects. One is possessed, the other the possessor.[29]

The ideology of male domination cannot be separated from capitalist social and economic relations. While the symbolic power of 'man' is determined by his possessions, these symbolic objects are themselves first and foremost commodities produced and consumed in the marketplace. The commodity production of cars has

26. Game, A., Pringle R., *Gender At Work*, Allen and Unwin, Sydney, 1983, p. 89.

27. Eisenstein, H., *Contemporary Feminist Thought*, Unwin, Sydney, 1984, p. 85.

28. Chambers, D., 'Symbolic Equipment and the Objects of Leisure Images', *Leisure Studies*, 2, 1983, p. 311.

29. ibid., p. 312.

been of fundamental importance to the 'health' of postwar capitalism. Time, space and patterns of social life have changed in varying degrees with the postwar housing construction 'boom' and the widespread use of motor vehicles. Leisure activities, for which the car or motorbike are an essential attribute, have become increasingly commodified. A system that generates class inequalities also limits access to the commodity market. Working class males who are unemployed, underemployed or lowly paid simply do not have the immediate accessibility to such an important commodity as a vehicle. The importance of that particular commodity is twofold: symbolically it defines masculine power and success; practically it is necessary because the availability of all kinds of resources is predicated on ownership and structured so as to make ownership indispensable.

To take the above two points further, one can argue that certain cultural practices develop around vehicle ownership and the working class. I have mentioned the relationship of sexual domination, power and machines. There is also the power over the 'environment' involved with vehicles. There is a sense in which the power felt in the vehicle is a displacement for the lack of power in other spheres of life: the workplace in particular. At this point it is necessary to remember that power is far from simply symbolic, it is real, it is exercised in daily life. Thus the symbolic power over women used in the commodity sale of vehicles finds its 'reality' in the practice of rape in cars — particularly of teenage girls who are dependent on males for transport. There is also a 'reality' in the 'freedom' that vehicles offer to males, however transitory and dependent it may be. At this point the symbolic and the practical completely intertwine.

Two 17 year old boys steal a car and drive to Sydney. They are arrested in Kings Cross. Why did they steal the car? They were sick of living in Yass. They didn't have the train fare anyway. There was a car left unlocked, so fuck it they took it. Anything to get out of Yass. I met these two boys as they were about to be flown in the police aeroplane back to Canberra and then transported to Yass to face charges. They were philosophical. They had got out of Yass for a couple of days, been to the Cross and got a ride in a plane. Two 17 year old boys and a 16 year old girl steal a car in Blacktown on a Friday night. They decide to go to Melbourne to visit a friend. In the early hours of Saturday morning they reach Albury. No money and no petrol left. They pull into an all-night self-serve garage, fill up and drive off. Ten minutes later the Highway Patrol pull them over after a high speed chase. Fortunately this time no one is killed. The cops find a .22 rifle in the boot. Charges for armed hold-up are serious. A guilty plea on a string of lesser offences is recognised as a better bargain. The girl is committed to an institution on the charge of being in moral danger, the boys are sent away on motor vehicle larceny, theft and driving offences.

Stealing cars, motorbikes and related motor vehicle offences are a significant part of juvenile male crime. Studies back to 1959 indicate that it has remained a major activity.[30] What I have tried to indicate is that specific instances of crime need to be carefully related to the dominant power structures of society. Motor vehicles as commodities fulfill particular functions — both symbolic and real. The 'illegal' use of that commodity by young working class males can only be understood in the light of certain class and gender practices. Like much 'crime', capital has its own direct responsibility. Several studies have shown the role of big business in facilitating car theft. Both car manufacturers and insurance corporations have nothing to lose through the sale of vehicles which are relatively easy to steal.[31] Like much petty crime it disproportionately affects the working class through higher insurance premiums and vehicle loss. The most likely car to be stolen in N.S.W. is a Holden that is about eight years old.[32]

In analysing the interstices of gender and class in the criminalisation of working class youth it is constantly necessary to refer to the material conditions under which people live and the practices in which they are engaged. The explanations of male delinquency discussed at the beginning of this paper dehistoricize and depoliticize the behaviour they describe. Little wonder then that the explanations they offer are ideological. Masculinity, like class, is descriptive of practices under particular historical conditions.

---

30. Kraus, J., 'Trends in the Rates of Non-Capital Offences Among Male Juveniles in N.S.W., 1959-1969', *Australian and N.Z. Journal of Criminology*, 3, 4, Dec. 1970, pp. 196-213.

31. Brill, H., 'Auto Theft and the Role of Big Business', *Crime And Social Justice*, 18, Winter 1982, pp. 62-68; Karmen, A.A., 'Auto Theft and Corporate Irresponsibility', *Contemporary Crises*, 5, 1981, pp. 63-81.

32. N.S.W. Bureau of Crime Statistics, op. cit.

THE SOCIAL CONSTRUCTION OF AUSTRALIAN PEACE MOVEMENT DEMANDS

Brian Martin

The Australian peace movement in the 1980s has emphasised a number of demands for change in government policy or action. Some of the most important of these are
* the Australian government should take a stronger international stand against nuclear war;
* visits by nuclear-powered or nuclear-armed ships and aircraft to Australia should be banned;
* U.S. military and intelligence bases in Australia should be removed or internationalised;
* uranium mining and export should be halted;
* the Australian government should establish a more independent foreign policy in relation to defence;
* there should be a nuclear-free zone in the Pacific region and a zone of peace in the Indian Ocean region;
* programs in peace education and research should be established.

Many people assume that these demands are the self-evident and 'natural' avenues for rhetoric and action for members of a peace movement. This is by no means the case. Peace movement demands, like other parts of social reality, are socially constructed. That is, they reflect the prevailing social, economic and political structures, and also the social position of peace activists.[1]

There are a large number of possible peace movement demands and activities, but only a small fraction of these actually become the focus for mass attention. This can be seen by listing some of the areas which have received less attention from the peace movement:
* ending Australian military collaboration with repressive Third World regimes;
* establishing a defence system based on nonviolent community resistance to aggression (social defence);
* disarmament of Australian military forces;
* conversion of Australian military production and labour to socially useful purposes (peace conversion);

1. This is a standard view within the sociology of knowledge. See for example Peter L. Berger and Thomas Luckmann: *The Social Construction of Reality* (Garden City, NY: Doubleday, 1966).

* pursuing social justice, including reduction of inequalities in wealth and of oppression of women and ethnic minorities;
* challenging major institutional frameworks, such as capitalism and the state, and replacing them with more participatory and democratic alternatives.

Some of the areas on this second list have received more attention than others. In particular, there has been considerable opposition to Australian military aid to the Philippines. Also, the women's peace movement has emphasised the links between patriarchy and the war system. But this does not affect my basic point that the priority demands of the peace movement are selected out of a considerable range of potential demands.

The key question I want to address in this article is, why does the Australian peace movement focus on some demands and not on others? I assume that there is more to the question than simply a rational assessment that some issues are 'better' than others. By delving into the social factors influencing the choices of peace movement demands, some insight may be provided to improve peace movement effectiveness. To address the question, I will first look briefly at the nature of the Australian peace movement and its recent history. Then I'll examine some of the implicit themes underlying peace movement demands. In this examination, some attention will be placed on the social origins of different sections of the peace movement. Finally I'll mention a few alternative directions for the peace movement. To avoid misunderstanding, I should emphasise that I support the major demands of the Australian peace movement such as removing U.S. bases. But I see major limitations in the range and type of initiatives taken by the peace movement, as I will describe later.

What is the Peace Movement?

To speak of 'the peace movement' can give a false impression of the social dynamics of activity on peace issues. Before proceeding further, I will outline some of the features of participation and support for peace initiatives and demands in Australia. To begin, what is a **peace** issue? This has varied historically. The issues typically taken up under this banner have involved either opposition to particular wars (such as the Vietnam War), opposition to particular types of war (such as nuclear war) or opposition to all war. Groups with such aims are conventionally called peace groups, although it would be more accurate to refer to them as antiwar groups — especially since everyone, including the military, speaks out in favour of 'peace'.

What then is the peace **movement**? At the core of things are the key activists and spokespeople. This includes those who hold top positions in the larger peace organisations, those who frequently give public talks and make statements to the media, and many of those who devote a large fraction of their time towards peace movement activities. A few of the latter group are paid full-time or part-time, though usually at only a nominal salary. The next layer consists of active members of peace groups. Being 'active' can range from occasional attendance at meetings to regular efforts towards raising funds, organising meetings and rallies, writing letters and articles, circulating petitions and raising the issues in a diversity of forums. Also in this layer might be included those who participate in major direct actions, such as the women's action at Pine Gap in November 1983. Defining a 'peace group' is a problem. Many peace activists act within churches, trade unions, professional groups, political parties, artistic groups and schools. They may not be members of any formal peace groups, yet it seems reasonable to include them in the peace movement. A third layer can be called occasional participants. This includes those who sometimes attend films, talks, rallies or other functions organised by peace groups. It also includes many of the less active members of peace groups — those who attend a few meetings now and again — and perhaps those who write letters to the paper or to politicians, or make regular donations to peace groups. A final layer consists of passive supporters: those who do not take part in organised actions but who support the goals and efforts of the peace movement. Some passive supporters may keep their opinions to themselves, but many will discuss or argue the issues with their friends and neighbours, sign petitions or vote for 'peace candidates'. Thus there is a range in the degree of 'passivity' of these supporters. I have used the imagery of 'layers', as if the peace movement were like an onion, but the actual dynamics are more fluid and changing. A person's level of activism can change markedly from time to time, and often does. There is also a considerable complexity to the type of involvement. Aside from participating in formal peace groups and activities, there are for example many 'independents' who act in their own personal way towards the goals of the peace movement, perhaps by writing letters, providing professional services to peace groups, introducing ideas into classrooms or withholding taxes, with little or no connexion with the organised peace movement.

It should be clear that 'the peace movement' can be defined in a variety of ways. It seems to me that the most useful boundary will include active members and exclude passive supporters. Occasional participants can be considered members of the peace movement when they participate — as at a rally — but not otherwise. I will use this definition here. But the important thing is to remember the complexity and diversity of activity on peace issues — and the diversity of what are considered peace issues. My concern here is with the priorities for goals and actions by those active in the peace movement. Some of these priorities are reflected in formal demands, such as the contents of the Australian nuclear disarmament declaration. But in other cases the priorities are found in the personal views of the individual members of the peace movement. At this stage it is only fair that I mention my own involvement in the peace movement. In the early 1970s in Sydney I was an occasional participant in moratorium marches. In 1979 I helped to set up Canberra Peacemakers, a small activist peace group. Since then I have remained an active member of that group. Until 1982, Canberra Peacemakers was the only specifically peace group in Canberra, but since then many new groups have been established. Canberra Peacemakers mainly works on social defence as part of an overall emphasis on challenging and replacing the institutions underlying the war system. These experiences of course influence my perspective on the peace movement and my analysis in this article.

Recent Peace Movement History[2]

The large size and strength of the Australian peace movement in the mid-1980s is unusual. For most of the time in the past, peace movements around the world have been small and inconspicuous. However, there have been times of peace movement strength, such as the World War One anti-conscription campaign in Australia, the antiwar movement in Britain and the U.S. in the 1930s, and the Campaign for Nuclear Disarmament in Britain in the late 1950s to the early 1960s. The last time the Australian peace movement had a major public profile was during the Australian military participation in the Vietnam War. In the late 1960s and early 1970s the Vietnam moratorium movement generated mass involvement, most visibly in a series of major demonstrations. The moratorium movement drew considerable strength from involvement of university students and major trade unions. It was strongly supported by large sections of the Labor Party. The Australian government's military participation in the Vietnam War was never more than a token one, designed to provide legitimation for the U.S. military role in Vietnam. Even so, by 1972 the Liberal-Country Party government had withdrawn almost all Australian troops from Vietnam.[3] Because the moratorium movement focused almost entirely on Australian military participation in the Vietnam War, it had little staying power as a general antiwar movement. After 1972 the organisational base of the peace movement dwindled to a small core in the major cities, mainly in Sydney and Melbourne.

The moratorium days left a strong stamp on peace movement demands in the decade 1972 to 1981. Many of those most active in the moratorium movement had supported the National Liberation Front and North Vietnam in the Vietnam War, and were very much anti-U.S. and anti-capitalist. Hence, demands for removal of U.S. bases, ending or renegotiating the ANZUS treaty and establishing a non-aligned foreign policy were high on the priority list for key peace movement activists. Because the

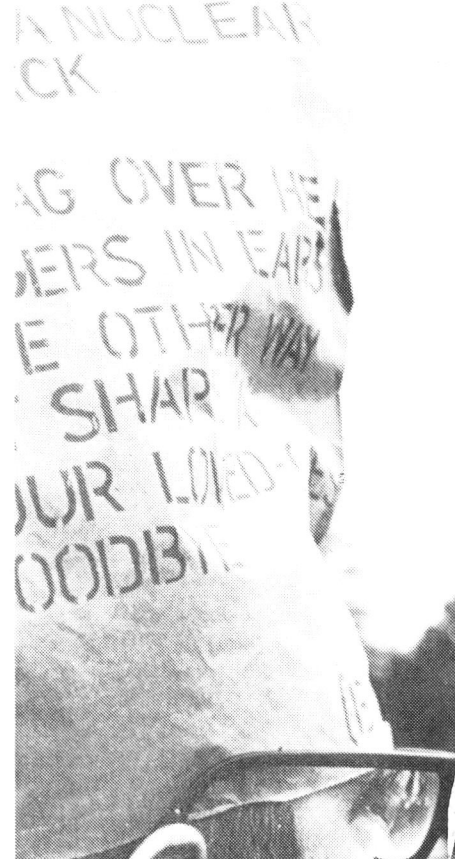

2. Ralph V. Summy: 'Militancy and the Australian peace movement, 1960-1967', *Politics*, volume 5, number 2, (November 1970), pp. 148-162; Malcolm Saunders and Ralph Summy: 'Salient themes of the Australian peace movement', *Social Alternatives*, volume 3, number 1 (Octobeer 1982), pp. 23-32; Harry Redner and Jill Redner: *Anatomy of the World: The Impact of the Atom on Australia and the World* (Melbourne: Fontana, 1983), chapter 11. Also of relevance, though I have not seen it, is a major two-part article by Malcolm Saunders and Ralph Summy on the history of the Australian peace movement, to be published in *Peace and Change* in 1985.

3. Malcolm Saunders: 'Australia's withdrawal from Vietnam: the influence of the peace movement', *Social Alternatives*, volume 1, numbers 6/7 (June 1980), pp. 56-62.

movement was so small, peace movement demands closely reflected the views of key activists. There was also a strong pro-Soviet minority in the Australian peace movement who supported criticisms of capitalist militarism and opposed any criticisms of state socialist militarism. Aside from the pro-Vietnam and pro-Soviet figures in the peace movement, the other major voice was simply antiwar. In this latter group fell for example many of the church-based peace activists. But the pro-Vietnam and pro-Soviet voices discouraged many possible initiatives. Moreover, the financial base of the movement was largely provided by trade unions, whose leaders held pro-Vietnam sentiments, hence much of what was done was compatible with a pro-Vietnam stance and a non-hostile stance towards the Soviet Union. All this helped to make opposition to U.S. bases, questioning of ANZUS and support for a non-aligned foreign policy into priority issues for the peace movement. These were areas on which almost all activists in the movement could agree, and for which a political base for implementing the demands seemed to exist — namely the left wing of the Labor Party.

This narrow base for the organised peace movement in the 1970s then saw the rise of the mass-based anti-uranium movement[4] which paralleled the rise of other anti-nuclear power movements around the world in the mid-1970s. While the base of the 1970s peace movement was provided by trade unions, the new anti-uranium movement depended to a far greater extent on middle class radicals, often connected with the left of the Labor Party. In the peak years of the anti-uranium movement, 1976-1978, there was major participation from the labour movement, students and unemployed, professions, churches and other groups. As in other countries, opposition to uranium cut across usual party-political lines. But unlike most other countries, where the movement had some of its strongest roots in rural or middle-class communities — often with conservative politics — the anti-uranium movement in Australia came to include a strong working-class involvement. There were also strong links with the Aboriginal land rights movement. Because Australia's role in the nuclear fuel cycle was solely as an exporter of uranium, the issue of proliferation of nuclear weapons via the 'peaceful' nuclear fuel cycle became a major issue. Thus, much more than in most countries, the issue of nuclear power was strongly linked at an early stage to the issue of nuclear war. However, the links between the anti-uranium movement and the peace movement took a while to develop. Traditional peace movement activists saw that the anti-uranium movement was where the popular strength lay, and tried in the late 1970s to use that strength to promote their own issues, such as opposition to nuclear weapons and to U.S. bases. At that time, for example, Hiroshima Day focused almost entirely on uranium mining and nuclear power rather than on traditional peace issues. Quite a few anti-uranium activists did not want to 'contaminate' the anti-uranium message with traditional peace movement demands. Like many single-issue groups, they preferred to use their strength for specific and narrow ends.

Ironically, by 1982, the relation between the anti-uranium and peace movements was reversed. The peace movement was now the stronger. For a year or two the anti-uranium movement tried to get uranium discussed at major peace movement functions, while some people in the peace movement preferred just to talk about nuclear war and not to 'confuse' the discussion with the uranium issue. But this resistance to including opposition to uranium mining on the peace movement agenda did not last long. The continuing strength of the anti-uranium movement, and its continuing influence especially within the labour movement, has meant that opposition to uranium mining has become one of the main demands of the peace movement.

The 1979 NATO decision to deploy cruise and Pershing missiles was a crucial factor which stimulated the enormous expansion of the Western European peace movement. This movement gradually spread to other Western countries, and to a limited degree has penetrated state socialist and Third World countries.[5] The infectious explosion of the Western peace movement reached Australian cities in 1981 and 1982. The immediate consequence was the formation of new groups and the organisation of large rallies. The process has continued with the formation of many suburban and occupational groups, and with the initiation of direct action

4. Jim Falk: *Global Fission: The Battle Over Nuclear Power* (Melbourne: Oxford University Press, 1982); Brian Martin, 'The Australian anti-uranium movement', *Alternatives*, volume 10, number 4 (Summer 1982), pp. 26-35.

5. See especially the journal *Disarmament Campaigns* for an ongoing account of worldwide peace movement activities.

(notably the women's action at Pine Gap in 1983). The existence of a strong movement has enabled much more frequent and favourable news coverage of peace issues.

The rise of the 1980s peace movement caught the old peace activists largely by surprise. In the 1970s there was no planning of avenues for involvement and action should there be a quick upsurge of interest in peace issues. The 'old guard' from the 1970s has largely been swamped by new members and new groups. However, since a large fraction of the new participants have been completely new to political action, they have brought few new ideas and demands to supplement or replace the traditional demands of the earlier peace movement. The new people have largely accepted the stand against U.S. bases and ship visits, but they have brought a change of emphasis. There is now more ritual declaiming against nuclear war. As a demand, this often translates into requests that the Australian government take a stronger line for nuclear disarmament in world forums. The other new emphasis has been on peace education, which is partly a consequence of the large number of teachers and academics who have become active in the movement, and also the more active and prominent role of women in the 1980s movement.

Themes

The effectiveness of social action groups can be judged on two levels. One level is external impact: making changes in policies and practices which are causing harm. The other level is encouraging the development of skills, understanding and commitment among the members of the movement. Both these levels are important.

Most peace groups seem to act in an expressive way: they act in ways which help to express the moral outrage or social concern of the group members.[6] Such actions — which include demonstrations, letters to newspapers and civil disobedience — can be quite powerful. But in many cases they are not effective in actually affecting policies or practices concerning war, and indeed external effectiveness is often not a major consideration. Quite simply, there is little analysis and little strategic thinking about how to achieve even those peace movement goals which are clearly articulated.

While external effectiveness has not been a strong point for peace groups, in the past the development of capabilities of members has not been either. Many groups have been strongly task oriented. They have done little to try to develop patterns of group interaction that are satisfying, and devoted little effort towards spreading skills and knowledge and the opportunities to apply them. For example, public speaking or group representation at conferences often is left to the same experienced activists. There has been some change in the past few years towards emphasising the development of talents and commitment of group members. This is often termed 'empowerment'. This has been especially important in the women's peace movement, many of whose members have been alienated by patterns of male dominance and internal power hierarchies in the mainstream groups.

To return to analyses of the war system: although only a few members of peace movements have developed a coherent analysis and strategy, nevertheless there are implicit analyses and strategies underlying a great number of peace movement activities. Because these analyses are mostly implicit, it is not easy to examine them. What I will do here is describe some themes which seem to me to be common in the implicit analyses behind the approaches taken by many active members of the peace movement. I use the word 'themes' to suggest that approaches to the problem of war are organised around particular guiding images. The six themes I will discuss are:
* nuclear weapons are the primary danger;
* war is due to elite decision-making;
* Australia's military alliance is the basic problem;
* capitalism is the root of war;
* patriarchy is the root of war;
* the war system is a complex social system tied into major social institutions.

6. Bob Overy: *How Effective are Peace Movements?*(London: Housmans, 1982); Frank Parkin: *Middle Class Radicalism: The Social Bases of the British Campaign for Nuclear Disarmament* (Manchester: Manchester University Press, 1968).

There are other analyses of the causes of war. One, for example, is that war results from a biologically rooted drive for human aggression.[7] This belief is widely held among the general public, but also has some currency within the peace movement, especially among new members. Nor are the themes discussed here entirely independent either logically or in terms of individual beliefs. Theme 6, for example, overlaps with themes 4 and 5. In terms of personal beliefs, some people would see nuclear weapons as a primary danger, but also recognise the role of capitalism or patriarchy in promoting the nuclear threat. The significance of the six themes is that they try to encompass the rationales behind the major public demands and actions of peace activists.

Theme 1: Nuclear Weapons Are the Primary Danger

It is evident that the majority of antiwar campaigning in the 1980s focuses on nuclear war. This is obvious from reading literature produced by peace groups, or indeed from the daily press. The major umbrella peace organisation in Australia is called People for Nuclear Disarmament. A recent political manifestation of this emphasis is the Nuclear Disarmament Party. (Incidentally, it should be mentioned that the Nuclear Disarmament Party did not grow out of established peace groups, and at the December 1984 election was not endorsed by most of the major peace groups. It therefore cannot be considered to be the political wing of the peace movement, though it is certainly part of that movement by the definition I have adopted.)

Many of the demands made by the Australian peace movement link closely with this analytic theme: opposition to nuclear ships and aircraft; pressure for a stronger Australian government stand against the nuclear policies of the superpowers; support for genuine nuclear-free zones; and opposition to uranium mining, which is seen as a contributor to the risk of nuclear war. Looking more closely at policies of major peace groups, one will find explicit opposition to other types of war, in particular chemical and biological war and outer space war — though not so often conventional war. But the bulk of campaigning focuses on nuclear war.

The alternative vision associated with this theme is of a world without nuclear weapons, but otherwise basically the same. To be fair, many peace activists would want to do much more than remove nuclear weapons. But for many, removal of nuclear weapons would eradicate the primary evil. The major group of people who respond to this theme are from the middle class, the great mass of people newly involved in the peace movement since 1981, such as housewives, public servants and professionals. Many people join the peace movement because they read about nuclear war and become concerned, for themselves or their children, about the terrible looming disaster. Many of those who stay in the movement then discuss, read and think more about the issues and develop more sophisticated perspectives. Others continue to focus entirely on nuclear war, or drop out. In any case, there are a large number of people in the peace movement who subscribe to the analysis that nuclear weapons are the primary danger, and this strongly influences the demands made by the movement.

Theme 2: War Is Due to Elite Decision-Making

The underlying idea here is that national leaders are ignorant, misled (for example by their military advisers) or tied to vested interests. It is a widespread belief within peace groups that if elites only came to understand the true danger, and realised that war is counterproductive for all humans, then they would change national policies. However, some elites are too tied to vested interests to be convinced to change

7. For a refutation of this view, see Ashley Montague: *The Nature of Human Aggression* (New York: Oxford University Press, 1976).

policies; it is thought that these elites need to be pressured to change their actions or, alternatively, outnumbered and replaced. This analysis leads to an emphasis on demands made on the elites themselves. Removal of U.S. bases, stopping of uranium mining, or establishment of a nuclear-free zone are all seen as initiatives which need to be implemented by governments. This theme thus underlies the whole conception of making **demands**, namely demands for government action.

In terms of political practice, an emphasis on disseminating information and on lobbying is the usual approach used to convince elites. If the elites are too tied to vested interests to be convinced then the approach used is to apply pressure on governments via letters, media coverage and demonstrations, or to work through the Labor Party to 'get the numbers'. Finally, there is the alternative of replacing the elites, which means electing sympathetic politicians and promoting anti-nuclear political parties. Even direct action is often seen as a way of applying pressure on elites or of replacing them, as in the case of the Southwest Tasmania blockade. There are some other themes related to this one, for example that war is due to evil elites, or that war is due to powerless elites who will not confront their own bureaucracies. The basic orientation is the same: the making of demands for altered action by the elites, or for replacement of the elites by others.

The solution to the problem of war from the perspective of this analysis is rational elites, achieved either by conversion of present elites to rationality or by outnumbering, outflanking or replacing present elites by rational ones. As in the case of the first theme, social structures would remain basically the same. Also as in the case of the first theme, the major group involved here is the middle class, and especially members who are relatively new to the peace movement.

Theme 3: Australia's Military Alliance Is the Basic Problem

The idea here is that Australia's military alliance, notably the connexion with the U.S., ties the country into the system of military spending, confrontation and dependence on power bloc politics. It is thought that if the Australian government could break free of the alliance and establish a non-aligned or neutral foreign policy, then this would contribute to the weakening of the hegemony of the dominant military powers — especially by providing an example to other countries — and provide the freedom to take independent initiatives in many areas relating to disarmament. New Zealand's stand against nuclear ship visits is seen as a welcome step in this direction.

This theme is part of what lies behind opposition to U.S. bases and to visits by nuclear ships and aircraft, and is the immediate rationale for pushing a more independent foreign policy. The alternative to Australian military alliance with the U.S. is a greater degree of independence. Some activists would like a neutral foreign policy, similar to that of Sweden or Switzerland, which rules out any military alliance or collaboration. Others would prefer non-alignment, which does not automatically rule out military or political collaboration on specific issues or for specific purposes. Yet others would simply wish to redefine the ANZUS agreement or the ongoing military collaboration between Australia and the U.S. in order to give the Australian government more autonomy and independence. One common feature of these alternatives is continued reliance on Australian military forces. Indeed, less dependence on U.S. military capabilities might well imply greater Australian military expenditure. Hence it is to be expected that many Australian military and political elites might support this alternative, at least once it mustered more political strength.

Within the peace movement, a primary focus on the alliance is not nearly as common as focus on nuclear weapons. Yet there are a number of key figures who have raised the issue of the alliance for many years, and many activists focus on this theme, though seldom exclusively. Quite a number of those who emphasise this theme are involved with the left of the labour movement.

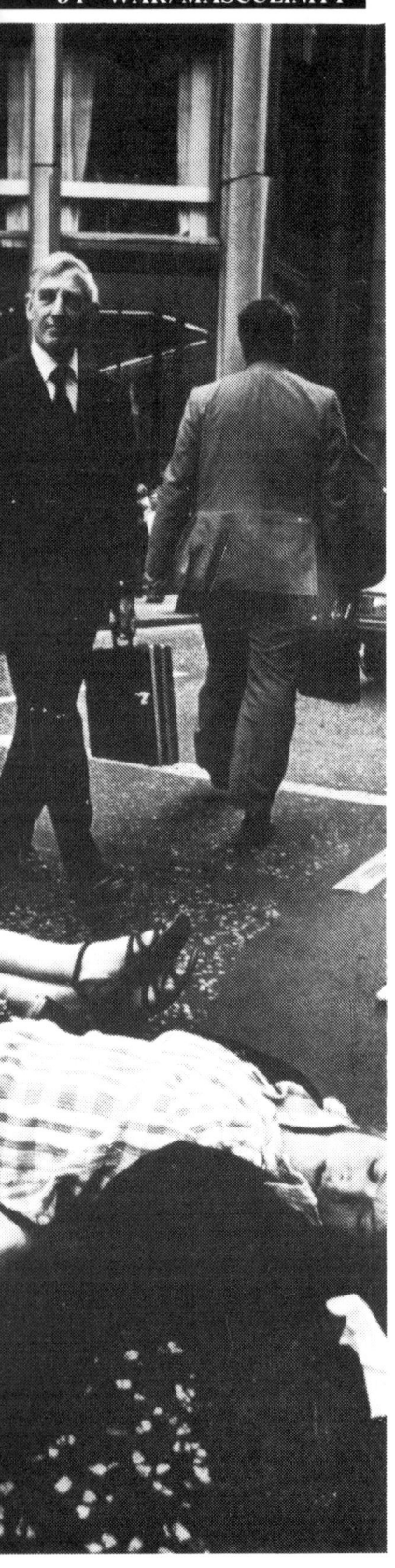

Theme 4: Capitalism Is the Root of War

This theme is closely related to the previous one. But here the emphasis is not on the alliance *per se* but on the system of private production for profit. Military spending in the West is seen as a means by which states protect their exploitative economic systems against threats from inside and outside. Military spending in state socialist countries is seen on the other hand as a necessary — if unfortunate — response to Western military threats. (Alternatively, state socialism is conceptualised as state capitalism, which necessarily engenders militarism.) This theme also lies behind opposition to any connexion with the U.S. military or U.S. foreign policy. The alternative, from the perspective of this theme, is a socialist Australia. This might be either socialism in the social democratic mould (such as Sweden), or in some other mould. Undoubtedly the typical vision would be of a specifically Australian socialism. But in any case there would probably be a need for an Australian military, if only to prevent capitalist military threats.

The left of the labour movement, plus a number of Marxist groups, form the main force linked to this analysis. This theme was quite prominent within the peace movement in the 1950s and 1960s and, to a somewhat lesser extent, during the 1970s. With the wave of new participants in the 1980s, it has become very much a minority view.

Theme 5: Patriarchy Is the Root of War

Growing out of the feminist movement and the feminist analysis of social institutions, this view sees warfare as closely linked to domination of and violence against women by men. Many feminists see male domination as predating and as more fundamental than domination associated with capitalism, the state or the military. The extreme male chauvinism fostered in military training is seen as a manifestation of male violence against women used to sustain other institutions. Also important is the role of rape as a means for domination both in peace and war.

There are a number of different views about alternatives to patriarchy. One is that of a world in which women are treated like men, and occupy an equal share of positions in all spheres, including elite positions. But many feminists in the peace movement would take a more radical position, seeing the necessity to reconstruct or abolish many social institutions entirely — such as the military, which cannot be reformed simply by an influx of women soldiers and generals. The feminist analysis of war has had little overt impact on the normal list of peace movement demands. Its greatest impact has been on the actions undertaken: in particular, attempts to join Anzac Day marches, and the civil disobedience actions at Pine Gap and Cockburn Sound.

Theme 6: The War System Is a Complex Social System Tied Into Major Social Institutions

The idea behind this theme is that militarism is deeply embedded in a number of institutions such as the state, capitalism, patriarchy and the military. The theme as a whole is one which does not trace war to a single cause, but rather looks at a set of social institutions which have ramifications throughout society, for example in the education system, in individual psychology, in centralised economic production, and in the use of soldiers and police for repressing threats to the dominant social order. For example, some feminists might begin with a focus on the link between patriarchy and violence. There are connexions with patriarchy involved in the way military forces mobilise masculinity for the purpose of violence, and the direct support that women provide to the military as wives, prostitutes, nurses and workers. But in looking at war feminists might also examine the role of the state in organising military forces and the role of capitalism in military production. For example, state bureaucracies are controlled by men, and operate on the bureaucratic principles of hierarchy and the division of labour, thereby structurally downgrading characteristics such as co-operation and emotional support which are conventionally assigned to women. Bureaucracies foster the instrumental rationality which enables social resources to be allocated to the development of weapons of mass destruction and enables business as usual to be conducted with (or within) repressive regimes. The role of ideology might also be examined: the mobilisation of mass support for the state in wartime via propaganda, peer group pressure, schooling and cultural traditions. Conventional gender roles apply at all these levels. Pursuing such an analysis can lead to the conclusion that patriarchy is tied to the war system in a multitude of ways — and also that patriarchy is not the only important institution linked to the war system. A similar conclusion might be reached by beginning the analysis with the state, capitalism or the military rather than patriarchy. Examples of this theme include some of the initiatives for peace education, and some of the motivation for civil disobedience actions.

The alternative vision in this case would be institutional reconstruction. For example, this might include decentralisation of power to local communities via more local economic production and local political control. Male domination would be removed, and this would undercut the mobilisation of male violence in the military and elsewhere. Involved here are portions of the feminist movement and the environmental movement, some members of left groups, some radical Christians, and a miscellany of others.

Oligarchy and Democracy

With the 1980s resurgence of the Australian peace movement, there have been large numbers of new activists who have had no previous involvement in social action. Most of these people have no particular sympathy with the anti-U.S. and anti-capitalist analysis underlying much of the opposition to U.S. bases and the Australian-U.S. alliance. Their initial concern — often stimulated by media accounts of the horrors of nuclear war — is with nuclear weapons, and hence the analysis that nuclear weapons are the primary danger seems to be a common one. Those who have a sophisticated anti-U.S. and anti-capitalist analysis are greatly outnumbered, and yet their orientation remains strongly influential, if not dominaant. Partly this is historically rooted in the social location of the 1970s antiwar movement, as described above; and partly it derives from the continuing presence of the U.S. bases, the U.S. alliance, and visits by nuclear vessels and aircraft. But, as I have argued here, the 'obviousness' of these targets is to a considerable degree socially constructed. There are other possible targets, such as Australian military forces, which in physical terms are at least as 'obvious', but which have not become the target of significant peace movement activity.

It can be argued that the reason for emphasis on U.S. bases, on visits by nuclear ships and on the U.S. alliance is the new perception that they are part of a first strike strategy by the U.S. military which has been coming into being for some years. But the U.S. bases and alliance were a primary focus in the 1970s, well before the first strike analysis became widely touted. As I see it, the first strike analysis was used to justify and sustain an emphasis which had already been established. I am not saying that analyses of the 'real threat' are irrelevant to the development of peace movement focuses, simply that they are only one factor, and not so often the dominant one.

The way peace groups are organised can also help to maintain the hegemony of certain demands and orientations. Let me broach this delicate topic by making some general comments about social action groups. Many groups have been and are dominated by experienced activists, are hierarchical in de facto if not official ways, and are heavily task-oriented rather than convivial and participatory in their style. What this means is that much of the running in such meetings is made by the experienced and politically sophisticated 'heavies'. When there are full-time staff, they are usually prominent among this core of influential activists. Quite a few people who are new to the issue feel alienated and unwelcome in such groups. Often they feel that they are being used for the purposes of others rather than being genuine participants. While the 'heavies' are undoubtedly sincere, concerned, and hard-working, the style of their commitment discourages many others who might otherwise become involved.

Who are these experienced activists? Many of them are also the people who prefer to work through the Labor Party, or to work to apply pressure on the Labor Party. Indeed many are experienced Labor activists. It is their political savvy in the cut and thrust of party politics that informs their analysis and shapes their political styles, and this is what often alienates newcomers. In this way the orientation of social movement demands towards top-down solutions by governments can be sustained by elements of a top-down organisation of the social movement itself.

This critique has often been made of 'left' groups. One stimulus behind the development of the 1960s feminist movement was the hierarchy and manipulation within many left groups, and in particular the exploitation and marginalisation of women in those groups. Since then, portions of the feminist movement, the nonviolent action movement and the environmental movement have consciously fostered egalitarian group dynamics, consensus decision-making, the sharing of tasks and skills, and the development of campaigns designed to encourage participation.[8]

In the period of quiescence in the Australian peace movement in the 1970s, the features of hierarchy and de facto domination by 'heavies' were common. This reinforced the priorities of key activists: in particular, the anti-capitalist emphasis. Since 1981, with the large influx of new people, a decentralisation of activity has been forced on the movement: lots of independent groups have sprung up and done their own thing. Furthermore, many of the major groups have decentralised their operations and organisations, thus providing opportunities for new members via relatively unthreatening avenues.

Nevertheless, actual and de facto hierarchies still play a significant role. This especially applies at 'peak' councils and other key decision-making meetings at state and national levels. While decisions made at state meetings or national conferences are not binding on peace groups, many of the decisions strongly orient local action, such as plans for national rallies or signature drives. In as much as key figures play a disproportionate role in the decision-making process, this helps to sustain and promote certain emphases in peace movement demands. The major effect is twofold. First, there is an emphasis on the more 'radical' demands — for example, opposition to U.S. bases rather than rhetorical concern about nuclear war — but only the more radical demands drawn out of the reservoir of standard demands. Second, many of the major actions are oriented towards pressuring government in one way or another. For example, one of the principal goals of mass rallies is to show the government that people are concerned.

Both of these emphases help to sustain the influence of key activists within the movement. The key activists are the ones more knowledgeable about the more radical demands. But only radical demands that are 'on the agenda' provide opportunities for these activists to influence the directions for action by large numbers of people. Second, the orientation towards pressuring government implies the need for centrally decided-upon, large-scale actions, such as national rallies. This also gives the key activists more of a say about movement directions than would an orientation more towards decentralised and independent actions.

Is the disproportionate influence of the 'heavies' harmful? It is when large numbers of potential new activists feel unwelcome. But to be fair, there must be a balance between catering for new members at the lowest common denominator, and developing campaigns with a cutting edge. In addition, there are many experienced peace activists who make every attempt to democratise the movement while at the

---

8. See for example Virginia Coover, Ellen Deacon, Charles Esser and Christopher Moore: *Resource Manual for a Living Revolution* (Philadelphia: New Society Press, 1981).

same time arguing for their own favoured lines of action. Compared to organisations such as the military or corporations, the peace movement is a model of participation, decentralisation and democracy. Indeed, in some circles there is strong antagonism towards any form of overt hierarchy, and a distrust of some experienced activists who are spokespeople for the movement.

Nevertheless, the processes I have outlined can play a restraining role on the development of the movement. There is no guarantee that widespread participation in the peace movement will last, and going by past history a downturn is virtually inevitable.[9] When that process begins to occur, then the organisation of the movement will play a big role in its long-term survival and effect. A movement that is too oriented to government for solutions to social problems, and too dependent on key activists for providing directions and organisational skills, will be vulnerable to both attack and co-option.

This suggests that a high priority for the movement is to increase the opportunities for members of independent groups to develop their skills, understanding and commitment. At the moment, the main demands made by the peace movement and the campaigns to promote them do not provide many opportunities for local groups to act in ways that are both independent of central co-ordination and immediately relevant to peace movement goals. Most major rallies for example require central co-ordination, while organising suburban street stalls is beneficial but hardly sufficient for challenging the war system. Some initiatives, such as the women's civil disobedience actions, satisfy both these requirements. Other such initiatives are needed which can be taken up by different parts of the wide diversity of groups in the peace movement.

The Failure of Theory

The social origins of the peace movement agenda also help explain the failure of most theorising about war and peace to provide any useful directions for peace movement action. Of course, to analyse 'the failure of theory' is to make an analysis from a particular theoretical viewpoint. My own stance falls into this category that 'The war system is a complex social system tied into major social institutions'. In particular, I see war as a manifestation of the power of states within a system of states. States are founded on a monopoly of what is claimed to be the legitimate use of violence. This is used not only to protect against external threats but, just as important, to defend against internal challenges to state power. Power in the modern state also depends crucially on centralised economic management and extraction of resources from the national economy, which sustains the state and in particular the military. The organisational form of modern state power is bureaucracy, which facilitates top-down control, disciplines the work-force (in particular the military), and undermines self-managing alternatives. Patriarchy is closely linked to the state, bureaucracy and the military via a process of mutual mobilisation: men use formal positions, such as in bureaucracies, to maintain male power, while elite bureaucracies mobilise male support for bureaucratic hierarchy by measures such as the gender division of labour. Also tied into the war system are a number of other institutions such as capitalism, racism and the domination of nature.[10]

From the point of view of such an analysis, the themes focusing on the dangers of nuclear weapons and on elite decision-making mistake symptoms for causes. Nuclear weapons are the product of the war system, not its driving force. Likewise, the attitudes and actions of elites reflect their position in social systems which are integral to the war system. They are not irrational, but rather behave according to the rationality of the system they serve: a rationality deadly to wider human interests, to be sure, but nevertheless a rationality deriving from the interests of particular social groups. Because elites are constrained by the structures in which they operate, applying pressure on them or replacing them by 'better' elites can go only a limited way towards addressing the structural roots of war. Orientations towards nuclear weapons and towards elites reflect the lack of social critique by large numbers of those in the peace movement.

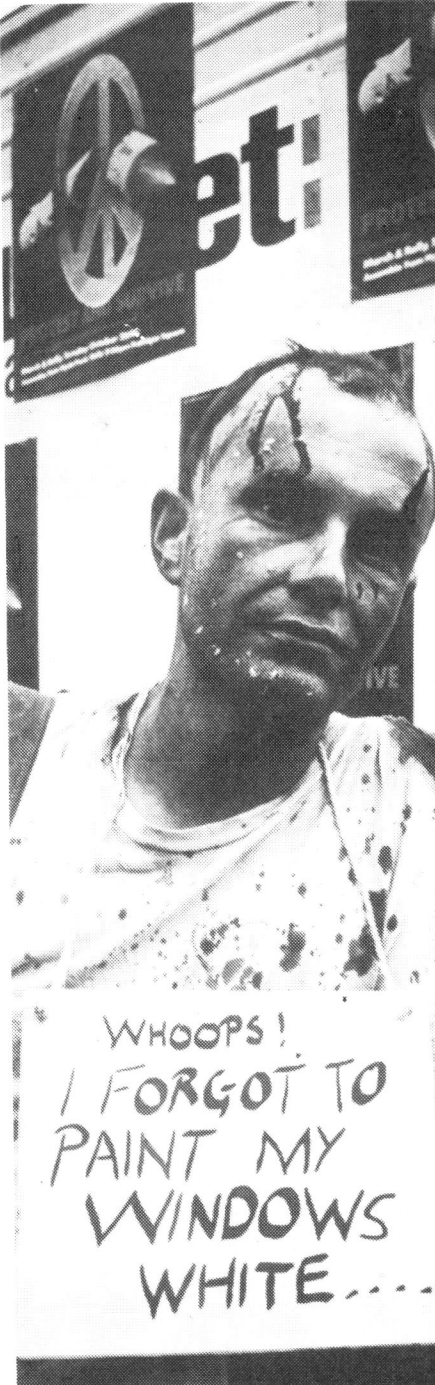

9. Nigel Young: 'Why peace movements fail', *Social Alternatives*, volume 4, number 1 (March 1984), pp. 9-16.

10. Brian Martin: *Uprooting War* (London: Freedom Press, 1984).

11. Martin Shaw: *Socialism and Militarism* (Nottingham: Bertrand Russell Peace Foundation, n.d.).

12. Seymour Melman: *Pentagon Capitalism: The Political Economy of War* (New York: McGraw-Hill, 1970).

13. Paul Joseph: *Cracks in the Empire: State Politics in the Vietnam War* (Boston: South End Press, 1981).

14. One of the more sophisticated feminist treatments of war is Penny Strange: *It'll Make a Man of You: A Feminist View of the Arms Race* (Nottingham: Mushroom Books and Peace News, 1983).

The themes of anti-alignment and anti-capitalism derive from the dominant analysis used by the orthodox left, which is an analysis of capitalism. Most anti-capitalist analysis does not provide a critique of the state or of the state system as institutions to be challenged, destroyed and fundamentally reconstructed. It is the capitalist state, not the state *per se*, which is the subject of major examination. Indeed, anti-capitalist analysis largely looks to the state as the location for resolution of social contradictions, for example via nationalisation or via redistribution of social benefits. It is for this reason, in my opinion, that since World War One until recently there has been an almost total absence of analysis of the problems of war — not to mention organised anti-militarism — coming from Marxists.[11]

The problem is that the usual categories used in the Marxist critique of capitalism do not throw much light on the problem of war. Modern war is never a direct battle between classes: it is always violent conflict channelled through the state. (This is not to deny the many bloody clashes between capitalists and workers.) Historically, workers have lined up behind their governments and militaries rather than supporting their class allies in 'enemy' countries. Before World War One the peace movement and the international socialist movement were strong, solidly connected and well organised. Yet both fell to bits with the outbreak of war.

The reason for this collapse can be traced to the underlying driving forces for the war, which — while they involved capitalist competition to some extent — were founded on state rivalries. The organisation and use of military forces depend mainly on the degree and organisation of state power and on the economic resources at the state's disposal. Any economic system that enables a surplus to be extracted by the state for central allocation — and this certainly includes both capitalism and state socialism — is compatible with the creation and maintenance of professional military forces. In short, the military is a feature of the state, not simply the capitalist state. Socialists before World War One did not oppose the state system or their own states to any significant degree; their opposition to war, founded on working class solidarity, collapsed in the face of nationalism.

Since World War Two, the 'peacetime' role of corporations in war production has become extensive, as analysis of the military-industrial complex has shown. This development reflects the increasingly tight link between economic production and state policy in capitalist societies. But these links in themselves show that capitalism drives the state's military policy. Just as convincing is the argument that the state ties capitalist production to military priorities.[12] For example, Paul Joseph[13] argues in favour of the thesis that the U.S. state intervention in Vietnam was carried out primarily to serve capitalism. However, his own evidence seems more convincingly interpreted as showing that this militaristic enterprise was neither controlled by nor very much in the interests of the U.S. capitalist class as a whole, much less the global capitalist class. The many wars and confrontations between socialist states in recent decades show that war cannot be attributed solely to a capitalist economic base — unless of course existing socialist states are categorised as state capitalism.

These considerations suggest that opposing capitalism is insufficient as a basis for opposing war. But it is also clear that capitalism is tightly linked to the war system, and so opposition to war must include opposition to many if not all aspects of capitalism.

It is only in the past few years that Marxists have begun to readdress the issue of war, in response to the rise of the 1980s peace movement. Their orientation by and large remains one of finding solutions through rather than against the state. Other theoretical approaches have not done much better than Marxism. Liberal theorists seldom provide an analysis of institutions, and even more seldom relate their insights to strategy for social movements. Anarchists certainly have a critique of the state, but have not been able to develop their insights and apply them to practical organising in a major way. Feminists in the 1980s have again begun addressing the issue of war, but the connexion between feminist analysis and political practice is only beginning to be made.[14] Most importantly, most of the non-Marxist theoretical perspectives lack any development of strategy for social movements aside from working to influence policies of the state. They are often as tied to state-based solutions as conventional socialists. (The alternative option of building autonomous self-managed institutions, often adopted by anarchists and sometimes by feminists, suffers from the problem of not providing a serious challenge to dominant institutions such as the state and capitalism.) This theoretical gap is a reflection of the social factors which have shaped the development of the conventional list of peace movement demands.

Future Directions

The first major limitation I see in the main demands of the Australian peace movement is that they are a limited selection of possible demands. The second major limitation is exactly that they are **demands** made of the government. If state power is centrally implicated in the war system, then it is insufficient to rely on state elites to implement solutions. Some governments, such as the Swedish and Yugoslav governments, will support limited movement out of the dominant military paradigm. But this path cannot be relied upon, any more than the good will of some 'enlightened' capitalists towards their workers means that capitalists can be relied upon to implement workers' control. The alternative is not to ignore the state, but rather to **supplement** the conventional demands and the lobbying and pressuring of elites by grassroots initiatives which do not depend on action from above. The following areas provide many opportunities for grassroots involvement.

* Promotion of social defence: dissemination of the idea of nonviolent resistance as an alternative to military defence, and local organising and training in methods and organisations of nonviolent resistance. This can be done, for example, by groups of workers, students or suburbanites. The methods and skills developed and practised can also be used in other campaigns. For example, workers would need to learn how to halt or take over production to be effective in social defence; this same ability clearly could be used in campaigns against employers or the government.

* Peace conversion: promotion of the idea of conversion of military forces and production to socially useful purposes, and local organising with military personnel and workers to develop plans and programs of action to implement conversion. Again, the capabilities developed in peace conversion campaigns could be used for other campaigns, such as conversion of transport or energy systems.

* Links with other social movements: greater liaison and development of joint initiatives with those in the feminist movement, the environmental movement, the Aboriginal movement, the gay movement, human rights movement, the unemployed workers' movement, the workers' control movement, etc.

* International initiatives: development of ways to encourage grassroots antiwar activism in other countries, especially under regimes where such activism is actively repressed, such as Indonesia and the Soviet Union. This might involve distributing information, making personal contacts, and developing radio links. For example, a church group might invite foreign church workers to Australia, and provide them with information and training in struggle against oppression.

* Institutional reconstruction: development of grassroots challenges to dominant institutions which are tied to the war system, such as the system of centrally regulated economic production which provides resources for state-funded military activities, and promotion of alternatives such as community control of decentralised economic activities.

It may sound contradictory to analyse the social construction of peace movement demands and then to advocate a different set of directions, as if a free choice could be made. But social movements are neither fully determined nor entirely autonomous. Individuals and groups are conditioned by their history and their social environment, but within this a measure of choice and opportunity exists. There is quite a bit of room for independent initiative and innovation. Indeed, often it is such initiatives, such as the Greenham women's actions, which enlarge the scope for participation and for further initiative. Furthermore, there has been a gradual increase — though the level is still quite low — in organised analysis and long-term planning within peace groups. this provides some hope that future antiwar initiatives will be less reactive and will be based to a larger extent on awareness of opportunities and limitations. This will not guarantee success, but it may improve the chance of it.

Acknowledgements:

Phil Anderson, Mark Diesendorf, David Purnell and Jacki Quilty offered useful comments on a draft of this article. Janet Hunt provided many detailed, incisive and critical suggestions. Ralph Summy offered valuable corrections and comments, and Paul Patton provided useful suggestions.

THE POLITICAL ECONOMY OF ARMS AND DISARMAMENT

Brian Pinkstone

The dominant radical paradigm used to analyse militarism in capitalist societies has been that of the underconsumptionist tradition — extending from J.A. Hobson to Rosa Luxemburg, and Baran and Sweezy.[1] In the post World War II period this approach was linked to Keynes' theories on aggregate demand and sub-optimal equilibrium, with the central argument being that military expenditure (M.E.) is used by the capitalist state to boost aggregate demand because large capitalist corporations are the chief beneficiaries of increased armament production, whereas other forms of pump-priming expenditure, such as social welfare, health, etc. benefit the working class.[2]

More recently it has been pointed out while a permanent crisis of underconsumption/overproduction might have seemed plausible during the postwar boom decades of capitalism, declining profits and declining growth rates since, have raised serious doubts about the validity of the general paradigm.[3]

The alternative view that M.E. is largely disfunctional for a capitalist economy, has mainly been put by political economists working within a more orthodox framework. Seymour Melman pioneered this approach in 1974 and he has been followed more recently by Mary Kaldor, and Dan and Ron Smith.[4] This paper will argue that the latter view is correct and entirely consistent with the value analysis originally developed by Marx. However, because the above authors remain largely within an orthodox framework they fail to comprehend the most important disfunctional aspect of M.E., that is, its structural reinforcement of the precise factors which bring about a long term tendency for the rate of profit to decline (T.R.P.D.) in capitalist countries.[5]

The central concern of Part I of this paper will be to illustrate the principal long term economic effects of M.E. using Marxian reproduction schemes, and in the light of that analysis, Part II will compare and assess the various forms which disarmament programs might take.

PART I: The Economic Consequences of Military Expenditure in Capitalist Economies

The structure of a capitalist economy can be treated as an input/output system in which material inputs of means of production and workers' wage goods are transformed by the application of human labour power into a physical output. Using Marx's notation, the production process can be thought of in terms of physical units,

---

1. J.A. Hobson: *Imperialism: A Study* (Ann Arbor: University of Michigan Press, 1965). Rosa Luxemburg: *The Accumulation of Capital* (London: Routledge & Kegan Paul Ltd., 1951). P. Baran, P. Sweezy: *Monopoly Capital* (New York: Monthly Review Press, 1965). The underconsumptionist argument — that unproductive consumption is necessary to cope with realisation problems is based essentially on the idea that the surplus (profits) is constantly tending to rise under capitalism. See E.O. Wright: 'Alternative Perspectives in Marxist Theory of Accumulation and Crisis' in Jesse Swartz (ed.) *The Subtle Anatomy of Capitalism* (Santa Monica: Goodyear Publishing Co., 1977) pp. 210-216.

2. See M. Reich: 'Military Spending and the U.S. Economy', in S. Rosen (ed.): *Testing the Theory of the Military Industrial Complex* (Lexington: D.C. Heath & Co., 1974), pp. 85-101, for a concise statement of this position.

3. Donald Mackenzie: 'Militarism and Socialist Theory' *Capital and Class*, Spring, 1983, pp. 33-73. Also in the same issue, George Georgiou: 'The Political Economy of Military Expenditure', pp. 183-205.

4. S. Melman: *The Permanent War Economy: American Capitalism in Decline*, (New York: Simon and Shuster, 1974); Mary Kaldor: *The Baroque Arsenal* (London: Abacus, 1983); Dan Smith and Ron Smith: *The Economics of Militarism* (London: Pluto Press, 1983); D. Mackenzie, op. cit., pp. 54-63 for an overview and defence of this position.

5. For attempts at theoretical and empirical analysis of these crisis theories see T.E. Weisskopf: 'Marxian Crisis Theory and the Rate of Profit in the Postwar U.S. Economy' *Cambridge Journal of Economics*, December 1979, 3, pp. 341-378; and E.N. Wolff: 'The Rate of Surplus Value, the Organic Composition of Capital and the General Rate of Profit in the U.S. Economy 1947 — 1967' *American Economic Review*, June 1979, pp. 329-341. Some problems of structural rigidity are analysed in Amit Bhaduri and Joan Robinson: 'Accumulation and Exploitation: An Analysis in the Tradition of Marx, Sraffa and Kalecki' *Cambridge Journal of Economics*, April, 1980, 4, pp. 103-115. Also see A. Lowe: *The Path of Economic Growth*, (New York: Cambridge Univ. Press, 1976).

units of embodied and living labour time, or monetary units — the transformations in these 'forms' of value are analysed by Marx in Vol. 2 of *Capital*.[6] In order to deal with the phenomena of technological change in a comprehensible manner, it is necessary to refer to both physical and labour time quantities in our model, which will follow Marx's well known formula: C + V + S = W. C denotes the flow of capital (fixed capital goods and raw materials) used up in production each year — for simplicity we assume that all capital stock is expended and reproduced during each production period. V denotes the share of social product obtained by labour. S denotes the social surplus product appropriated by Capitalists. W represents the gross output of the system, while V + S together in physical terms represent the net product Y; in labour terms they represent the sum of newly added labour power in a given production period, denoted by L. And again for the sake of simplicity we begin with the assumption that one average unit of social product embodies one average unit of labour time. We can then ascribe suitable quantitive values to the model in order to comprehend basic economic phenomena, such as growth and productivity, e.g.

Figure 1

C + V + S = W   Y = V + S in physical terms
100 + 100 + 100 = 300 L = V + S in labour-time terms

in which 100 physical units of capital combined with 200 hours of labour time produce 300 physical units of output.

To grasp this intuitively we might imagine that the physical product is corn, and all physical capital inputs are seed corn — so that 100 units of seed corn planted and harvested produce 300 units of corn as gross output. The ratio $\frac{Y}{C}$ gives us a measure of the nett productivity of capital inputs, which is 2/1 in this example. Likewise the ratio $\frac{Y}{L}$ gives us a measure of the productivity of labour, which in this case is $\frac{200}{200}$ or one unit of seed corn per unit of living labour-time.

Such relationships vary with technical change depending on whether the change economises on capital or labour inputs, or involves the substitution of one type of input for another. These issues will be dealt with in depth at a later stage. For the present however, we will discuss the concept of simple extensive growth, in which no technical change takes place (i.e. the ratios $\frac{Y}{C}$ and $\frac{Y}{L}$ remain constant) and examine the impact of M.E. on such growth.

Returning to the model in Figure 1 we can see that if capitalists consume all of the surplus product each year, then there will be only 200 units of product left to outlay on seed corn and wages for the next year's production, so that the system will simply reproduce itself. However, if capitalists do not consume all of the surplus, they can invest in new, expanded production and with fixed technical coefficients the system will expand in proportion to the amount of new investment. For example, if at the end of production period 1, capitalists invested the total surplus product in new production, then C would rise by 50 units in the next production period, given the fixed productivity of capital ($\frac{Y}{C}$ = 2) net output would rise to 300 units, while the need for extra labour would also rise proportionately so that 50 extra units would have to be outlayed by capitalists on labour power. An illustration of what would happen if this process was repeated for three years is given in Figure 2 (p.p. indicates production period).

Figure 2

	C	V	S	=	W
p.p.1	100	100	100	=	300
p.p.2	150	150	150	=	450
p.p.3	225	225	225	=	675

6. K. Marx: *Capital* Vol. 2, (Moscow: Progress Publishers, 1967) Part I.

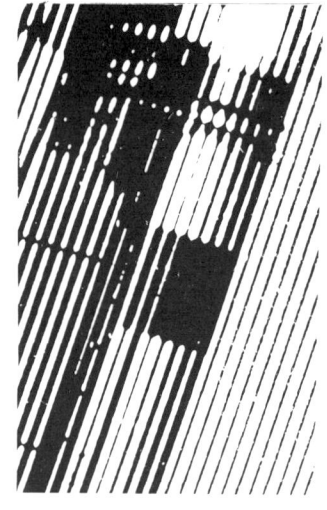

If we define the rate of growth, as the percentage increase in gross output each year ($G = \frac{W_n}{W_{n-1}} \times \frac{100}{1}$), then we will note from this model that the rate of growth of an economy is directly dependent upon the proportion of the surplus which is invested in new production each year (with constant technology and no problems of new labour supply). This means that the more capitalists spend on luxury goods, i.e. real estate, Rolls Royces, rare stamps, caviar, antiques, etc., the less capital there is available to invest in new production. This is true despite the fact that people may be employed in the production of luxury goods, for if capitalists raise their spending on luxury goods, then they must proportionately decrease their spending on investment goods — consequently in total no more people are employed. When they invest in new productive equipment which can be used for producing more goods, then totally new employment possibilities are opened up.

Now, weapons expenditure is clearly of the luxury goods type. In political terms, the means of violent coercion are used by the capitalist state to uphold the property rights of capital. They are therefore a necessary, though unproductive expense and form part of the capitalists' consumption goods bundle. Moreover, weapons are as physically unproductive as rare stamps: they cannot be used to produce new output. In this they are unlike capital goods, raw materials or workers' consumption goods, all of which are used to create new output (workers' consumption goods are transformed into labour power).

Once this central point is understood it becomes clear that 'pump priming' M.E. will not lead to any sustained long term growth, for not only are the products of M.E., weapons, incapable of use in new production, but also military personnel are unproductive — shining belt buckles and playing war games does not add anything to national output. In the short run an increase in M.E. may fuel some extra growth by lifting the level of aggregate demand (i.e. through Keynesian multiplier effects) but in the long run expenditure on M.E. represents a diversion of resources away from the accumulation of new productive capital. Thus several studies have shown that an inverse relationship exists between the amounts spent by governments on military spending and the amount of capital directed towards new fixed capital investment. Dan and Ron Smith argue that in general there is a one-to-one relationship, such that an increase of one per cent in the share of national output devoted to military spending results in a fall of one per cent in the share going to fixed capital formation; and they show that rates of growth in the leading capitalist countries have tended to be inversely related to rates of military spending in the postwar period.[7]

In the analysis so far we have only dealt with extensive growth, that is, growth based on the expansion of production through the use of more inputs. However, intensive growth is of far more significance for capitalist economies, because such growth is based on getting more output from given inputs and thereby entails technological change.

Theoretically, we can distinguish five possible forms which technological change can take: pure capital-saving innovation; pure labour saving innovation; neutral factor saving innovation (which saves equally on capital and labour inputs); capital-saving labour-intensive innovation; and capital-using labour-saving innovation (i.e. the substitution of capital for labour). As space precludes a thoroughgoing analysis of each of these, we will concentrate here on the two forms of most importance for the long-term development of capitalism: pure capital-saving and capital-using labour-saving innovations.

Pure capital-saving innovation raises the productivity of capital and, in Marxian terms, tends to lower the organic composition of capital (i.e. the ratio between labour-time embodied in means of production and that embodied in workers' wage goods). This raises both the rate of profit R, which is the percentage return to capital on input costs (i.e. $\frac{S}{C+V} \times \frac{100}{1}$), and the rate of growth. How this occurs is illustrated in Figure 3.

7. D. Smith and R. Smith: op. cit., pp. 87-89.

Figure 3

	C	V	S	=	W		
p.p.1	100	100	100	=	300	$\frac{Y}{C} =$	$\frac{2}{1}$

Now an innovation takes place whereby $\frac{Y}{C}$ rises to $\frac{3}{1}$

	C	V	S	=	W		
p.p.2	100	150	150	=	400	$\frac{Y}{C} =$	$\frac{3}{1}$

Here we see that the net product has risen by 50% so that, with constant labour productivity, 50 per cent more labour must be employed. The wage bill rises to 150 units and consequently capitalists are left with a surplus of 150 units. The rate of profit rises to $\frac{150}{200} \times \frac{100}{1} = 60\%$, and total output has grown by 33⅓ per cent. Hence with capital-saving innovation, even if capitalists consume all of the surplus, the economy will still grow. However, in fact, the rising surplus (expressed in rising rates of profit) would encourage capitalists to invest in expanded production, so that capital-saving intensive growth also generates extensive growth.[8]

It was precisely this type of growth which fuelled the postwar boom. Capital-saving innovations were developed during and immediately after World War II in response to the collapse of international trade and the sudden shortage of vital raw materials. This resulted in the rapid development of new or previously little used products such as plastic and aluminium. Moreover, more efficient processes for refining petroleum were quickly adopted and increased research and development (R and D) spending saw major breakthroughs in the creation of new alloys, high speed machine tools, and chemical production.[9]

These advances were made possible by the imperatives of wartime mobilization in which the whole economy becomes geared to raising economic output to a maximum under intensive state direction. After World War II, however, wartime controls were largely relaxed and the capitalist economies gradually returned to the class struggle dynamics of the free market under which capitalists exhibit a preference for investment in capital-intensive labour-displacing innovation — illustrated by the current obsession with computers and micro-chip technology.

Several reasons were suggested by Marx for this obsession, including the pressures on labour-supply induced when extensive growth runs up against the finite quantity of available labour, the general war between capitalists as each tries to reduce the labour-value of his output in order to undermine his rivals, and most importantly, the micro-economic experience of the individual capitalists in the class struggle against labour, wherein the substitution of physical capital for labour power allows him to undermine the strength of labour. This last aspect is particularly important because unlike other commodity suppliers the suppliers of labour-power, workers, are directly involved in the production process. They can therefore use tactics such as strikes, 'go slows' or setting up 'closed shops'. These often allow workers to cut a particular firm off from the total labour market and thereby raise their wage above that which would be determined by a competitive market for labour-power. Such strategies are not generally available to the suppliers of physical commodities.

In dealing with capital intensive labour-saving innovation, it is necessary to use a value analysis to show exactly why rates of profit will fall with such technologies. Much has been written on this subject, with various economists, particularly neo-Ricardians, offering proofs that the Tendency for the Rate of Profit to Decline (T.R.P.D.) cannot be shown as theoretically possible, given the profit maximizing incentive of capitalists. These authors, without exception, base their 'proofs' on the assumption that real wages are held constant.[10] This of course was not what Marx assumed. He assumed that the labour time value of wages remained constant.[11] The difference is that, if the value of wages remain constant, then real wages will rise as the productivity of labour rises since a set labour time value of wages will command an increasing number of goods. This can be revealed using value analysis. For example, returning to our original Marxian model, we shall assume that real wages are held constant and capitalists introduce a new technique at the end of

---

8. Marx extensively analyses the results of capital-saving innovation in Volume 3 of *Capital* (Moscow: Progress Publishers, 1974), Chapters 5-7.

9. The capital-saving innovations which led to the long boom are analysed in my unpublished Honours Thesis 'The Intersectoral Dynamics of Technological Change and Class Struggle in the Post-War U.S. Economy: Theoretical Considerations and Empirical Evidence' (Macquarie University, 1983).

10. See, N. Okishio: 'Technical Change and the Rate of Profit', *Kobe University Economic Review*, 7 (1961), pp. 85-99; Ian Steedman: *Marx After Sraffa* (London, 1977), pp. 116-136; Phillipe van Parijs: 'The Falling Rate of Profit: An Obituary', *Review of Radical Political Economics*, Vol. 12, No. 1 (1980), pp. 1-17.

11. 'The level of the necessaries of life whose total value constitutes the value of labour-power can itself rise or fall ... In practice, as in theory, the point of departure is the *value* of labour-power regarded as a given quantity.' K. Marx: *Capital* Vol. 1 (London: Penguin 1979) pp. 1068-1069. This is precisely the assumption used by Marx for his hypothetical model of the T.R.P.D. in *Capital* Vol. 3, op. cit., p. 211.

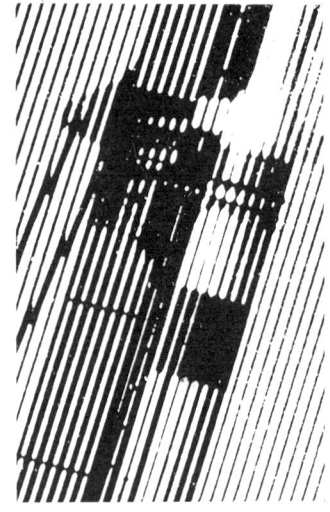

p.p.1, which in cost terms allows them to save 50 per cent of their requirements for living labour (and thus initially halve their wage bill) while only increasing the size (and costs) of constant capital by 25 per cent. At the end of p.p.1 it is assumed that each good sells at its new labour-embodied value. These values may be arrived at by dividing the value of output at p.p.2 by the value of output at p.p.1. This provides us with a value multiplier index (denoted by x) which determines the price paid for physical capital and real wages at the beginning of the next production period. This iterative method allows us to arrive at the new equilibrium value constitution of the system as it goes through several production cycles. Although theoretically it would take an infinite number of production cycles before values stopped changing, in practice the equilibrium level becomes obvious between 5 and 7 iterations.[12] Once equilibrium is known one can determine the effect on the rate of profit using the standard formula $R = \frac{S}{C+V} \times \frac{100}{1}$. For simplicity we assume here that capitalists consume all S, i.e. there is no investment in expanded production.

Figure 4

	C	V	S	=	W	
pp.1	100	100	100	=	300	
pp.2	125	50	50	=	225	$x = \frac{225}{300} = 0.75$
pp.3	(125 x 0.75)	(50 x 0.75)	(100 — V)	=	193.5	
	93.75	37.5	62.5	=	193.5	$x = \frac{193.5}{225} = 0.86$
pp.4	80.625	32.25	67.75	=	180.625	$x = 0.9335$
pp.5	75.26	30.11	69.89	=	175.26	$x = 0.97$
pp.6	73.02	29.2	70.8	=	173.02	$x = 0.99$
pp.7	72.29	28.9	71.1	=	172.29	$x = 1$

as pp.n $\to \infty$ C$\to$71.43   V$\to$28.57   S$\to$71.43

i.e. at equilibrium $R = \frac{S}{C+V} \times \frac{100}{1} = 71.43\%$

Figure 4 shows that the new equilibrium rate of profit will be higher when real wages are held constant and capital-intensive labour-saving innovation is introduced. This results from the fact that as the value of each unit of output falls, the capitalists' outlays for both capital and labour are reduced. This process can also be understood in physical terms: in the original system 100 surplus units were produced with an outlay of 100 units on capital and 100 units on labour. If a new system is employed which produces 300 physical units for an outlay of 125 units on capital and only 50 units on labour, then the surplus in physical terms is 125 units, accordingly the rate of profit is $\frac{125}{125+50} \times \frac{100}{1} = 71.43\%$.

If, however, we follow Marx and hold the value level of wages constant, so that real wages rise as commodity values fall, we find that the final equilibrium rate of profit is less than the rate prior to the change in technique, e.g.

Figure 5

	C	V	S	=	W	
pp.1	100	100	100	=	300	
pp.2	125	50	50	=	225	$x = 0.75$
pp.3	(125 x 0.75)	50	50	=	193.75	$x = 0.86$
pp.4	80.625	50	50	=	180.625	$x = 0.934$
pp.5	75.26	50	50	=	175.26	$x = 0.97$
pp.6	73.02	50	50	=	173.02	$x = 0.99$
etc.						

as pp.n $\to \infty$ C $\to$ 71.43   V = 50   S = 50

i.e. at equilibrium $R = \frac{S}{C+V} \times \frac{100}{1} = 41.18\%$

---

12. This iterative method is a simplified application of the technique developed by Anwar Shaikh to solve the transformation problem, see his 'Marx's Theory of Value and the Transformation Problem' in Jesse Swartz (ed.): op. cit., pp. 106-139.

In physical terms, capitalists expect that the rate of profit will rise to 71.43 per cent, on the basis of the real wage existing at the time the new technique is introduced, however, the final distribution of physical product is of the form

$$\begin{array}{cccc} C & V & S & = W \\ 125 & 87.5 & 87.5 & = 300 \quad R = 41.18\% \end{array}$$

In other words, capitalists eventually have to pay 87.5 units of physical product to obtain labour power instead of the 50 which obtained when the decision was first made to adopt the capital intensive technique. It may be noted that the general rise in employed workers real wages is $\frac{87.5-50}{50} \times \frac{100}{1} = 75\%$, which is equivalent to the rise in their net productivity from 200 units of product in 200 hours, to 175 units in 100 hours.[13]

Consequently, Marx's argument that a rising organic composition of capital will produce a declining rate of profit is theoretically vindicated. It can also be empirically vindicated, for there is plenty of statistical evidence to show that the productivity of capital goods and capital investment has fallen in the advanced capitalist countries in the period since the mid-1960s. For example, figures provided by U.S. government and semi-government bodies show a distinct fall in both the general rate of profit and output-capital ratios for the main elements of fixed capital during the post-war period.[14] The pre-tax, rate of return for U.S. non-financial corporations was 15.6% in 1948, but by 1976 it was down to 9.4% (a fall of 38%). In the same period, output capital ratios for construction, electrical and non-electrical machinery had fallen by an average of 32%.

Further evidence is provided by Table 1 which compares average incremental capital-output ratios (I.C.O.R.s) for 1960-1970 with those for 1970-1981 in the U.S., the U.K., West Germany, Japan and Australia. I.C.O.R.s are the ratio of annual new investment to annual growth rates. They therefore give a measure of the percentage of national output which must be directed to fixed capital formation to produce a one percentage increase in national output.

13. For simplicity, we assume here that all capitalists instantaneously take up the new technique. Hence in pp.2 the value rate of profit immediately falls. However, if a more complex and realistic model is used, where there is a gradual introduction of the new technique over several production periods, it is found that until more than 50 per cent of the capitalists have innovated, the initial innovators enjoy a transitional rate of profit higher than the original general rate of profit. This is because the innovators produce at costs below the general value level of commodities. The last capitalists using the labour intensive earlier technique are also forced to adopt the new technique because it becomes *relatively* more profitable as the level of real wages rises.

14. For rates of return on Capital Stock of Non-Financial Corporations 1945-1976 see R. Lindsay (et al.): *The Nation's Capital Needs* (Washington D.C., Committee for Economic Development 1979). Output-capital ratios for basic elements of fixed capital are derived from data in J. Kendrick and E. Grossman: *Productivity in the United States* (Baltimore: Johns Hopkins U.P., 1980).

Table 1

Average Annual Percentage Rates of Investment and Growth for 1960-1981 and I.C.O.R.s in the Advanced Capital Countries and Australia

| Country | 1960 — 1970 | | 1970 — 1981 | | I.C.O.R.s | |
	(1) Gross Domestic Investment	(2) Growth Rate	(3) Gross Domestic Investment	(4) Growth Rate	1960 — 1970 (1)/(2)	1970 — 1981 (3)/(4)
	%	%	%	%		
U.S.	19.1	4.3	18.6	2.9	4.4	6.4
U.K.	19.4	2.9	19.0	1.7	6.7	11.2
W.Germany	24.0	4.4	24.0	2.6	5.4	9.2
Japan	29.6	10.4	33.3	4.5	2.8	7.4
Australia	26.5	5.6	24.1	3.3	4.7	7.3

Sources: Rate of Capital Formation from *National Accounts of OECD Countries*, Vols. 1 and 2.
Growth Rate from *World Development Report 1983* (World Bank 1983).

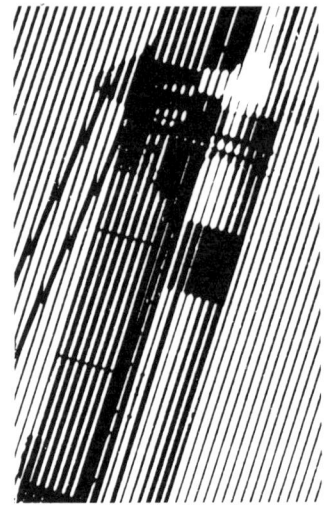

On average, for the countries in Table 1, it required 70 per cent more capital investment to produce one percentage point of economic growth in the 1970s than it had in the previous decade. This phenomena was accompanied by rising levels of unemployment throughout the western world. Levels of unemployment, however, are secondary effects of the impact of technological change on capital accumulation. With constant labour productivity any growth of the economy as a whole will create a corresponding increase in employment; long term trends in unemployment therefore depend on the difference between the rate of growth of labour productivity (i.e. labour displacement) and the overall rate of economic growth, other things being equal. If labour productivity grows at a slower rate than the economy, then unemployment will fall. However, if, as has happened, labour productivity grows at a higher rate than the whole economy, then unemployment must rise. Now, as the previous analysis has indicated it is precisely these phenomena (falling rates of economic growth with constantly rising labour productivity) which can result from capital-intensive labour-displacing innovation.

There is thus considerable evidence given by the behaviour of rates of capital productivity, rates of economic growth, unemployment levels and general rates of profit, that a qualitative change took place in the overall thrust of technological and general economic development in advanced capitalism beginning in the late 1960s. These changes are all consistent with a re-assertion of the tendency for the rate of profit to fall, as a result of a rising organic composition of capital.

Such contradictions are intensified by the diversion of investment into armament production which results from increased M.E., precisely because armament production takes place in the heartland of the capitalist economy: the capital goods sector. The immediate impact on simple extensive growth of diverting resources from the production of capital goods to armaments has already been described. However, far more important in the long run is its effect on intensive growth. For in the production of modern weapon systems a conjuncture of structurally related characteristics has brought about a concentrated development of capital-intensive technologies, the effects of which have permeated the entire framework of capitalist production and reinforced the already existing processes encouraging a general rise in the organic composition of capital. In order then to appreciate the crucial economic disfunctionality of arms production it is necessary to examine the peculiarities of its structural location and the implications of this for the development of the productive forces.

Arms Production and the Development of the Productive Forces

Military goods are the most important of capitalists' consumption goods as they provide the final guarantee of capitalist social relations. Hence they are assigned a very high priority in social output, so high in fact that all capitalists recognise the right of the state to interfere in, and give overall direction to, the process of armament production. The priority which weapons enjoy also means that they embody technologies which not only reflect but tend to lead tendencies inherent in the wider economy. For example, the complexity, scale, power and speed of production processes has been enormously increased during the development of capitalism and this is perhaps nowhere better manifested than in the technology of destruction.

Since World War II attempts to increase the power and speed of weapons has placed enormous demands on the service personnel who must operate them, particularly in terms of the reaction time available for decision making. This factor has been a driving force behind the military's support for research and development into electronic technologies. Most major developments in this field came as a direct result of military backed research. The first computer was built for the Manhattan project, the development of transistors was stimulated by the need for less fragile components than vacuum tubes, and the military stimulated the development of integrated circuits by underwriting the research program of Westinghouse. While it is true that many research programs initiated by the U.S. military have not proved viable for commercial uses, and that Japanese corporations have shown greater capacity than American corporations in the development of commercial microprocessor applications, nevertheless, the basic processes are still largely developed by U.S. military oriented companies.[15]

A further consequence of the scale and complexity of production processes has been an increase in the requirement for workers who perform purely administrative and co-ordinative functions, i.e. white collar workers. This tendency in the capitalist economy has its counterpart in the structure of the armed forces, thus in the U.S.:

... fewer than one out of every six persons in uniform — 360,000 out of 2,200,000 — currently serve in combat specialty. By way of historical comparison; better than nine of every ten persons serving in the Union forces during the American Civil War had combat specialties.[16]

Consequently micro-electronic technologies which could increase the speed and precision of control and communication functions have had a particular relevance to military operations, but once the basic processes were developed, non-military applications aimed at displacing civilian white-collar labour were soon found.

The priority given to the development of military technology during the postwar period is revealed by the concentration of scientific personnel found in such industries. For example, in 1970 weapons producers employed 7.4 scientists, engineers and technicians for every 100 production workers, while in the rest of manufacturing industry only one such person was employed per 100 production workers.[17] Knowledge is an essential element in human labour power and an integral part of society's productive forces. Such figures therefore represent an enormous diversion of capitalism's intellectual resource base.

This diversion and the capital intensive nature of modern armaments has also been encouraged by the role of the state as the only significant buyer (particularly in the U.S.). This factor means that there is a relative lack of competitive demand forces, with virtually no independent decision making bodies outside the state whose buying behaviour could provide some sort of objective yardstick. Once a decision to buy is made therefore, the state is stuck with the consequences and no real means to ascertain how good or bad those consequences are. Mary Kaldor has pointed out that the peculiar nature of the market has meant that competition between firms is not on the basis of complexity; exotic weapons systems appeal to the military who are little concerned with price, and contracts are won by firms offering technological gimickry (creating what Mary Kaldor has described as a *Baroque Arsenal*), while cheapness and efficiency in the production process itself becomes a very secondary criterion.

Some attempt is made by the state to keep prices down through writing quite low rates of profit (around four to five per cent) into defence contracts. However, in reality, the low rates are quite reasonable for big capital, since the profits are guaranteed and realised rates may be considerably higher since much capital equipment is supplied free of charge or at cost, by the state. Furthermore, there are many indirect benefits from defence contracts; for example, the results of state funded R and D, can be fully exploited for non-military uses — this is clearly important for the large diversified corporations which make up the bulk of prime contractors, e.g. Boeing, General Dynamics, General Electric, Westinghouse, General Motors, etc.[18] Perhaps the most insidious inflationary effect, however, is the fact that once a contract is won competition between contractors ceases and as products such as missiles, tanks, or submarines, take around a decade to develop,

15. Mary Kaldor: op. cit. pp. 68-71; R.N. Noyce: 'Microelectronics', *Scientific American* vol. 237, no. 3 (September 1974), pp. 62-70.

16. Mary Kaldor: op. cit., p. 9.

17. S. Melman: 'Twelve Propositions on Productivity and the War Economy', *Challenge* 7, March-April 1975, p. 8.

18. D. Mackenzie: op. cit., p. 38.

no realistic final price can be given. Consequently contracts are on a cost plus basis which gives corporations an incentive to raise the volume of their profits by allowing their costs to rise. Jaques Gansten, former Deputy Assistant Secretary of Defence in the U.S., has reported that contracts usually end up costing 50 to 100 per cent more than initial estimates.[19]

In other words the unique relationship between the state and arms producers (which is itself given by the political priority of defence goods) has encouraged capital-wasting technologies both in the production of weapons and in the weapons themselves. Since capital-intensive labour-displacing technologies are seen as appropriate weapons in the class struggle with labour, such technologies have been adapted to the needs of all capital. Hence the armaments producing industries have an economic significance which goes beyond simple quantitative measures — they have not only absorbed productive and intellectual resources in basically unproductive activity, they have also stimulated and reinforced the development of technologies which cause the organic composition of capital to rise — which in turn has led to falling rates of profit, falling rates of economic growth and a long downward slide into stagnation for the capitalist system throughout the world.

Given the structural links between M.E. and the T.R.P.D. what position should socialists take? On the one hand we might argue that it is all to the good, i.e., as it heightens the tendency towards crisis in the capitalist system it will speed on the triumph of socialism. Few socialists, however, could seriously take such a position. Clearly, the more intensive the military build up of capital, the more probabl becomes nuclear war. Since socialists are basically concerned with the development of a non-exploitative and humane society, such a prospect is anathema. Nevertheless, as Ernest Mandel has argued, it is only in a united socialist world in which capitalism, competitive individualism and the sovereign nation state have been transcended, that the human race will be able collectively to remove the threat of racial annihilation by banning the production of weapons of extermination.[20]

Consequently, the long term struggle for disarmament is only realistic if it also involves a struggle for socialism. Socialists must therefore not only support and defend socialist revolutions whenever they take place, they must also constantly point out the structural links between third world military adventurism, the arms build up and the ongoing crisis of imperial capital. Since these structural links are forged through political and not economic necessity it is in fact possible to attack M.E. on the grounds of economic rationality. Such attacks are clearly of use in winning over those people who may be objectively progressive in their sympathies with the peace movement but worried by the economic consequence of disarmament. However, this means that it is also necessary to go beyond mere criticism of the current arms build up and engage in a discussion of the positive benefits which could be expected to flow from well thought out disarmament programs.

PART II: The Political Economy of Disarmament

Unilateralism: If M.E. is disfunctional for a capitalist economy then clearly the most 'economically' rational response is unilateral disarmament. Many on the left have pointed to the increases in social services which could be realised from a significant reduction in M.E. The current crisis in capitalism has once again made unemployment and its consequence, poverty, an integral part of working class life. Unilateral disarmament could therefore be used as a method for mitigating the worst effects of capitalism on the working class and redistributing income towards those who have, in various ways, been denied access to the social product.

19. ibid.

20. E. Mandel: 'The Threat of War and the Struggle for Socialism' *New Left Review*, September 1983, p. 49.

However, the scope for such action is limited. In Australia for example, while M.E. accounts for around 10% of the Federal Government's budget, social security and welfare payments already account for around 30%. In the medium term probably a more effective approach would be to redirect M.E. into employment creating production. This could be achieved at least partly through the conversion of existing defence industries to the production of socially useful products with an emphasis on labour intensive production processes.

Research on such conversion programs has been carried out by various groups in Europe, in particular, by the German Union I.G. Metall — Europe's largest union.[21] The most publicised of conversion programs, however, was that drawn up by the workers at Lucas Aerospace in Britain, when this multinational decided to close down its British factory. Workers at Lucas Aerospace developed designs for alternative, socially useful products, which could be produced using existing technology and production facilities.[22] Such products included the 'Hobcart', a small mobile vehicle for children suffering from spina bifida; an ambulance life-support system; a vehicle capable of travelling by road or rail; gaseous hydrogen energy storage cells and advanced electric generators powered by wind and using the latest knowledge of aerodynamics. It is significant that the workers and technicians tended to develop not only socially useful but also capital-saving devices when they were free from the direction of capital.

Conversion programs would require careful planning and effective market research. However, given a concurrent increase in R & D funds (which could be directed towards conversion programs) this type of project would have the potential for not only raising standards of living but also for promoting employment growth, particularly if the emphasis was placed on capital-saving rather than labour-saving innovation. Gains could, of course, be more equitably distributed if the benefits of capital-saving went to the state rather than to private capital, but this would require nationalisation of defence industries and a redirection of M.E. into the expansion of state-owned industry.

Given the fact that the hegemonic class structure of capitalism has not yet been discredited or disorganised in the advanced capitalist countries, it is unlikely that any social democratic parties would proceed with what could amount to an assault on the commanding heights of capital — and thereby provoke the type of ruling class mobilisation and probable electoral defeat which any such challenge usually entails. Nevertheless, such programs are being discussed in Britain, and Dan and Ron Smith have pointed out that they would be compatible with the Alternative Economic Strategy being promoted by the Left of the British Labour Party.[23]

If the primary goal, however, is to promote peace and undermine the international imperialist alliance this may be more effectively achieved by disarmament programs which do not promote massively hostile responses on the part of national capitalist ruling classes. Indeed, it may be possible to construct disarmament programs which could appeal to fractions of national capital and thereby cut across existing class loyalties — helping to build a movement of the 'people' against the arms build up. So, for example, if unilateral disarmament were adopted, then a program which substantially redirected M.E. into new productive fixed capital formation and increased non-military R & D (rather than increased social welfare) would directly reinforce capital accumulation and help to stabilise the process of expanded reproduction in any country which adopted such a program.

Japan, which spends 1% of its GNP on M.E. has maintained rates of new investment of over 30% of GNP. The U.S., spending 8% of GNP on M.E. (during the late 70s it fell to 5%, but Reagan has lifted it back to 8%) re-invested only 18% to 19% of GNP. Theoretically, if the U.S. reduced its M.E. to that of Japan it could raise its rate of new capital formation by close to one third. The redirection of resources from M.E. would take some time and existing weapons manufacturers would have to be encouraged to convert their plants to non-military output. However, the evidence referred to earlier of a one-to-one inverse relationship between general capital goods production and armament production indicates that this problem would be less

21. M. Kaldor: op. cit., p. 163.

22. The history of the workers' struggle at Lucas is in Mike Cooley: *Architect or Bee* (Sydney: Transnational Co-op. Ltd., 1980). See pp. 67-74 for a sample of the type of alternative products developed by the Lucas work force.

23. Dan Smith and Ron Smith: op. cit., pp. 102-119 contains an extensive discussion of a left labour party oriented disarmament program for the U.K.

troublesome than it might at first sight appear. There would also be a problem with running down the number of military personnel without adding to mass unemployment, nevertheless if capital formation increased by one third, rates of economic growth should pick up by similar amounts thereby creating new (productive) employment opportunities. As part of a conservative programme one would require the new capital formation to take place in the private sector of the economy. This could be achieved through various taxation incentives, such as accelerated or exaggerated depreciation allowances. Moreover, a fall in government borrowing due to reduced M.E. would cause a fall in interest rates on financial markets, thus increasing the relative return on new capital investment and further stimulating increased capital accumulation.

This program would not, of course, remove the T.R.P.D., given the preference of each capitalist for capital-intensive labour-displacing technologies. Consequently, the long-term problems of capitalist development would not be removed. However, if the capitalist state were to redirect some part of the savings from reduced M.E. towards non-military (preferably capital-saving) oriented R & D, then it is possible that the T.R.P.D. could be offset to some degree, and any country which adopted such a strategy would, over time, increase its international comparative advantage. To some extent Japan has followed such a course, spending over two percent of GNP on R & D, with only a negligible amount going to military research; and from the mid-1970s the state has orchestrated a campaign to cut energy and raw material costs.[24] In the U.S. a similar percentage of GNP goes to R & D, but the 50% of R & D which is government funded goes primarily to National Defence and Space Research.[25]

Australia spends only 2.5% of GNP on defence but less than 1% on R & D. If these figures were reversed considerable benefits would be attained by Australian capital — particularly given that our major export industries are extractive and agricultural. Such industries have been the site of major capital-saving innovations in the past (e.g. surface mining and increased yield/seed ratios) and research may suggest other areas in which the productive efficiency of Australian capital could be raised. For example, Australia has a natural advantage in many of the raw materials used in the chemicals industries. In the U.S. this industry has experienced a declining capital-to-output ratio throughout almost the entire post-war period.[26] In Australia, the chemicals, petroleum and coal products industries have proved themselves as earners of export income — the share of this group in exports of manufactures rose from just over 10% in the late 1960s to 25% by 1975-6 and to 44% in 1983-4.[27] Chemicals have also clearly provided savings in working capital for other domestic Australian industries as the price of chemicals rose less than that of any other producer good from 1968 to 1984 (293% against an average rise of 409%).[28]

Much ado has also been made recently about so-called 'sunrise' industries, particularly those based on micro-chip technology. This technology at first glance appears to be highly capital-saving in nature. Costs of computing capacity for example have been falling at about 30% p.a. for several years.[29] For large scale computer systems though, which are primarily installed in order to save on labour costs, many ex-ante capital-savings may be lost due to the installation of excess or inappropriate capacity — especially if the equipment undergoes an accelerated depreciation due to the introduction of newer generation technologies which rapidly induce technological obsolescence in this field. On the other hand, use of small-scale micro-chip technology has certainly proven effective and investigations into small-scale applications of 'high' technology could be a cost effective direction in which to encourage Australian R & D.

While the largest funds for projects such as the above would become available under a unilateral disarmament programme, there is no doubt that most Australians would not approve of any strategy which left Australia without any means of defence at all. Consequently, in the final section I will examine some of the ways in which a strategy of armed neutrality (which removed Australia from the international imperialist alliance) could be put into effect, while minimising the inherently wasteful and disfunctional aspects of M.E.

24. Such measures in Japan however have been offset to a considerable extent by the adoption of highly capital-intensive labour-displacing fixed capital. See Norio Iwahshi Katsuhiko Hosoi and Brian Pinkstone: 'Economic Change and Education in Japan 1945-1983', in R. Sharp (ed.): *Economic Crisis, the State and Schooling: Comparative Studies in the Politics of Education*. (London: MacMillan, 1985.)

25. This is indicated by figures in E. Mansfield: 'Technology and Productivity in the United States', in Martin Feldstein (ed.): *The American Economy in Transition* (Chicago, 1980), pp. 563-596.

26. See Pinkstone: 'The Intersectoral Dynamics ...', op. cit., pp. 70-74; c.f. Kendrick and Grossman; op. cit., p. 149.

27. E.A. Boehm: *Twentieth Century Economic Development in Australia*, Second edition (Melbourne: Longman Cheshire Pty. Ltd., 1979) p. 209; and A.B.S. Catalogue No. 5404 (Canberra: A.G.P.S. 1984).

28. See A.B.S. Catalogue 5406 (Canberra: A.G.P.S. 1985).

29. Professor Shir Nyssen of Queensland University, cited in Barry Jones: *Technology, Development and Unemployment* (Sydney: Sixth National Conference of Labor Economists, 1983).

Armed Neutrality: In his book *Armed Neutrality for Australia* David Martin argues in favour of a small, highly mobile set of armed forces which would rely on high techology weaponry to make up for its lack of numbers.[30] Despite his general acknowledgement of the vulnerability of heavy attack weapon-systems, he still advocates what amounts to a fairly conventional system of forward oriented defence — which would include mini-destroyers, frigates, corvettes, mine layers, possibly an aircraft carrier and a sizeable submarine fleet, combined with an airforce capable of making 'an actual or potential aggressor to look to defence of his [sic.]own air space to ward off retaliatory strikes'.[31]

While Martin recognises the ineffectivity of heavy weapons systems and therefore proposes that Australia concentrate on the use of new generation light defensive weapons, he nevertheless argues in favour of raising the level of defence spending, and for the establishment of a largely independent defence industry in Australia. Indeed Graham Oke, who provides a chapter in Martin's book, on 'The Economic Back-up", envisages Australia developing an efficient arms producing sector which could export arms to the rest of the world.[32]

This is a path which the experience of Sweden has shown can be followed by a small high-wage capitalist economy. Using high technology and skilled labour and specialising in the production of heavy tracked vehicles, artillery and short-range missiles, Sweden now exports around half the output of its defence linked industry.[33] However, Sweden is a country close to the enormous European market and Swedish capital (i.e. Volvo, S.K.F., Saab-Scania etc.) has concentrated on the production of heavy capital equipment during the post-war period. In 1981, for example, such equipment accounted for $U.S.11.45 billion of merchandise export income for Sweden (or 40% of all exports). In Australia, by contrast, such equipment accounted for $U.S.1.4 billion or 7% of all merchandise export income.[34] These figures reflect the essentially dependent capitalist development which has taken place in Australia — with much of Australia's fixed capital (apart from construction) being imported. In 1982/3, for example total new fixed capital investment in equipment amounted to $17,942 m., while imports of machinery and transport equipment totalled $8,017 m.[35]

For purely practical reasons (let alone the moral questions involved in promoting the export of armaments) it is unlikely that Australia could emulate the Swedish experience in the near future. If armed neutrality were to be put into practice in Australia then, rather than the development of an expensive and wasteful domestic arms producing sector, it would be better to adopt a simple territorial defence strategy supported by a policy of importing the most cost-effective defensive weaponry from overseas.

Territorial Defence is defence which is clearly not provocative to other States but indicates to them that any attempt at invasion would face unacceptably high costs. Such a defence policy for Australia would involve a renunciation of all types of Forward Defence — in particular Australia's current commitment to maintain an overseas military presence, demonstrated by the Butterworth R.A.A.F. base in Malaysia. Similarly, all Australian military aid used to help prop-up militaristic anti-socialist states in Asia should be halted.

In economic terms the major benefit of a purely defensive strategy is that as far as equipment is concerned the technology of modern defensive weapons is cheaper and more cost effective than the technology involved in heavy attack weaponry. Precision Guided Munitions (P.G.M.s) use micro-electronics to guide various types of missiles to their targets with a very high degree of accuracy.[36] Given the increases in the destructive power of conventional explosives which have been made over the last two decades, such weapons can be used to destroy large complex attack systems — as the Exocet demonstrated in the Falklands War. The relative cheapness of such weapons can be illustrated by the fact that an anti-tank P.G.M. can be acquired for less than 1% of the cost of a tank.[37]

30. David Martin: *Armed Neutrality for Australia* (Melbourne: Dove Communications, 1984).

31. ibid., pp. 152-155.

32. ibid., pp. 175-176.

33. World Bank *World Development Report* (New York: Oxford U.P. 1983) pp. 165-167.

34. ibid.

35. Figures from A.B.S. catalogues 5204.0 and 5406.0 (Canberra A.G.P.S. 1984).

36. Mary Kaldor: op. cit., pp. 128-129.

37. Peter Tatchell: 'Unilateral Disarmament and the Case for an Alternative Defense Strategy' in Mike Cole (ed.): *Up Against the State: Young People in the 1980's,* (unpublished). Peter Tatchell's ideas will be developed at length in his book *Democratic Defense — a Non-Nuclear Alternative* to be published by Heretic Books in 1985.

Australia also has several territorial defense advantages; any mass invasion force must cross large areas of open ocean during which time they would be highly vulnerable to anti-ship missile attacks. Anti-ship missiles can be either based on land or carried by small surface ships. Moreover, unless an invasion army wanted to cross huge areas of inland Australian desert (with all the supply problems that would involve) the attack would have to be made by sea or air on the south-eastern coastline. Whichever element was used the invading force would remain exposed to anti-aircraft or anti-ship missile attack for an inordinately long period. If a successful landing was made P.G.M.'s again would lend themselves to use by partisan type resistance. Such resistance could be organised along the lines that Peter Tatchel as put forward in Britain. That is, a part-time volunteer people's army, decentralised and structured around parliamentary constituencies. The latter means that the members would have 'the military advantage of defending an area they knew intimately and the morale advantage of the passionate commitment which goes with defending one's own "hearth and home" '.[38]

Another alternative would be to use the Voluntary Latent Forces System (V.L.F.S.) proposed by Dr Ross Babbage for Australia. This system is more conventionally oriented and involves having about 20,000 to 30,000 volunteers trained in the armed forces each year for 8 to 12 months. After 8 years of operation in Australia would be in the position of being able to mobilise just under one quarter of a million combatants. David Martin argues that this system would be more cost effective than the existing Citizens Military Forces which has a drop-out rate of 30% p.a.[39] Highly motivated citizens' armies have enabled small countries such as Switzerland, Sweden, Yugoslavia and Cuba to maintain their independence despite their proximity to very powerful neighbours. Likewise, Vietnam won its independence from the most powerful military machine in the world using small-scale, labour-intensive, decentralised strategies.

There is nothing in such approaches that necessitates the establishment of a huge defence industry or massive increases in military R & D. For Australia it would be far more rational to buy our territorial defence technologies from overseas and concentrate an increased amount of Australian R & D in directions which would benefit productive Australian capital. This is an objective which is clearly achievable for the Australian State given the fact that it already funds around four fifths of the R & D in Australia.[40] At present 94% of Australian technological royalties go overseas and much private manufacturing is carried out under licence.[41] This reflects the small-scale of Australian capital and its domination by international capital, however, the situation has been exacerbated by the R & D policies of the Australian State. For example, the O.E.C.D. report on R & D in Australia found that 30% of funds for government laboratories went to defence research, while industrial research received only 20% and primary industry research 18%.[42] Obviously, from the perspective of the argument in this paper, there is considerable space for a re-structuring of R & D priorities by the state in ways that could only benefit Australian national capital.

Conclusion: Disarmament programs which aim at strengthening National Capital may not have much appeal for many on the Left (including myself). Nonetheless such programs probably have a greater chance of success precisely because they cut across class polarities. Ultimately, the struggle to prevent nuclear war must condition and take priority over immediate struggles for socialism.

As has been indicated, a conservative disarmament program could be developed which still contained progressive elements in it, i.e. the avoidance of a mini-Australian military industrial complex and the creation of a democratically structured defence force. On balance it would be worth seeing Australian capital temporarily strengthened if it meant advancing the world prospects for peace and socialism by facilitating achievements such as the abolition of U.S. bases, the banning of nuclear weapons in Australia and the undermining of the international imperialist alliance.

38. ibid.

39. David Martin: op. cit., pp. 144-145.

40. *Industrial R & D in Australia*, report from the Senate Standing Committee on Science and the Environment (Canberra: A.G.P.S. 1979) p. 52.

41. David Martin, op. cit., p. 164.

42. *O.E.C.D. Examiners Report on Science and Technology in Australia* (Canberra: A.G.P.S. 1974) p. 11.